The *New* Daily Study Bible

The Gospel of
John
Volume I

The *New* Daily Study Bible

The Gospel of
John

Volume I

William Barclay

WESTMINSTER
JOHN KNOX PRESS
LOUISVILLE · KENTUCKY

Originally published in 1955 as *The Daily Study Bible: The Gospel of John, Volume 1* by Saint Andrew Press, 121 George Street, Edinburgh EH2 4YN

Revised and updated by Saint Andrew Press, 2001

Published in the United States by
Westminster John Knox Press
Louisville, Kentucky

Cover design by McColl Productions Ltd., by courtesy of Saint Andrew Press

PRINTED IN THE UNITED STATES OF AMERICA

04 05 06 07 08 09 10 — 10 9 8 7 6

A catalog card for this book is available at the Library of Congress.

ISBN 0-664-22489-X

CONTENTS

JOHN

JOHN

SERIES FOREWORD
(by Ronnie Barclay)

My father always had a great love for the English language and its literature. As a student at the University of Glasgow, he won a prize in the English class – and I have no doubt that he could have become a Professor of English instead of Divinity and Biblical Criticism. In a pre-computer age, he had a mind like a computer that could store vast numbers of quotations, illustrations, anecdotes and allusions; and, more remarkably still, he could retrieve them at will. The editor of this revision has, where necessary, corrected and attributed the vast majority of these quotations with considerable skill and has enhanced our pleasure as we read quotations from Plato to T. S. Eliot.

There is another very welcome improvement in the new text. My mother was one of five sisters, and my grandmother was a commanding figure as the Presbyterian minister's wife in a small village in Ayrshire in Scotland. She ran that small community very efficiently, and I always felt that my father, surrounded by so many women, was more than somewhat overawed by it all! I am sure that this is the reason why his use of English tended to be dominated by the words 'man', 'men' and so on, with the result that it sounded very male-orientated. Once again, the editor has very skilfully improved my father's English and made the text much more readable for all of us by amending the often one-sided language.

It is a well-known fact that William Barclay wrote at breakneck speed and never corrected anything once it was on paper – he took great pride in mentioning this at every possible opportunity! This revision, in removing repetition and correcting the inevitable errors that had slipped through, has produced a text free from all the tell-tale signs of very rapid writing. It is with great pleasure that I commend this revision to readers old and new in the certainty that William Barclay speaks even more clearly to us all with his wonderful appeal in this new version of his much-loved *Daily Study Bible*.

Ronnie Barclay
Bedfordshire
2001

GENERAL INTRODUCTION

(by William Barclay, from the 1975 edition)

The Daily Study Bible series has always had one aim – to convey the results of scholarship to the ordinary reader. A. S. Peake delighted in the saying that he was a 'theological middle-man', and I would be happy if the same could be said of me in regard to these volumes. And yet the primary aim of the series has never been academic. It could be summed up in the famous words of Richard of Chichester's prayer – to enable men and women 'to know Jesus Christ more clearly, to love him more dearly, and to follow him more nearly'.

It is all of twenty years since the first volume of *The Daily Study Bible* was published. The series was the brain-child of the late Rev. Andrew McCosh, MA, STM, the then Secretary and Manager of the Committee on Publications of the Church of Scotland, and of the late Rev. R. G. Macdonald, OBE, MA, DD, its Convener.

It is a great joy to me to know that all through the years *The Daily Study Bible* has been used at home and abroad, by minister, by missionary, by student and by layman, and that it has been translated into many different languages. Now, after so many printings, it has become necessary to renew the printer's type and the opportunity has been taken to restyle the books, to correct some errors in the text and to remove some references which have become outdated. At the same time, the Biblical quotations within the text have been changed to use the Revised Standard Version, but my own original translation of the New Testament passages has been retained at the beginning of each daily section.

There is one debt which I would be sadly lacking in courtesy if I did not acknowledge. The work of revision and correction has been done entirely by the Rev. James Martin, MA, BD, Minister of High Carntyne Church, Glasgow. Had it not been for him this task would never have been undertaken, and it is impossible for me to thank him enough for the selfless toil he has put into the revision of these books.

It is my prayer that God may continue to use *The Daily Study Bible* to enable men better to understand His word.

William Barclay
Glasgow
1975
(Published in the 1975 edition)

GENERAL FOREWORD

(by John Drane)

I only met William Barclay once, not long after his retirement from the chair of Biblical Criticism at the University of Glasgow. Of course I had known about him long before that, not least because his theological passion – the Bible – was also a significant formative influence in my own life and ministry. One of my most vivid memories of his influence goes back to when I was working on my own doctoral research in the New Testament. It was summer 1971, and I was a leader on a mission team working in the north-east of Scotland at the same time as Barclay's Baird Lectures were being broadcast on national television. One night, a young Ph.D. scientist who was interested in Christianity, but still unsure about some things, came to me and announced: 'I've just been watching William Barclay on TV. He's convinced me that I need to be a Christian; when can I be baptized?' That kind of thing did not happen every day. So how could it be that Barclay's message was so accessible to people with no previous knowledge or experience of the Christian faith?

I soon realised that there was no magic ingredient that enabled this apparently ordinary professor to be a brilliant communicator. His secret lay in who he was, his own sense of identity and purpose, and above all his integrity in being true to himself and his faith. Born in the far north of Scotland, he was brought up in Motherwell, a steel-producing town south of Glasgow where his family settled when he was only five, and this was the kind of place where he felt most at home. Though his association with the University of Glasgow provided a focus for his life over almost fifty years, from his first day as a student in 1925 to his retirement from the faculty in 1974, he never became an ivory-tower academic, divorced from the realities of life in the real world. On the contrary, it was his commitment to the working-class culture of industrial Clydeside that enabled him to make such a lasting contribution not only to the world of the university but also to the life of the Church.

He was ordained to the ministry of the Church of Scotland at the age of twenty-six, but was often misunderstood even by other Christians. I doubt that William Barclay would ever have chosen words such as 'missionary' or 'evangelist' to describe his own ministry, but he accomplished what few others have done, as he took the traditional Presbyterian emphasis on spirituality-through-learning and transformed it into a most effective vehicle for evangelism. His own primary interest was in the history and language of the New Testament, but William Barclay was never only a historian or literary critic. His constant concern was to explore how these ancient books, and the faith of which they spoke, could continue to be relevant to people of his own time. If the Scottish churches had known how to capitalize on his enormous popularity in the media during the 1960s and 1970s, they might easily have avoided much of the decline of subsequent years.

Connecting the Bible to life has never been the way to win friends in the world of academic theology, and Barclay could undoubtedly have made things easier for himself had he been prepared to be a more conventional academic. But he was too deeply rooted in his own culture – and too seriously committed to the gospel – for that. He could see little purpose in a belief system that was so wrapped up in arcane and complicated terminology that it was accessible only to experts. Not only did he demystify Christian theology, but he also did it for working people, addressing the kind of things that mattered to ordinary folks in their everyday lives. In doing so, he also challenged the elitism that has often been deeply ingrained in the twin worlds of academic theology and the Church, with their shared assumption that popular culture is an inappropriate vehicle for serious thinking. Professor Barclay can hardly have been surprised when his predilection for writing books for the masses – not to mention talking to them on television – was questioned by his peers and even occasionally dismissed as being 'unscholarly' or insufficiently 'academic'. That was all untrue, of course, for his work was soundly based in reliable scholarship and his own extensive knowledge of the original languages of the Bible. But like One many centuries before him (and unlike most of his peers, in both Church and academy), 'the common people heard him gladly' (Mark 12:37), which no doubt explains why his writings are still inspirational – and why it is a particular pleasure for me personally to commend them to a new readership in a new century.

John Drane
University of Aberdeen
2001

EDITOR'S PREFACE
(by Linda Foster)

When the first volume of the original *Daily Bible Readings*, which later became *The Daily Study Bible* (the commentary on Acts), was published in 1953, no one could have anticipated or envisaged the revolution in the use of language which was to take place in the last quarter of the twentieth century. Indeed, when the first revised edition, to which William Barclay refers in his General Introduction, was completed in 1975, such a revolution was still waiting in the wings. But at the beginning of the twenty-first century, inclusive language and the concept of political correctness are well-established facts of life. It has therefore been with some trepidation that the editing of this unique and much-loved text has been undertaken in producing *The New Daily Study Bible*. Inevitably, the demands of the new language have resulted in the loss of some of Barclay's most sonorous phrases, perhaps best remembered in the often-repeated words 'many a man'. Nonetheless, this revision is made in the conviction that William Barclay, the great communicator, would have welcomed it. In the discussion of Matthew 9:16–17 ('The Problem of the New Idea'), he affirmed the value of language that has stood the test of time and in which people have 'found comfort and put their trust', but he also spoke of 'living in a changing and expanding world' and questioned the wisdom of reading God's word to twentieth-century men and women in Elizabethan English. It is the intention of this new edition to heed that warning and to bring

William Barclay's message of God's word to readers of the twenty-first century in the language of their own time.

In the editorial process, certain decisions have been made in order to keep a balance between that new language and the familiar Barclay style. Quotations from the Bible are now taken from the New Revised Standard Version, but William Barclay's own translation of individual passages has been retained throughout. Where the new version differs from the text on which Barclay originally commented, because of the existence of an alternative reading, the variant text is indicated by square brackets. I have made no attempt to guess what Barclay would have said about the NRSV text; his commentary still refers to the Authorized (King James) and Revised Standard Versions of the Bible, but I believe that the inclusive language of the NRSV considerably assists the flow of the discussion.

For similar reasons, the dating conventions of BC and AD – rather than the more recent and increasingly used BCE (before the common era) and CE (common era) – have been retained. William Barclay took great care to explain the meanings of words and phrases and scholarly points, but it has not seemed appropriate to select new terms and make such explanations on his behalf.

One of the most difficult problems to solve has concerned monetary values. Barclay had his own system for translating the coinage of New Testament times into British currency. Over the years, these equivalent values have become increasingly out of date, and often the force of the point being made has been lost or diminished. There is no easy way to bring these equivalents up to date in a way that will continue to make sense, particularly when readers come from both sides of the Atlantic. I have therefore followed the only known yardstick that gives any feel for the values concerned, namely that a *denarius* was a day's wage for a working man, and I have made alterations to the text accordingly.

One of the striking features of *The Daily Study Bible* is the range of quotations from literature and hymnody that are used by way of illustration. Many of these passages appeared without identification or attribution, and for the new edition I have attempted wherever possible to provide sources and authors. In the same way, details have been included about scholars and other individuals cited, by way of context and explanation, and I am most grateful to Professor John Drane for his assistance in discovering information about some of the more obscure or unfamiliar characters. It is clear that readers use *The Daily Study Bible* in different ways. Some look up particular passages while others work through the daily readings in a more systematic way. The descriptions and explanations are therefore not offered every time an individual is mentioned (in order to avoid repetition that some may find tedious), but I trust that the information can be discovered without too much difficulty.

Finally, the 'Further Reading' lists at the end of each volume have been removed. Many new commentaries and individual studies have been added to those that were the basis of William Barclay's work, and making a selection from that ever-increasing catalogue is an impossible task. It is nonetheless my hope that the exploration that begins with these volumes of *The New Daily Study Bible* will go on in the discovery of new writers and new books.

Throughout the editorial process, many conversations have taken place – conversations with the British and American publishers, and with those who love the books and find in them both information and inspiration. Ronnie Barclay's contribution to this revision of his father's work has been invaluable. But one conversation has dominated the work, and that has been a conversation with William Barclay himself through the text. There has been a real sense of listening to his voice in all the questioning and in the searching for new words to convey the meaning of that text. The aim of *The New Daily Study Bible* is to make clear his message, so that the distinctive voice, which has spoken to so many in past years, may continue to be heard for generations to come.

Linda Foster
London
2001

INTRODUCTION

(by John Drane)

John has always been recognized to be different in character from the other three gospels. At the time that William Barclay was himself a student, it was fashionable to explain this by supposing that John's account is an essentially fictional narrative, loosely based on the synoptic gospels, but concerned more with defending early Christian beliefs than with providing any sort of independent testimony to the life and teaching of Jesus. By the time that Barclay wrote this volume, the idea that John's gospel should be rehabilitated as a credible historical account had been proposed by several leading scholars, but was still a matter of considerable ongoing debate. Barclay unhesitatingly accepted this 'new look' on John, not only affirming the essential trustworthiness of the gospel as an authentic presentation of the life and teaching of Jesus, but also connecting its composition with the apostle John himself. His proposal that the finished gospel was not actually written down by the apostle himself, but reflected the life and faith of a 'Johannine community' that flourished in Ephesus towards the end of the first century, has been more fully explored since Barclay's time, and is now widely accepted among New Testament scholars, though some would be inclined to date the gospel itself a little earlier than AD 100.

Some aspects of this commentary would certainly be expressed differently today, especially Barclay's descriptions of the 'opponents' whom he believed John was countering.

He scarcely noticed the anti-Jewish tone of some passages which has been the subject of heated debate, and the description of Gnosticism at 1:3 as 'an intellectual and philosophical approach to Christianity' is by no means the whole story. Texts written by Gnostics themselves have shown that Gnosticism was not an exclusively Christian phenomenon, while some doubt that 'Gnosticism' as such really was a definable entity, preferring to see it as a more loosely formulated 'attitude', much like today's 'New Age', with which it has much in common.

In characteristic Barclay style, this volume is concerned with the wider meaning of the text to Christian life and witness. He has a good deal to say about what would now be called contextualization, the relevant expression of the Christian message in different cultures. The recurrence of this theme throughout not only reveals Barclay's own underlying concern for effective mission, but also highlights an issue which continues to be a key challenge for the Church at the beginning of this new century.

John Drane
University of Aberdeen
2001

INTRODUCTION TO
THE GOSPEL OF JOHN

The Gospel of the Eagle's Eye

For many Christian people, the Gospel according to St John is the most precious book in the New Testament. It is the book on which above all they feed their minds and nourish their hearts, and in which they rest their souls. Very often on stained-glass windows and the like, the gospel writers are represented in symbol by the figures of the four animals that the writer of the Revelation saw around the throne (Revelation 4:7). The emblems are variously distributed among the gospel writers, but a common allocation is that the *man* stands for Mark, which is the plainest, the most straightforward and the most human of the gospels; the *lion* stands for Matthew, for he specially saw Jesus as the Messiah and the Lion of the tribe of Judah; the *ox* stands for Luke, because it is the animal of service and sacrifice, and Luke saw Jesus as the great servant of men and women and the universal sacrifice for all people; and the *eagle* stands for John, because it alone of all living creatures can look straight into the sun and not be dazzled, and, of all the New Testament writers, John has the most penetrating gaze into the eternal mysteries and the eternal truths and the very mind of God. Many people find themselves closer to God and to Jesus Christ in John than in any other book in the world.

The Gospel that is Different

But we have only to read the Fourth Gospel in the most cursory way to see that it is quite different from the other three. It omits so many things that they include. The Fourth Gospel has no account of the birth of Jesus, of his baptism, of his temptations; it tells us nothing of the Last Supper, nothing of Gethsemane and nothing of the ascension. It has no word of the healing of any people possessed by devils and evil spirits. And, perhaps most surprising of all, it has none of the parable stories Jesus told which are such a priceless part of the other three gospels. In these other three gospels, Jesus speaks either in these wonderful stories or in short, epigrammatic, vivid sentences which stick in the memory. But in the Fourth Gospel, the speeches of Jesus are often a whole chapter long and are often involved, argumentative pronouncements quite unlike the pithy, unforgettable sayings of the other three.

Even more surprising, the account in the Fourth Gospel of the facts of the life and ministry of Jesus is often different from that in the other three.

(1) John has a different account of the *beginning* of the ministry of Jesus. In the other three gospels, it is quite definitely stated that Jesus did not emerge as a preacher until after John the Baptist had been imprisoned. 'Now after John was arrested, Jesus came to Galilee, proclaiming the good news of God' (Mark 1:14; cf. Luke 3:18, 20; Matthew 4:12). But in John there is a quite considerable period during which the ministry of Jesus overlapped with the activity of John the Baptist (John 3:22–30, 4:1–2).

(2) John has a different account of the *scene* of Jesus' ministry. In the other three gospels, the main scene of the ministry is Galilee, and Jesus does not reach Jerusalem until

the last week of his life. In John, the main scene of the
ministry is Jerusalem and Judaea, with only occasional with-
drawals to Galilee (2:1–13, 4:35–5:1, 6:1–7:14). In John,
Jesus is in Jerusalem for a Passover which occurred at the
same time as the cleansing of the Temple, as John tells the
story (2:13); he is in Jerusalem at the time of an unnamed
feast (5:1); he is there for the Feast of Tabernacles (7:2, 10);
he is there at the Feast of Dedication in the wintertime
(10:22). In fact, according to the Fourth Gospel, Jesus never
left Jerusalem after that feast; after chapter 10 he is in
Jerusalem all the time, which would mean a stay of months,
from the wintertime of the Feast of the Dedication to the
springtime of the Passover at which he was crucified.

In point of fact, in this particular matter John is surely right.
The other gospels show us Jesus mourning over Jerusalem as
the last week came on. 'Jerusalem, Jerusalem, the city that
kills the prophets and stones those who are sent to it! How
often have I desired to gather your children together as a hen
gathers her brood under her wings, and you were not willing!'
(Matthew 23:37 = Luke 13:34). It is clear that Jesus could not
have said that unless he had paid repeated visits to Jerusalem
and made repeated appeals to it. It was impossible for him to
say that on a first visit. In this, John is unquestionably right.

It was in fact this difference of scene which provided the
great Church historian Eusebius with one of the earliest
explanations of the difference between the Fourth Gospel and
the other three. He said that in his day (about AD 300) many
people who were scholars held the following view. Matthew
at first preached to the Hebrew people. The day came when
he had to leave them and go to other nations. Before he went,
he set down his story of the life of Jesus in Hebrew, 'and thus
compensated those whom he was obliged to leave for the
loss of his presence'. After Mark and Luke had published

3

their gospels, John was still preaching the story of Jesus orally. 'Finally he proceeded to write for the following reason. The three gospels already mentioned having come into the hands of all and into his hands too, they say that he fully accepted them and bore witness to their truthfulness; *but there was lacking in them an account of the deeds done by Christ at the beginning of his ministry . . .* They therefore say that John, being asked to do it for this reason, gave in his gospel an account of the period which had been omitted by the earlier evangelists, and of the deeds done by the Saviour during that period; that is, of the deeds done before the imprisonment of John the Baptist . . . John therefore records the deeds of Christ which were performed *before* the Baptist was cast into prison, but the other three evangelists mention the events which happened *after* that time . . . The *Gospel according to John* contains the *first* acts of Christ, while the others give an account of the *latter* part of his life' (Eusebius, *The Ecclesiastical History*, 5:24).

So then according to Eusebius there is no contradiction at all between the Fourth Gospel and the other three; the difference is due to the fact that the Fourth Gospel is describing a ministry in Jerusalem, at least in its earlier chapters, which preceded the ministry in Galilee, and which took place while John the Baptist was still at liberty. It may well be that this explanation of Eusebius is at least in part correct.

(3) John has a different account of the *duration* of Jesus' ministry. The other three gospels, on the face of it, imply that it lasted only one year. Within the ministry, there is only one Passover Feast. In John, there are *three* Passovers: one at the cleansing of the Temple (2:13), one near the feeding of the 5,000 (6:4), and the final Passover at which Jesus went to the cross. According to John, the ministry of Jesus would take a

minimum of two years, and probably a period nearer three years, to cover its events. Again, John is unquestionably right. If we read the other three gospels closely and carefully, we can see that he is right. When the disciples plucked the ears of corn (Mark 2:23), it must have been springtime. When the 5,000 were fed, they sat down on the *green grass* (Mark 6:39); therefore it was springtime again, and there must have been a year between the two events. There follows the tour through Tyre and Sidon, and the transfiguration. At the transfiguration, Peter wished to build three booths and to stay there. It is most natural to think that it was the time of the Feast of Tabernacles or Booths and that that is why Peter made the suggestion (Mark 9:5). That would make the date early in October. There follows the space between that and the last Passover in April. Therefore, behind the narrative of the other three gospels lies the fact that Jesus' ministry actually did last for at least three years, as John represents it.

(4) It sometimes even happens that John differs in matters of fact from the other three. There are two outstanding examples. First, John puts the cleansing of the Temple at the *beginning* of Jesus' ministry (2:13–22); the others put it at the *end* (Mark 11:15–17; Matthew 21:12–13; Luke 19:45–6). Second, when we come to study the narratives in detail, we will see that John dates the crucifixion of Jesus on the day before the Passover, while the other gospels date it on the day of the Passover.

We can never shut our eyes to the obvious differences between John and the other gospels.

John's Special Knowledge

One thing is certain – if John differs from the other three gospels, it is not because of ignorance and lack of information.

5

The plain fact is that, if he omits much that they tell us, he also tells us much that they do not mention. John alone tells of the marriage feast at Cana of Galilee (2:1–11); of the coming of Nicodemus to Jesus (3:1–15); of the woman of Samaria (4); of the raising of Lazarus (11); of the way in which Jesus washed his disciples' feet (13:1–17); of Jesus' wonderful teaching about the Holy Spirit, the Comforter, which is scattered through chapters 14–17. It is only in John that some of the disciples really come alive. It is in John alone that Thomas speaks (11:16, 14:5, 20:24–9); that Andrew becomes a real personality (1:40–1, 6:8–9, 12:22); that we get a glimpse of the character of Philip (6:5–7, 14:8–9); that we hear the carping protest of Judas at the anointing at Bethany (12:4–5). And the strange thing is that these little extra touches are intensely revealing. John's pictures of Thomas and Andrew and Philip are like little cameos or vignettes in which the character of each man is etched in a way we cannot forget.

Further, again and again John has little extra details which read like the memories of one who was there. The loaves which the young boy brought to Jesus were *barley* loaves (6:9); when Jesus came to the disciples as they crossed the lake in the storm, they had rowed between three and four miles (6:19); there were six stone water pots at Cana of Galilee (2:6); it is only John who tells of the four soldiers gambling for the seamless robe as Jesus dies (19:23); he knows the exact weight of the myrrh and aloes which were used to anoint the dead body of Jesus (19:39); and he remembers how the perfume of the ointment filled the house at the anointing at Bethany (12:3). Many of these things are such apparently unimportant details that they are inexplicable unless they are the memories of someone who was there.

6

However much John may differ from the other three gospels, that difference is to be explained not by ignorance but rather by the fact that he had more knowledge or better sources or a more vivid memory than the others.

Further evidence of the specialized information of the writer of the Fourth Gospel is his *detailed knowledge of Palestine and of Jerusalem*. He knows how long it took to build the Temple (2:20); that the Jews and the Samaritans had a permanent quarrel (4:9); the low Jewish view of women (4:9); and how the Jews regard the Sabbath (5:10, 7:21–3, 9:14). His knowledge of the geography of Palestine is intimate. He knows of two Bethanys, one of which is beyond Jordan (1:28, 12:1); he knows that Bethsaida was the home of some of the disciples (1:44, 12:21); that Cana is in Galilee (2:1, 4:46, 21:2); and that Sychar is near Shechem (4:5). He has what one might call a street-by-street knowledge of Jerusalem. He knows the sheepgate and the pool near it (5:2); the pool of Siloam (9:7); Solomon's Porch (10:23); the brook Kidron (18:1); the pavement which is called Gabbatha (19:13); and Golgotha, which is like a skull (19:17). It must be remembered that Jerusalem was destroyed in AD 70 and that John did not write until around AD 100; and yet from his memory he knows Jerusalem like the back of his hand.

The Circumstances in which John Wrote

We have seen that there are very real differences between the Fourth Gospel and the other three gospels; and we have seen that, whatever the reason, it was not lack of knowledge on John's part. We must now go on to ask, what was the aim with which John wrote? If we can discover this, we will discover why he selected and treated his facts as he did.

The Fourth Gospel was written in Ephesus around AD 100. By that time, two special features had emerged in the situation of the Christian Church. First, *Christianity had gone out into the Gentile world.* By that time, the Christian Church was no longer predominantly Jewish; it was in fact overwhelmingly Gentile. The vast majority of its members now came not from a Jewish but a Greek background. That being so, *Christianity had to be restated.* It was not that the truth of Christianity had changed; but the terms and the categories in which it found expression had to be changed.

Take but one instance. A Greek might take up the Gospel according to St Matthew and immediately on opening it would be confronted with a long genealogy. Genealogies were familiar enough to Jews, but quite unintelligible to Greeks. Moving on, the reader would be confronted with a Jesus who was the Son of David, a king of whom the Greeks had never heard, and the symbol of a racial and nationalist ambition which had no significance for the Greeks. The picture presented was of Jesus as the Messiah, a term of which Greeks had never heard. Must Greeks who wished to become Christians be compelled to reorganize their entire thinking into Jewish categories? Must they learn a good deal about Jewish history and Jewish apocalyptic literature (which told about the coming of the Messiah) before they could become Christians? As the biblical scholar E. J. Goodspeed phrased it: 'Was there no way in which [they] might be introduced directly to the values of Christian salvation without being for ever routed, we might even say, detoured, through Judaism?' Greeks were among the world's greatest thinkers. Was it necessary for them to abandon all their own great intellectual heritage in order to think entirely in Jewish terms and categories of thought?

John faced that problem fairly and squarely. And he found one of the greatest solutions which ever entered the human mind. Later on, in the commentary, we shall deal much more fully with John's great solution. At the moment, we touch on it briefly. The Greeks had two great conceptions.

(a) They had the conception of the *Logos*. In Greek, *logos* means two things – it means *word* and it means *reason*. Jews were entirely familiar with the all-powerful word of God. 'God said, "Let there be light"; and there was light' (Genesis 1:3). Greeks were entirely familiar with the thought of reason. They looked at this world; they saw a magnificent and dependable order. Night and day came with unfailing regularity; the year kept its seasons in unvarying course; the stars and the planets moved in their unaltering path; nature had her unvarying laws. What produced this order? Greeks answered unhesitatingly: the *Logos*, the mind of God, is responsible for the majestic order of the world. They went on: what is it that gives human beings power to think, to reason and to know? Again they answered unhesitatingly: the *Logos*, the mind of God, dwelling within an individual makes that person a thinking rational being.

John seized on this. It was in this way that he thought of Jesus. He said to the Greeks: 'All your lives you have been fascinated by this great, guiding, controlling mind of God. The mind of God has come to earth in the man Jesus. Look at him and you see what the mind and thought of God are like.' John had discovered a new category in which Greeks might think of Jesus, a category in which Jesus was presented as nothing less than God acting in human form.

(b) They had the conception of two worlds. The Greeks always conceived of two worlds. The one was the world in which we live. It was a wonderful world in its way but a world of shadows and copies and unrealities. The other was the real world, in which the great realities, of which our earthly things are only poor, pale copies, stand for ever. To the Greeks, the unseen world was the real one; the seen world was only shadowy unreality.

Plato systematized this way of thinking in his doctrine of forms or ideas. He held that in the unseen world there was the perfect pattern of everything, and the things of this world were shadowy copies of these eternal patterns. To put it simply, Plato held that somewhere there was a perfect pattern of a table of which all earthly tables are inadequate copies; somewhere there was the perfect pattern of the good and the beautiful of which all earthly goodness and earthly beauty are imperfect copies. And the great reality, the supreme idea, the pattern of all patterns and the form of all forms was God. The great problem was how to get into this world of reality, how to get out of our shadows into the eternal truths.

John declares that that is what Jesus enables us to do. He *is* reality come to earth. The Greek word for *real* in this sense is *alēthinos*; it is very closely connected with the word *alēthēs*, which means *true*, and *alētheia*, which means *the truth*. The Authorized and Revised Standard Versions translate *alēthinos* as *true*; they would be far better to translate it as *real*. Jesus is the *real* light (1:9); Jesus is the *real* bread (6:32); Jesus is the *real* vine (15:1); to Jesus belongs the *real* judgment (8:16). Jesus alone has reality in our world of shadows and imperfections.

Something follows from that. Every action that Jesus did was, therefore, not only an act in time but a window which allows us to see into reality. That is what John means when he talks of Jesus' miracles as *signs* (*sēmeia*). The wonderful works of Jesus were not simply wonderful; they were windows opening on to the reality which is God. This explains why John tells the miracle stories in a quite different way from the other three gospel writers. There are two differences.

(a) In the Fourth Gospel, we miss the note of compassion which is in the miracle stories of the others. In the others, Jesus is moved with compassion for the leper (Mark 1:41); his sympathy goes out to Jairus (Mark 5:22); he is sorry for the father of the epileptic boy (Mark 9:14); when he raises to life the son of the widow of Nain, Luke says with an infinite tenderness: 'He gave him to his mother' (Luke 7:15). But in John the miracles are not so much deeds of compassion as deeds which demonstrate the glory of Christ. After the miracle at Cana of Galilee, John comments: 'Jesus did this, the first of his signs, in Cana of Galilee, *and revealed his glory*' (2:11). The raising of Lazarus happens *'for God's glory'* (11:4). The blind man's blindness existed to allow a demonstration of the glory of the works of God (John 9:3). To John, it was not that there was no love and compassion in the miracles; but in every one of them he saw the glory of the reality of God breaking into time and into human affairs.

(b) Often the miracles of Jesus in the Fourth Gospel are accompanied by a long discourse. The feeding of the 5,000 is followed by the long discourse on the bread of life (chapter 6); the healing of the blind man springs from the saying that Jesus is the light of the world (chapter 9); and the raising of Lazarus leads up to the saying that Jesus is the resurrection and the life (chapter 11). To John, the miracles were not simply single events in time; they were insights into what God is always doing and what Jesus always is; they were windows into the reality of God. Jesus did not merely once feed 5,000 people; that was an illustration that he is forever the real bread of life. Jesus did not merely once open the eyes of a blind man; he is forever the light of the world. Jesus did not merely once raise Lazarus from the dead; he is forever and for everyone the resurrection and the life. To John, a miracle was never an isolated act; it was always a window into the reality of what Jesus always was and always is and always did and always does.

It was with this in mind that the great scholar Clement of Alexandria (about AD 230) arrived at one of the most famous and true of all verdicts about the origin and aim of the Fourth Gospel. It was his view that the gospels containing the genealogies had been written first – that is, Luke and Matthew; that then Mark, at the request of many who had heard Peter preach, composed his gospel, which embodied the preaching material of Peter; and that then 'last of all, John, perceiving that what had reference to the bodily things of Jesus' ministry had been sufficiently related, and encouraged by his friends, and inspired by the Holy Spirit, wrote *a spiritual gospel*' (quoted in Eusebius, *The Ecclesiastical History*, 6:14). What Clement meant was that John was interested not so much in the mere facts as in the meaning of the facts, that it was not facts he was after but truth. John did not see the events of Jesus' life simply as events in time; he saw them as windows looking into eternity, and he pressed towards the spiritual meaning of the events and the words of Jesus' life in a way that the other three gospels did not attempt.

That is still one of the truest verdicts on the Fourth Gospel ever reached. John did write, not a historical, but a spiritual gospel.

So, first of all, John presented Jesus as the mind of God in a person come to earth, and as the one person who possesses reality instead of shadows and is able to lead men and women out of the shadows into the real world of which Plato and the great Greeks had dreamed. The Christianity which had once been clothed in Jewish categories had taken to itself the greatness of the thought of the Greeks.

The Rise of the Heresies

The second of the great facts confronting the Church when the Fourth Gospel was written was *the rise of heresy*. It was now about seventy years since Jesus had been crucified. By this time, the Church was an organization and an institution. Theologies and creeds were being thought out and stated; and inevitably the thoughts of some people went down mistaken ways, and heresies resulted. A heresy is seldom a complete untruth; it usually results when one facet of the truth is unduly emphasized. We can see at least two of the heresies which the writer of the Fourth Gospel sought to combat.

(a) There were certain Christians, especially Jewish Christians, who gave too high a place to John the Baptist. There was something about him which had an inevitable appeal to the Jews. He walked in the prophetic succession and talked with the prophetic voice. We know that in later times there was an accepted sect of John the Baptist within the orthodox Jewish faith. In Acts 19:1–7, we come upon a little group of twelve on the fringe of the Christian Church who had never got beyond the baptism of John.

Over and over again, the Fourth Gospel quietly, but definitely, relegates John to his proper place. Over and over again, John himself denies that he has ever claimed or possessed the highest place, and without qualification yields that place to Jesus. We have already seen that in the other gospels the ministry of Jesus did not begin until John the Baptist had been put into prison, but that in the Fourth Gospel their ministries overlap. The writer of the Fourth Gospel may well have used that arrangement to show John and Jesus in actual meeting and to show that John used these meetings to admit, and to urge others to admit, the supremacy of Jesus. It is carefully pointed out that John is not 'that light' (1:8). He is shown as quite definitely disclaiming all messianic aspirations (1:20ff., 3:28, 4:1, 10:41). It is not even permissible to think of him as the highest witness (5:36). There is no criticism at all of John the Baptist in the Fourth Gospel; but there is a rebuke to those who would give him a place which ought to belong to Jesus and to Jesus alone.

(b) A certain type of heresy which was very widely spread in the days when the Fourth Gospel was written is called by the general name of Gnosticism. Without some understanding of it, much of John's greatness and much of his aim will be missed. The basic doctrine of Gnosticism was that matter is essentially evil and spirit is essentially good. The Gnostics went on to argue that on that basis God himself cannot touch matter and therefore did not create the world. What he did was to put out a series of emanations. Each of these emanations was further from him, until at last there was one so distant from him that it could touch matter. That emanation was the creator of the world.

By itself that idea is bad enough, but it was made worse by an addition. The Gnostics held that each emanation knew less and less about God, until there was a stage when the emanations were not only ignorant of God but actually hostile to him. So they finally came to the conclusion that the creator god was not only different from the real God, but was also quite ignorant of and actively hostile to him. Cerinthus, one of the leaders of the Gnostics, said that 'the world was created, not by God, but by a certain power far separate from him, and far distant from that Power who is over the universe, and ignorant of the God who is over all'.

The Gnostics believed that God had nothing to do with the creating of the world. That is why John begins his gospel with the ringing statement: 'All things came into being

through him, and without him not one thing came into being'
(1:3). That is why John insists that 'God so loved the *world*'
(3:16). In face of the Gnostics who so mistakenly spiritualized
God into a being who could not possibly have anything to do
with the world, John presented the Christian doctrine of the
God who made the world and whose presence fills the world
that he has made.

The beliefs of the Gnostics impinged on their ideas of Jesus.

(a) Some of the Gnostics held that Jesus was one of the
emanations which had proceeded from God. They held that
he was not in any real sense divine; that he was only a kind
of demi-god who was more or less distant from the real God;
that he was simply one of a chain of lesser beings between
God and the world.

(b) Some of the Gnostics held that Jesus had no real body.
A body is matter and God could not touch matter; therefore
Jesus was a kind of phantom without real flesh and blood.
They held, for instance, that when he stepped on the ground
he left no footprint, for his body had neither weight nor
substance. They could never have said: 'The Word became
flesh' (John 1:14). St Augustine tells how he had read much
in the work of the philosophers of his day; he had found
much that was very like what was in the New Testament, but,
he said: '"The Word was made flesh and dwelt among us" I
did not read there.' That is why John in his First Letter insists
that Jesus came *in the flesh*, and declares that anyone who
denies that fact is moved by the spirit of the antichrist (1
John 4:3). This particular heresy is known as *Docetism*.
Docetism comes from the Greek word *dokein* which means
to seem; and the heresy is so called because it held that Jesus
only *seemed* to be a man.

(c) Some Gnostics held a variation of that heresy. They
held that Jesus was a man into whom the Spirit of God came

at his baptism; that the Spirit remained with him throughout his life until the end; but since the Spirit of God could never suffer and die, it left him before he was crucified. They gave Jesus' cry on the cross as: 'My power, my power, why have you forsaken me?' And in their books they told of people talking on the Mount of Olives to a form which looked exactly like Jesus while the man Jesus died on the cross.

So then the Gnostic heresies were expressed in two possible alternative beliefs. They believed either that Jesus was not really divine but simply one of a series of emanations from God, or that he was not in any sense human but a kind of phantom in the shape of a man. The Gnostic beliefs at one and the same time destroyed the real godhead and the real humanity of Jesus.

The Humanity of Jesus

The fact that John is out to correct both these Gnostic tendencies explains a curious paradoxical double emphasis in his gospel. On the one hand, there is no gospel which so uncompromisingly stresses the real humanity of Jesus. Jesus was angry with those who bought and sold in the Temple courts (2:15); he was physically tired as he sat by the well which was near Sychar in Samaria (4:6); his disciples offered him food in the way in which they would offer it to any hungry man (4:31); he had sympathy with those who were hungry and with those who were afraid (6:5, 20); he knew grief and he wept tears as any mourner might do (11:33, 35, 38); in the agony of the cross the cry of his parched lips was: 'I am thirsty' (19:28). The Fourth Gospel shows us a Jesus who was no shadowy, docetic figure; it shows us one who knew the weariness of an exhausted body and the wounds of a distressed mind and heart. It is the truly human Jesus whom the Fourth Gospel sets before us.

The Deity of Jesus

On the other hand, there is no gospel which sets before us such a view of the deity of Jesus.

(a) John stresses the *pre-existence* of Jesus. 'Before Abraham was,' said Jesus, 'I am' (8:58). He talks of the glory which he had with the Father before the world was made (17:5). Again and again he speaks of his coming down from heaven (6:33–8). John saw in Jesus one who had always been, even before the world began.

(b) The Fourth Gospel stresses more than any of the others the *omniscience* of Jesus. It is John's view that apparently miraculously Jesus knew the past record of the woman of Samaria (4:16–17); apparently without anyone telling him, he knew how long the man beside the healing pool had been ill (5:6); before he asked it, he knew the answer to the question he put to Philip (6:6); he knew that Judas would betray him (6:61–4); and he knew of the death of Lazarus before anyone told him of it (11:14). John saw in Jesus one who had a special and miraculous knowledge independent of anything which he might be told. He needed to ask no questions because he knew the answers.

(c) The Fourth Gospel stresses the fact, as John saw it, that Jesus always acted entirely on his own initiative and was not influenced by anyone else. It was not his mother's request which moved him to the miracle at Cana in Galilee; it was his own personal decision (2:4); the urging of his brothers had nothing to do with the visit which he paid to Jerusalem at the Feast of Tabernacles (7:10); no one took his life from him – no one could; he laid it down purely voluntarily (10:18, 19:11). As John saw it, Jesus had a divine independence from all human influence. He was self-determined.

To counter the Gnostics and their strange beliefs, John presents us with a Jesus who was undeniably human and who yet was undeniably divine.

The Author of the Fourth Gospel

We have seen that the aim of the writer of the Fourth Gospel was to present the Christian faith in such a way that it would commend itself to the Greek world to which Christianity had gone out, and also to combat the heresies and mistaken ideas which had arisen within the Church. We go on to ask: 'Who is that writer?' Tradition answers unanimously that the author was John the apostle. We shall see that beyond doubt the authority of John lies behind the gospel, although it may well be that its actual form and style of writing did not come from his hand. Let us, then, collect what we know about him.

He was the younger son of Zebedee, who possessed a fishing boat on the Sea of Galilee and was sufficiently well off to be able to employ hired servants to help him with his work (Mark 1:19–20). His mother was Salome, and it seems likely that she was the sister of Mary, the mother of Jesus (Matthew 27:56; Mark 16:1). With his brother James, he obeyed the call of Jesus (Mark 1:20). It would seem that James and John were in partnership with Peter in the fishing trade (Luke 5:7–10). He was one of the inner circle of the disciples, for the lists of the disciples always begin with the names of Peter, James and John, and there were certain great occasions when Jesus took these three specially with him (Mark 3:17, 5:37, 9:2, 14:33).

In character he was clearly a turbulent and ambitious man. Jesus gave to him and to his brother the name *Boanerges*, which the gospel writers take to mean *Sons of Thunder*. John and his brother James were completely exclusive and intolerant (Mark 9:38; Luke 9:49). So violent was their temper that they were prepared to blast a Samaritan village out of existence because it would not give them hospitality when they were on their journey to Jerusalem (Luke 9:54). Either they or their mother Salome had the ambition that when Jesus came into his kingdom, they might be his principal ministers of state (Mark 10:35; Matthew 20:20). In the other three gospels, John appears as a leader of the apostolic band, one of the inner circle, and yet a turbulent, ambitious and intolerant character.

In the Book of Acts, John always appears as the companion of Peter, and he himself never speaks at all. His name is still one of the three names at the head of the apostolic list (Acts 1:13). He is with Peter when the lame man is healed at the Beautiful Gate of the Temple (Acts 3:1ff.). With Peter, he is brought before the Sanhedrin and faces the Jewish leaders with a courage and a boldness that astonishes them (Acts 4:1–13). With Peter, he goes from Jerusalem to Samaria to survey the work done by Philip (Acts 8:14).

In Paul's letters, he appears only once. In Galatians 2:9, he is named as one of the pillars of the Church along with Peter and James, and with them is depicted as giving his approval to the work of Paul.

John was a strange mixture. He was one of the leaders of the Twelve; he was one of the inner circle of Jesus' closest friends; at the same time he was a man of temper and ambition and intolerance, and yet of courage.

We may follow John into the stories told of him in the early Church. Eusebius tells us that he was banished to Patmos in the reign of Domitian (Eusebius, *The Ecclesiastical History*, 3:23). In the same passage, Eusebius tells a characteristic story about John, a story which he received from Clement of Alexandria. John became a kind of bishop of Asia Minor and was visiting one of his churches near Ephesus. In the congregation, he saw a tall and exceptionally fine-looking young man. He turned to the elder in charge of the congregation and said to him: 'I commit that young man into your charge and into your care, and I call this congregation to witness that I do so.' The elder took the young man into his own house and cared for him and instructed him, and the day came when he was baptized and received into the Church. But very soon afterwards, he fell in with evil friends and embarked on such a career of crime that he ended up by becoming the leader of a band of murdering and pillaging brigands. Some time afterwards, John returned to the congregation. He said to the elder: 'Restore to me the trust which I and the Lord committed to you and to the church of which you are in charge.' At first the elder did not understand of what John was speaking. 'I mean', said John, 'that I am asking you for the soul of the young man whom I entrusted to you.' 'Alas!' said the elder, 'he is dead.' 'Dead?' said John. 'He is dead to God,' said the elder. 'He fell from grace; he was forced to flee from the city for his crimes and now he is a bandit in the mountains.' Immediately John went to the mountains. Deliberately he allowed himself to be captured by the robber band. They brought him before the young man, who was now the chief of the band; and, in his shame, the young man tried to run away from him. John, though an old man, pursued him. 'My son,' he cried, 'are you running away from your father? I am feeble and far advanced in age; have pity on me, my son; fear not; there is yet hope of salvation for you. I will stand for you before the Lord Christ. If need be, I will gladly die for you as he died for me. Stop, stay, believe! It is Christ who has sent me to you.' The appeal broke the heart of the young man. He stopped, threw away his weapons, and wept. Together he and John came down the mountainside and he was brought back into the Church and into the Christian way. There we see the love and the courage of John still in operation.

Eusebius (3:28) tells another story of John which he got from the works of the second-century theologian, Irenaeus. We have seen that one of the leaders of the Gnostic heresy was a man called Cerinthus. 'The apostle John once entered a bath to bathe; but, when he learned that Cerinthus was within, he sprang from his place and rushed out of the door, for he could not bear to remain under the same roof with him. He advised those who were with him to do the same. "Let us flee," he said, "lest the bath fall, for Cerinthus, the enemy of the truth, is within."' There we have another glimpse of the temper of John. Boanerges was not quite dead.

Writing in the fifth century, John Cassian tells another famous story about John. One day he was found playing with a tame partridge. A narrower and more rigid brother rebuked him for thus wasting his time, and John answered: 'The bow that is always bent will soon cease to shoot straight.'

It is the great biblical scholar Jerome who tells the story of the last words of John. When he was dying, his disciples asked him if he had any last message to leave them. 'Little children,' he said, 'love one another.' Again and again he repeated it; and they asked him if that was all he had to say. 'It is enough,' he said, 'for it is the Lord's command.'

Such then is our information about John; and he emerges as a figure of fiery temper, of wide ambition, of undoubted courage and, in the end, of gentle love.

The Beloved Disciple

If we have been following our references closely, we will have noticed one thing. All our information about John comes from the first three gospels. It is the astonishing fact that the Fourth Gospel never mentions the apostle John from beginning to end. But it does mention two other people.

First, it speaks of *the disciple whom Jesus loved*. There are four mentions of him. He was leaning on Jesus' breast at the Last Supper (John 13:23–5); it is into his care that Jesus committed Mary as he died upon his cross (19:25–7); it was Peter and he whom Mary Magdalene met on her return from the empty tomb on the first Easter morning (20:2); and he was present at the last resurrection appearance of Jesus by the lakeside (21:20).

Second, the Fourth Gospel has a kind of character whom we might call the *witness*. As the Fourth Gospel tells of the spear thrust into the side of Jesus and the issue of the water and the blood, there comes the comment: 'He who saw this has testified so that you also may believe. His testimony is true, and he knows that he tells the truth' (19:35). At the end of the gospel comes the statement that it was the beloved disciple who testified of these things, 'and we know that his testimony is true' (21:24).

Here we are faced with rather a strange thing. In the Fourth Gospel, John is never mentioned; but the beloved disciple is, and in addition there is a witness of some kind to the whole story. It has never really been doubted in tradition that the beloved disciple is John. A few have tried to identify him with Lazarus, for Jesus is said to have loved Lazarus (John 11:3, 5); or with the rich young ruler, of whom it is said that Jesus, looking on him, loved him (Mark 10:21). But although the gospel never says so in so many words, tradition has always identified the beloved disciple with John, and there is no real need to doubt the identification.

But a very real point arises – suppose John himself actually did the writing of the gospel, would he really be likely to speak of himself as the disciple whom Jesus loved? Would he really be likely to pick himself out like this, and, as it were, to say: 'I was his favourite; he loved me best of all'? It is surely very unlikely that John would confer such a title on himself. If it was conferred by others, it is a lovely title; if it was conferred by himself, it comes perilously near to an almost incredible self-conceit.

Is there any way, then, that the gospel can be John's own eyewitness story, and yet at the same time have been actually written down by someone else?

The Production of the Church

In our search for the truth, we begin by noting one of the outstanding and unique features of the Fourth Gospel. The most remarkable thing about it is the long speeches of Jesus. Often they are whole chapters long, and are entirely unlike the way in which Jesus is portrayed as speaking in the other three gospels. The Fourth Gospel, as we have seen, was written about the year AD 100, that is, about seventy years after the crucifixion. Is it possible after these seventy years to look on these speeches as word-for-word reports of what Jesus said? Or can we explain them in some way that is perhaps even greater than that? We must begin by holding in our minds the fact of the speeches and the question which they inevitably raise.

And we have something to add to that. It so happens that in the writings of the early Church we have a whole series of accounts of the way in which the Fourth Gospel came to be written. The earliest is that of Irenaeus, who was bishop of Lyons about AD 177; and Irenaeus was himself a pupil of the Bishop of Smyrna, Polycarp, who in turn had actually been a pupil of John. There is therefore a direct link between Irenaeus and John. Irenaeus writes:

> John, the disciple of the Lord, who also leant upon his
> breast, himself also *published* the gospel in Ephesus,
> when he was living in Asia.

The suggestive thing there is that Irenaeus does not merely
say that John *wrote* the gospel; he says that John *published*
(*exedōke*) it in Ephesus. The word that Irenaeus uses makes
it sound not like the private publication of some personal
memoir but like the public issue of some almost official
document.

The next account is that of Clement, who was head of the
great school of Alexandria about AD 230. He writes:

> Last of all, John perceiving that the bodily facts had
> been made plain in the gospel, *being urged by his
> friends*, composed a spiritual gospel.

The important thing here is the phrase *being urged by his
friends*. It begins to become clear that the Fourth Gospel is
far more than one man's personal production and that there is
a group, a community, a church behind it. On the same lines,
a tenth-century manuscript called the *Codex Toletanus*, which
prefaces the New Testament books with short descriptions,
prefaces the Fourth Gospel thus:

> The apostle John, whom the Lord Jesus loved most,
> last of all wrote this gospel, *at the request of the bishops
> of Asia*, against Cerinthus and other heretics.

Again we have the idea that behind the Fourth Gospel there
is the authority of a group and of a church.

We now turn to a very important document, known as the
Muratorian Canon. It is so called after a scholar Muratori
who discovered it. It is the first list of New Testament books
which the Church ever issued and was compiled in Rome
about AD 170. Not only does it list the New Testament books,

it also gives short accounts of the origin and nature and contents of each of them. Its account of the way in which the Fourth Gospel came to be written is extremely important and illuminating.

> At the request of his fellow-disciples and of his bishops, John, one of the disciples, said: 'Fast with me for three days from this time and whatsoever shall be revealed to each of us, whether it be favourable to my writing or not, let us relate it to one another.' On the same night it was revealed to Andrew that John should relate all things, *aided by the revision of all*.

We cannot accept all that statement, because it is not possible that Andrew, the apostle, was in Ephesus in AD 100; but the point is that it is stated as clearly as possible that, while the authority and the mind and the memory behind the Fourth Gospel are that of John, it is clearly and definitely the product, not of one man, but of a group and a community.

Now we can see something of what happened. About the year AD 100 there was a group living in Ephesus whose leader was John. They revered him as a saint and they loved him as a father. He must have been almost 100 years old. Before he died, they thought most wisely that it would be a great thing if the aged apostle set down his memories of the years when he had been with Jesus. But in the end they did far more than that. We can think of them sitting down and reliving the old days. One would say: 'Do you remember how Jesus said . . . ?' And John would say: 'Yes, and now we know that he meant . . .'

In other words, this group was not only writing down what Jesus *said*; that would have been a mere feat of memory. They were writing down what Jesus *meant*; that was the guidance of the Holy Spirit. John had thought about every word that Jesus had said; and he had thought under the guidance of the Holy Spirit who was so real to him. Professor W. M. Macgregor of Trinity College, Glasgow, had a sermon entitled: 'What Jesus becomes to a man who has known him long.' That is a perfect description of the Jesus of the Fourth Gospel. A. H. N. Green Armytage puts the point perfectly in his book *John Who Saw*. Mark, he says, suits the *missionary* with his clear-cut account of the facts of Jesus' life; Matthew suits the *teacher* with his systematic account of the teaching of Jesus; Luke suits the *parish minister or priest* with his wide sympathy and his picture of Jesus as the friend of all; but John is the gospel of the *contemplative*.

He goes on to speak of the apparent contrast between Mark and John. 'The two gospels are in a sense the same gospel. Only, where Mark saw things plainly, bluntly, literally, John saw them subtly, profoundly, spiritually. We might say that John lit Mark's pages by the lantern of a lifetime's meditation.' In his *Lyrical Ballads*, William Wordsworth defined poetry as 'Emotion recollected in tranquillity'. That is a perfect description of the Fourth Gospel. That is why John is unquestionably the greatest of all the gospels. Its aim is not to give us what Jesus said, like a newspaper report, but to give us what Jesus meant. In it, the risen Christ still speaks. John is not so much The Gospel according to St John; it is rather *The Gospel according to the Holy Spirit*. It was not John of Ephesus who wrote the Fourth Gospel; it was the Holy Spirit who wrote it through John.

The Writer of the Gospel

We have one question still to ask. We can be quite sure that the mind and the memory behind the Fourth Gospel is that of

John the apostle; but we have also seen that behind it is a witness who was the writer, in the sense that he was the one who actually wrote it all down. Can we find out who he was? We know from what the early Church writers tell us that there were actually two Johns in Ephesus at the same time. There was John the apostle; but there was another John, who was known as John the elder.

Papias, who loved to collect all that he could find about the history of the New Testament and the story of Jesus, gives us some very interesting information. He was Bishop of Hierapolis, which is quite near Ephesus, and his dates are from about AD 70 to about AD 145. That is to say, he was actually a contemporary of John. He writes how he tried to find out 'what Andrew said or what Peter said, or what was said by Philip, by Thomas, or by James, or by John, or by Matthew, or by any other of the disciples of the Lord; and what things Aristion and *the elder John*, the disciples of the Lord, say'. In Ephesus there was the *apostle* John and the *elder* John; and the elder John was so well-loved a figure that he was actually known as *The Elder*. He clearly had a unique place in the Church. Both Eusebius and Dionysius the Great tell us that even in their own days in Ephesus there were two famous tombs, the one of John the apostle and the other of John the elder.

Now let us turn to the two little letters, 2 John and 3 John. The *letters* come from the same hand as the gospel, and how do they begin? The *Second* Letter begins: 'The elder to the elect lady and her children' (2 John 1). The *Third* Letter begins: 'The elder to the beloved Gaius' (3 John 1). Here we have our solution. The one who actually penned the letters was John the elder; the mind and memory behind them was the aged John the apostle, the master whom John the elder always described as 'the disciple whom Jesus loved'.

The Precious Gospel

The more we know about the Fourth Gospel, the more precious it becomes. For seventy years, John had thought of Jesus. Day by day, the Holy Spirit had opened out to him the meaning of what Jesus said. So when John was near the century of life and his days were numbered, he and his friends sat down to remember. John the elder held the pen to write for his master, John the apostle; and the last of the apostles set down not only what he had heard Jesus say but also what he now knew Jesus had meant. He remembered how Jesus had said: 'I still have many things to say to you, but you cannot bear them now. When the Spirit of truth comes, he will guide you into all the truth' (John 16:12–13). There were many things which seventy years ago he had not understood; there were many things which in these seventy years the Spirit of truth had revealed to him. These things John set down even as the eternal glory was dawning upon him. When we read this gospel, let us remember that we are reading the gospel which of all the gospels is most the work of the Holy Spirit, speaking to us of the things which Jesus meant, speaking through the mind and memory of John the apostle and by the pen of John the elder. Behind this gospel is the whole church at Ephesus, the whole company of the saints, the last of the apostles, the Holy Spirit and the risen Christ himself.

JOHN

THE WORD

John 1:1–18

When the world had its beginning, the Word was already there; and the Word was with God; and the Word was God. This Word was in the beginning with God. He was the agent through whom all things were made; and there is not a single thing which exists in this world which came into being without him. In him was life and the life was the light of men; and the light shines in the darkness, and the darkness did not put it out. There emerged a man sent from God whose name was John. He came as a witness, in order to bear witness to the light, that through him all might believe. He himself was not the light; his function was to bear witness to the light. He was the real light, who, in his coming into the world, gives light to every man. He was in the world, and, although the world came into being through him, the world did not recognize him. It was into his own home that he came, and his own people did not welcome him. To all those who did receive him, to those who believe in his name, he gave the right to become the children of God. These were born not of blood, nor of any human impulse, nor of any man's will, but their birth was of God. So the Word of God became a person, and took up his abode in our being, full of grace and truth; and we

looked with our own eyes upon his glory, glory like the
glory which an only son receives from a father. John
was his witness and his statement still sounds out: 'This
is he of whom I said to you, he who comes after me has
been advanced before me, because he was before me.'
On his fullness we all of us have drawn, and from him
we have received grace upon grace, for it was the law
which was given by Moses, but grace and truth came
through Jesus Christ. No one has ever seen God. It is the
unique one, he who is God, he who is in the bosom of
the Father, who has told us all about God.

WE shall go on to study this passage in short sections and in
detail; but, before we do so, we must try to understand what
John was seeking to say when he described Jesus as *the Word*.

THE WORD BECAME FLESH

THE first chapter of the Fourth Gospel is one of the greatest
adventures of religious thought ever achieved.

It was not long before the Christian Church was confronted
with a very basic problem. It had begun in Judaism. In the
beginning, all its members had been Jews. By human descent
Jesus was a Jew; and, to all intents and purposes, except for
brief visits to the districts of Tyre and Sidon, and to the
Decapolis, he was never outside Palestine. Christianity began
among the Jews; and therefore inevitably it spoke in the
Jewish language and used Jewish categories of thought.

But although it was cradled in Judaism it very soon went
out into the wider world. Within thirty years of Jesus' death
it had travelled all over Asia Minor and Greece and had
arrived in Rome. By AD 60 there must have been 100,000
Greeks in the Church for every Jew who was a Christian.
Jewish ideas were completely strange to the Greeks. To take

but one outstanding example, the Greeks had never heard of
the Messiah. The very centre of Jewish expectation, the
coming of the Messiah, was an idea that was quite alien to the
Greeks. The very category in which the Jewish Christians
conceived and presented Jesus meant nothing to them. Here
then was the problem – how was Christianity to be presented
to the Greek world?

William Lecky, the nineteenth-century historian, once
said that the progress and spread of any idea depends not only
on its strength and force but on the predisposition to receive it
of the age to which that idea is presented. The task of the
Christian Church was to create in the Greek world a predisposition to receive the Christian message. As E. J. Goodspeed
put it, the question was: 'Must a Greek who was interested in
Christianity be routed through Jewish Messianic ideas and
through Jewish ways of thinking, or could some new approach
be found which would speak out of his background to his mind
and heart?' The problem was how to present Christianity in
such a way that it would be understandable to Greeks.

Round about the year AD 100, there was a man in Ephesus
who was fascinated by that problem. His name was John. He
lived in a Greek city. He dealt with Greeks to whom Jewish
ideas were strange and unintelligible and even uncouth.
How could he find a way to present Christianity to these
Greeks in a way that they would welcome and understand?
Suddenly the solution flashed upon him. In both Greek and
Jewish thought, there existed the conception of *the word*.
Here was something which could be worked out to meet the
double world of Greek and Jew. Here was something which
belonged to the heritage of both races and that both could
understand.

Let us then begin by looking at the two backgrounds of
the conception of *the word*.

The Jewish Background

In the Jewish background, four strands contributed something to the idea of the word.

(1) To Jews, a word was far more than a mere sound; it was something which had an independent existence and which actually did things. As Professor John Paterson, in his book *The Goodly Fellowship of the Prophets*, has put it: 'The spoken word to the Hebrew was fearfully alive . . . It was a unit of energy charged with power. It flies like a bullet to its billet.' For that very reason, the Hebrew language was sparing of words. Hebrew speech has fewer than 10,000; Greek speech has 200,000.

One poet tells how a certain man who had performed a heroic act found it impossible to tell it to his fellow tribesmen for lack of words – whereupon there arose another 'afflicted with the necessary magic of words', and he told the story in terms so vivid and so moving that 'the words became alive and walked up and down in the hearts of his hearers'. The words of the poet became a power. History has many an example of that kind of thing.

When John Knox preached in the days of the Reformation in Scotland, it was said that the voice of that one man put more courage into the hearts of his hearers than 10,000 trumpets braying in their ears. His words did things to people. In the days of the French Revolution, Rouget de Lisle wrote the 'Marseillaise', and that song sent men marching to revolution. The words did things. In the days of the Second World War, when Britain was bereft alike of allies and of weapons, the words of the Prime Minister, Sir Winston Churchill, as he broadcast to the nation, did things to people.

It was even more so in the middle east, and still is. To the people of this region, a word is not merely a sound; it is a power which does things. Once when the biblical scholar Sir George Adam Smith was travelling in the desert, a group of Muslims gave his party the customary greeting: 'Peace be upon you.' At first they failed to notice that he was a Christian. When they discovered that they had spoken a blessing to an infidel, they hurried back to ask for the blessing back again. The word was like a thing which could be sent out to do things and which could be brought back again. In 'The First Settler's Story', Will Carleton, the poet, expresses something like that:

> Boys flying kites haul in their white-winged birds;
> You can't do that way when you're flying words:
> 'Careful with fire,' is good advice we know,
> 'Careful with words,' is ten times doubly so.
> Thoughts unexpressed may sometimes fall back dead,
> But God himself can't kill them when they're said.

We can well understand how to the people of the middle east words had an independent, power-filled existence.

(2) The Old Testament is full of that general idea of the power of words. Once Isaac had been deceived into blessing Jacob instead of Esau, nothing he could do could take that word of blessing back again (Genesis 27). The word had gone out and had begun to act, and nothing could stop it. In particular, we see the word of God in action in the creation story. At every stage of it, we read: 'And God said . . .' (Genesis 1:3, 6, 11). The word of God is the creating power. Again and again we get this idea of the creative, acting, dynamic word of God. 'By the word of the Lord the heavens were made' (Psalm 33:6). 'He sent out his word and healed them' (Psalm 107:20). 'He sends out his command to the earth; his word runs swiftly' (Psalm 147:15). 'So shall my word be that goes out from my mouth; it shall not return to

me empty, but it shall accomplish that which I purpose, and succeed in the thing for which I sent it' (Isaiah 55:11). 'Is not my word like fire, says the Lord, and like a hammer that breaks a rock in pieces?' (Jeremiah 23:29). 'You spoke at the beginning of creation, and said on the first day, "Let heaven and earth be made," and your word accomplished the work' (4 Ezra [2 Esdras] 6:38). The writer of the Book of Wisdom addresses God as the one 'who have made all things by your word' (Wisdom 9:1). Everywhere in the Old Testament there is this idea of the powerful, creative word. Even human words have a kind of dynamic activity; how much more must it be so with God?

(3) There came into Hebrew religious life something which greatly accentuated the development of this idea of the word of God. For 100 years and more before the coming of Jesus, Hebrew was a forgotten language. The Old Testament was written in Hebrew, but the Jews no longer knew the language. The scholars knew it, but not the ordinary people. They spoke a development of Hebrew called Aramaic, which relates to Hebrew rather as modern English relates to Anglo-Saxon. Since that was so, the Scriptures of the Old Testament had to be translated into this language that the people could understand, and these translations were called the *Targums*. In the synagogue, the Scriptures were read in the original Hebrew, but then they were translated into Aramaic, and Targums were used as translations.

The Targums were produced in a time when people were fascinated by the transcendence of God and could think of nothing but the distance and the difference of God. Because of that, those who made the Targums were very much afraid of attributing human thoughts and feelings and actions to God. To put it in technical language, they made every effort to avoid *anthropomorphism* in speaking of him.

Now the Old Testament regularly speaks of God in a human way; and wherever they met a thing like that, the Targums substituted *the word of God* for the name of God. Let us see how this custom worked. In Exodus 19:17, we read that 'Moses brought the people out of the camp *to meet God*.' The Targums thought that was too human a way to speak of God, so they said that Moses brought the people out of the camp to meet *the word of God*. In Exodus 31:13, we read that God said to the people that the Sabbath 'is a sign between me and you throughout your generations'. That was far too human a way to speak for the Targums, and so they said that the Sabbath is a sign 'between *my word* and you'. Deuteronomy 9:3 says that God is a consuming fire, but the Targums translated it that *the word* of God is a consuming fire. Isaiah 48:13 has a great picture of creation: 'My hand laid the foundation of the earth, and my right hand spread out the heavens.' That was much too human a picture of God for the Targums, and they made God say: 'By *my word* I have founded the earth; and by my strength I have hung up the heavens.' Even so wonderful a passage as Deuteronomy 33:27 which in the Authorized and Revised Standard Versions speaks of God's 'everlasting arms' was changed, and became: 'The eternal God is thy refuge, and by his word the world was created.'

In the Jonathan Targum, the phrase *the word of God* occurs no fewer than about 320 times. It is quite true that it is simply a roundabout way of referring to the name of God; but the fact remains that *the word of God* became one of the commonest forms of Jewish expression. It was a phrase which any devout Jew would recognize because he heard it so often in the synagogue when Scripture was read. Every Jew was used to speaking of *the Memra*, *the word* of God.

(4) At this stage, we must look more fully at something we already began to look at in the introduction. The Greek

term for *word* is *Logos*; but *Logos* does not only mean *word*;
it also means *reason*. For John, and for all the great thinkers
who made use of this idea, these two meanings were always
closely intertwined. Whenever they used *Logos*, the twin ideas
of the word of God and the reason of God were in their minds.

The Jews had a type of literature called *The Wisdom
Literature* which was the concentrated wisdom of sages. It is
not usually speculative and philosophical, but practical
wisdom for the living and management of life. In the Old
Testament, the great example of Wisdom Literature is the
Book of Proverbs. In this book, there are certain passages
which give a mysterious life-giving and eternal power to
Wisdom (*Sophia*). In these passages Wisdom has been, as it
were, personified, and is thought of as the eternal agent and
co-worker of God. There are three main passages.

The first is Proverbs 3:13–26. Out of that passage we may
specially note:

> She is a tree of *life* to those who lay hold of her; those
> who hold her fast are called happy. *The Lord by wisdom*
> founded the earth; by understanding he established the
> heavens; by his knowledge the deeps broke open, and
> the clouds drop down the dew. (Proverbs 3:18–20)

We remember that *Logos* means *word* and also means *reason*.
We have already seen how the Jews thought of the powerful
and creative word of God. Here we see the other side
beginning to emerge. *Wisdom* is God's agent in enlightenment
and in creation; and *wisdom* and *reason* are very much the
same thing. We have seen how important *Logos* was in the
sense of *word*; now we see it beginning to be important in the
sense of *wisdom* or *reason*.

The second important passage is Proverbs 4:5–13. In it we
may notice:

> Keep hold of instruction; do not let go; guard her, for
> she is your life.

The *word* and *wisdom* are both seen as the *light of life* for
all people. The two ideas are amalgamating with each other
rapidly now.

The most important passage of all is Proverbs 8:1–9:2. In
it we may specially note:

> The Lord created me [Wisdom is speaking] at the
> beginning of his work, the first of his acts of long ago.
> Ages ago I was set up, at the first, before the beginning
> of the earth. When there were no depths I was brought
> forth, when there were no springs abounding with water.
> Before the mountains had been shaped, before the hills,
> I was brought forth – when he had not yet made earth
> and fields, or the world's first bits of soil. When he
> established the heavens, I was there, when he drew a
> circle on the face of the deep, when he made firm the
> skies above, when he established the fountains of the
> deep, when he assigned to the sea its limit, so that the
> waters might not transgress his command, when he
> marked out the foundations of the earth, then I was
> beside him, like a master worker; and I was daily his
> delight, rejoicing before him always. (Proverbs 8:22–
> 30)

When we read that passage, there is echo after echo of what
John says of the *word* in the first chapter of his gospel. *Wisdom*
had that eternal existence, that light-giving function, that
creative power which John attributed to the *word*, the *Logos*,
with which he identified Jesus Christ.

The development of this idea of *wisdom* did not stop here.
Between the Old and the New Testament, this kind of writing
called Wisdom Literature continued to be produced. It had so
much concentrated wisdom in it and drew so much from the

experience of the wise that it was a priceless guide for life. In particular, two very great books were written, which are included in the *Apocrypha* and which it will do anyone's soul good to read.

(a) The first is called 'The Wisdom of Jesus, the son of Sirach', or, as it is better known, Ecclesiasticus. It too makes much of this great conception of the creative and eternal wisdom of God.

> The sand of the sea, the drops of rain,
> and the days of eternity – who can count them?
> The height of heaven, the breadth of the earth,
> the abyss, and wisdom – who can search them out?
> *Wisdom was created before all other things,*
> and prudent understanding from eternity.
>
> (Ecclesiasticus 1:2–4)

> I came forth from the mouth of the Most High,
> and covered the earth like a mist.
> I dwelt in the highest heavens,
> and my throne was in a pillar of cloud.
> Alone I compassed the vault of heaven,
> and traversed the depths of the abyss.
>
> (Ecclesiasticus 24:3–5)

> Before the ages, in the beginning, he created me,
> and for all the ages I shall not cease to be.
>
> (Ecclesiasticus 24:9)

Here again we find wisdom as the eternal, creative power which was at God's side in the days of creation and the beginning of time.

(b) Ecclesiasticus was written in Palestine about the year 100 BC; and at almost the same time an equally great book was written in Alexandria in Egypt, called The Wisdom of Solomon. In it there is the greatest of all pictures of *wisdom*. *Wisdom* is the treasure which may be used to become the friend of God (7:14). *Wisdom* is personified as the creator of all things (7:22). She is the breath of the power of God and a pure stream flowing from the Almighty (7:25). She can do all things, and she makes all things new (7:27).

But the writer does more than talk about *wisdom*; he equates *wisdom* and the *word*. To him, the two ideas are the same. He can talk of the *wisdom of God* and the *word of God* in the same sentence and with the same meaning. When he prays to God, his address is:

> O God of my ancestors, and Lord of mercy, who have made all things by *your word*, and by *your wisdom* have formed humankind.
>
> (Wisdom 9:2)

He can speak of *the word* almost as John was to speak:

> For while gentle silence enveloped all things, and night in its swift course was now half gone, your all-powerful word leaped from heaven, from the royal throne, into the midst of the land that was doomed, a stern warrior carrying the sharp sword of your authentic command, and stood and filled all things with death, and touched the heaven while standing on the earth.
>
> (Wisdom 18:14–16)

To the writer of the Book of Wisdom, *wisdom* was God's eternal, creative, illuminating power; *wisdom* and *the word* were one and the same. It was *wisdom* and *the word* who were God's instruments and agents in creation and who continually bring the will of God to the minds and hearts of men and women.

So when John was searching for a way in which he could commend Christianity, he found in his own faith and in the record of his own people the idea of *the word*, the ordinary word which is in itself not merely a sound but a dynamic thing, the *word* of God by which God created the world, the *word* of the Targums which expressed the very idea of the action of God, the *wisdom* of the Wisdom Literature which was the eternal creative and illuminating power of God. So John said: 'If you wish to see that *word* of God, if you wish to see the creative power of God, if you wish to see that *word* which brought the world into existence and which gives light and life to everyone, *look at Jesus Christ*. In him the *word* of God came among you.'

The Greek Background

We began by seeing that John's problem was not that of presenting Christianity to the Jewish world, but of presenting it to the Greek world. How then did this idea of the *word* fit into Greek thought? It was already there waiting to be used. In Greek thought, the idea of the *word* began way back about 560 BC, and, strangely enough, in Ephesus where the Fourth Gospel was written.

In 560 BC, there was an Ephesian philosopher called Heraclitus whose basic idea was that everything is in a state of flux. Everything was changing from day to day and from moment to moment. His famous illustration was that it was impossible to step twice into the same river. You step into a river; you step out; you step in again; but you do not step into the same river, for the water has flowed on and it is a different river. To Heraclitus, everything was like that, everything was in a constantly changing state of flux. But if that is the case, why is life not complete chaos? How can there be any sense in a world where there is constant flux and change?

The answer of Heraclitus was: all this change and flux was not haphazard; it was controlled and ordered, following a continuous pattern all the time; and that which controlled the pattern was the *Logos*, the *word*, the *reason* of God. To Heraclitus, the *Logos* was the principle of order under which the universe continued to exist. Heraclitus went further. He held that not only was there a pattern in the physical world; there was also a pattern in the world of events. He held that nothing moved with aimless feet; in all life and in all the events of life there was a purpose, a plan and a design. And what was it that controlled events? Once again, the answer was *Logos*.

Heraclitus took the matter even nearer home. What was it that in us individually told us the difference between right and wrong? What made us able to think and to reason? What enabled us to choose aright and to recognize the truth when we saw it? Once again, Heraclitus gave the same answer. What gave to men and women reason and knowledge of the truth and the ability to judge between right and wrong was the *Logos* of God dwelling within them. Heraclitus held that in the world of nature and events 'all things happen according to the *Logos*', and that in the individual 'the *Logos* is the judge of truth'. The *Logos* was nothing less than the mind of God controlling the world and everyone in it.

Once the Greeks had discovered this idea, they never let it go. It fascinated them, especially the Stoics. The Stoics were always left in wondering amazement at the order of the world. Order always implies a mind. The Stoics asked: 'What keeps the stars in their courses? What makes the tides ebb and flow? What makes day and night come in unalterable order? What brings the seasons round at their appointed times?' And they answered: 'All things are controlled by the *Logos* of God.' The *Logos* is the power which puts sense into the world, the power which makes the world an order instead of a chaos, the power which set the world going and keeps it going in its perfect order. 'The *Logos*', said the Stoics, 'pervades all things.'

There is still another name in the Greek world at which we must look. In Alexandria, there was a Jew called Philo who had made it the business of his life to study the wisdom of two worlds, the Jewish and the Greek. No one ever knew the Jewish Scriptures as he knew them; and no Jew ever knew the greatness of Greek thought as he knew it. He too knew and used and loved this idea of the *Logos*, the *word*, the *reason* of God. He held that the *Logos* was the oldest thing in the world and the instrument through which God had made the world. He said that the *Logos* was the thought of God stamped upon the universe; he talked about the *Logos* by which God made the world and all things; he said that God, the pilot of the universe, held the *Logos* as a tiller and with it steered all things. He said that the human mind was stamped also with the *Logos*, that the *Logos* was what gave people reason, the power to think and the power to know. He said that the *Logos* was the intermediary between the world and God and that the *Logos* was the priest who set the soul before God.

Greek thought knew all about the *Logos*; it saw in the *Logos* the creating and guiding and directing power of God, the power which made the universe and kept it going. So John came to the Greeks and said: 'For centuries you have been thinking and writing and dreaming about the *Logos*, the power which made the world, the power which keeps the order of the world, the power by which we all think and reason and know, the power by which we come into contact with God. Jesus is that *Logos* come down to earth.' 'The word', said John, 'became flesh.' We could put it another way – 'The mind of God became a person.'

Both Jew and Greek

Slowly the Jews and Greeks had thought their way to the conception of the *Logos*, the mind of God which made the world and makes sense of it. So John went out to Jews and Greeks to tell them that in Jesus Christ this creating, illuminating, controlling, sustaining mind of God had come to earth. He came to tell them that men and women need no longer guess and grope; all that they had to do was to look at Jesus and see the mind of God.

THE ETERNAL WORD

John 1:1–2

> When the world had its beginning, the Word was already there; and the Word was with God; and the Word was God. This Word was in the beginning with God.

THE beginning of John's gospel is of such importance and of such depth of meaning that we must study it almost verse by verse. It is John's great thought that Jesus is none other than God's creative and life-giving and light-giving word, that Jesus is the power of God which created the world and the reason of God which sustains the world come to earth in human and bodily form.

Here at the beginning, John says three things about the word, which is to say that he says three things about Jesus.

(1) The word was already there at the very beginning of things. John's thought is going back to the first verse of the Bible: 'In the beginning when God created the heavens and the earth' (Genesis 1:1). What John is saying is this – the word is not one of the created things; the word was there *before creation*; the word is not part of the world which came

43

into being in time; the word is part of eternity and was there with God before time and the world began. John was thinking of what is known as *the pre-existence of Christ*.

In many ways, this idea of pre-existence is very difficult, if not altogether impossible, to grasp. But it does mean one very simple, very practical and very tremendous thing. If the word was with God before time began, if God's word is part of the eternal scheme of things, it means that *God was always like Jesus*. Sometimes we tend to think of God as stern and avenging; and we tend to think that something Jesus did changed God's anger into love and altered his attitude to human beings. The New Testament knows nothing of that idea. The whole New Testament tells us, this passage of John especially, that God has always been like Jesus. What Jesus did was to open a window in time that we might see the eternal and unchanging love of God.

We may well ask, 'What then about some of the things that we read in the Old Testament? What about the passages which speak about commandments of God to wipe out whole cities and to destroy men, women and children? What of the anger and the destructiveness and the jealousy of God that we sometimes read of in the older parts of Scripture?' The answer is this – it is not God who has changed; it is our knowledge of him that has changed. These things were written because people did not know any better; that was the stage which their knowledge of God had reached.

When children are learning any subject, they have to learn it stage by stage. They do not begin with full knowledge; they begin with what they can grasp and go on to more and more. When we begin music appreciation, we do not start with a Bach Prelude and Fugue; we start with something much more simple, and progress through stage after stage as our knowledge grows. It was that way with human beings and God. They could only grasp and understand God's nature and his ways in part. It was only when Jesus came that they saw fully and completely what God has *always* been like.

It is told that a little girl was once confronted with some of the more bloodthirsty and savage parts of the Old Testament. Her comment was: 'But that happened before God became a Christian!' If we may so put it with all reverence, when John says that the word was always there, he is saying that God was always a Christian. He is telling us that God was and is and ever shall be like Jesus; but that could not be known or realized until Jesus came.

(2) John goes on to say that *the word was with God*. What does he mean by that? He means that there has always been the closest connection between the word and God. Let us put that in another and a simpler way – there has always been the most intimate connection between Jesus and God. That means no one can tell us what God is like, what God's will is for us, what God's love and heart and mind are like, as Jesus can.

Let us take a simple human analogy. If we want to know what someone really thinks and feels about something, and if we are unable to approach the person ourselves, we do not go to a mere acquaintance who has known that person only a short time; we go to someone whom we know to be an intimate friend of many years' standing. We know that the friend will really be able to interpret the mind and the heart of the other person to us.

It is something like that that John is saying about Jesus. He is saying that Jesus has always been with God. Let us use very human language because it is the only language we can use. John is saying that Jesus is so intimate with God that God has no secrets from him; and that, therefore, Jesus is the

45

one person in all the universe who can reveal to us what God is like and how God feels towards us.

(3) Finally, John says that *the word was God*. This is a difficult saying for us to understand, and it is difficult because Greek, in which John wrote, had a different way of saying things from the way in which English expresses them. When Greek uses a noun, it almost always uses the definite article with it. The Greek for God is *theos* and the definite article is *ho*. When Greek speaks about God, it does not simply say *theos*; it says *ho theos*. Now when Greek does not use the definite article with a noun, that noun becomes much more like an adjective. John did not say that the word was *ho theos*; that would have been to say that the word was *identical* with God. He said that the word was *theos* – without the definite article – which means that the word was, we might say, of the very same character and quality and essence and being as God. When John said *the word was God*, he was not saying that Jesus was identical with God; he was saying that Jesus was so perfectly the same as God in mind, in heart and in being that in him we perfectly see what God is like.

So, right at the beginning of his gospel, John lays it down that in Jesus, and in him alone, there is perfectly revealed all that God always was and always will be, and all that he feels towards and desires for men and women.

THE CREATOR OF ALL THINGS

John 1:3

> He was the agent through whom all things were made; and there is not a single thing which exists in this world which came into being without him.

IT may seem strange to us that John so stresses the way in
which the world was created; and it may seem strange that he
so definitely connects Jesus with the work of creation. But he
had to do this because of a certain tendency in the thought of
his day.

In the time of John, there was a kind of heresy called
Gnosticism. Its characteristic was that it was an intellectual
and philosophical approach to Christianity. To the Gnostics,
the simple beliefs of the ordinary Christian were not enough.
They tried to construct a philosophic system out of
Christianity. They were troubled about the existence of sin
and evil and sorrow and suffering in this world, so they
worked out a theory to explain it. The theory was this.

In the beginning, two things existed – the one was God
and the other was matter. Matter was always there and was
the raw material out of which the world was made. The
Gnostics held that this original matter was flawed and
imperfect. We might put it that the world got off to a bad
start. It was made of material which had the seeds of
corruption in it.

The Gnostics went further. God, they said, is pure spirit,
and pure spirit can never touch matter at all, still less matter
which is imperfect. Therefore it was not possible for God to
carry out the work of creation himself. So he put out from
himself a series of emanations. Each emanation was further
and further away from God; and, as the emanations got further
and further away from him, they knew less and less about
him. About half-way down the series, there was an emanation
which knew nothing at all about God. Beyond that stage, the
emanations began to be not only ignorant of but actually
hostile to God. Finally in the series, there was an emanation
which was so distant from God that it was totally ignorant of
him and totally hostile to him – and that emanation was the

47

power which created the world, because it was so distant from God that it was possible for it to touch this flawed and evil matter. The creator god was utterly divorced from and utterly at enmity with the real God.

The Gnostics took one step further. They identified the creator god with the God of the Old Testament; and they held that the God of the Old Testament was quite different from, quite ignorant of and quite hostile to the God and Father of Jesus Christ.

In the time of John, this kind of belief was widespread. It was believed that the world was evil and that an evil God had created it. It is to combat this teaching that John here lays down two basic Christian truths. In point of fact, the connection of Jesus with creation is repeatedly laid down in the New Testament, just because of this background of thought which divorced God from the world in which we live. In Colossians 1:16, Paul writes: 'For in him all things in heaven and on earth were created . . . all things have been created through him and for him.' In 1 Corinthians 8:6, he writes of the Lord Jesus Christ 'through whom are all things'. The writer to the Hebrews speaks of the one who was the Son, 'through whom he also created the worlds' (Hebrews 1:2). John and the other New Testament writers who spoke like this were stressing two great truths.

(1) Christianity has always believed in what is called *creation out of nothing*. We do not believe that in his creation of the world God had to work with alien and evil matter. We do not believe that the world began with an essential flaw in it. We do not believe that the world began with God and something else. It is our belief that behind everything there is God and God alone.

(2) Christianity has always believed that this is *God's world*. So far from being so detached from the world that he

could have nothing to do with it, God is intimately involved in it. The Gnostics tried to put the blame for the evil of the world on the shoulders of its creator. Christianity believes that what is wrong with the world is due to human sin. But even though sin has injured the world and kept it from being what it might have been, we can never despise the world, because it is essentially God's. If we believe this, it gives us a new sense of the value of the world and a new sense of responsibility to it.

There is a story of a child from the back streets of a great city who was taken for a day in the country. When she saw the bluebells in the woods, she asked: 'Do you think God would mind if I picked some of his flowers?' This is God's world; because of that, nothing is out of his control; and because of that, we must use all things in the awareness that they belong to God. Christians do not belittle the world by thinking that it was created by an ignorant and hostile god; they glorify it by remembering that everywhere God is behind it and in it. They believe that the Christ who re-creates the world was the co-worker of God when the world was first created, and that, in the act of redemption, God is seeking to win back that which was always his own.

LIFE AND LIGHT

John 1:4

In him was life and the life was the light of men.

IN a great piece of music, the composer often begins by stating the themes which he or she is going to elaborate in the course of the work. That is what John does here. *Life* and *light* are two of the great basic words on which the Fourth Gospel is built up. They are two of the main themes which it is the aim of the gospel to develop and to expound. Let us look at them in detail.

The Fourth Gospel begins and ends with *life*. At the very beginning, we read that in Jesus was *life*; and at the very end we read that John's aim in writing the gospel was that everyone might 'believe that Jesus is the Messiah, the Son of God, and that through believing you may have *life* in his name' (John 20:31). The word is continually on the lips of Jesus. It is his wistful regret that people will not come to him that they might have *life* (5:40). It is his claim that he came that men and women might have *life* and that they might have it abundantly (10:10). He claims that he gives people *life* and that they will never perish because no one will snatch them out of his hand (10:28). He claims that he is the way, the truth and the *life* (14:6). In this gospel, the word *life* (*zōē*) occurs more than thirty-five times and the verb *to live* or *to have life* (*zēn*) more than fifteen times. What then does John mean by *life*?

(1) Quite simply, he means that *life* is the opposite of destruction, condemnation and death. God sent his Son that everyone who believes should not perish but have eternal *life* (3:16). Anyone who hears and believes has eternal *life* and will not come into judgment (5:24). There is a contrast between the resurrection to *life* and the resurrection to *judgment* (5:29). Those to whom Jesus gives *life* will never perish (10:28). There is in Jesus that which gives security in this life and in the life to come. Until we accept Jesus and take him as our Saviour and enthrone him as our King, we cannot be said to live at all. Those who live Christless lives *exist*, but they do not know what *life* is. Jesus is the one person who can make life worth living, and in whose company death is only the prelude to fuller life.

(2) But John is quite sure that, although Jesus is the bringer of this *life*, the giver of life is God. Again and again, John uses the phrase *the living God*, as indeed the whole Bible does. It is the will of the Father who sent Jesus that everyone who sees him and believes in him should have life (6:40). Jesus is the giver of life because the Father has set his own seal of approval upon him (6:27). He gives life to as many as God has given him (17:2). At the back of it all, there is God. It is as if God was saying: 'I created human beings that they should have real life; through their sin they have ceased to live and only exist; I have sent them my Son to enable them to know what real life is.'

(3) We must ask what this life is. Again and again, the Fourth Gospel uses the phrase *eternal life*. We shall discuss the full meaning of that phrase later. At present, we note this. The word John uses for *eternal* is *aiōnios*. Clearly, whatever else *eternal* life is, it is not simply life which lasts forever. A life which lasted forever could be a terrible curse; often the thing for which many people long is release from life. In eternal life, there must be more than *duration* of life; there must be a certain *quality* of life.

Life is not desirable unless it is a certain kind of life. Here we have the clue. *Aiōnios* is the adjective which is repeatedly used to describe God. In the true sense of the word, *only* God is *aiōnios*, *eternal*; therefore *eternal life is that life which God lives*. What Jesus offers us from God is God's own life. Eternal life is life which knows something of the serenity and power of the life of God himself. When Jesus came offering men and women *eternal life*, he was inviting them to enter into the very life of God.

(4) How, then, do we enter into that life? We enter into it *by believing in Jesus Christ*. The word *to believe* (*pisteuein*) occurs in the Fourth Gospel no fewer than seventy times.

'Whoever believes in the Son has eternal life' (3:36). 'Whoever believes', says Jesus, 'has eternal life' (6:47). It is God's will that those who see the Son should believe in him and have eternal life (5:24). What does John mean by *to believe*? He means two things.

(a) He means that we must be convinced that Jesus is really and truly the Son of God. He means that we must make up our minds about him. After all, if Jesus is only a man, there is no reason why we should give him the utter and implicit obedience that he demands. We have to think out for ourselves who he was. We have to look at him, learn about him, study him and think about him until we are driven to the conclusion that this is none other than the Son of God.

(b) But there is more than intellectual belief in this. To believe in Jesus means to take Jesus at his word, to accept his commandments as absolutely binding, to believe without question that what he says is true.

For John, belief means the conviction of the mind that Jesus is the Son of God, the trust of the heart that everything he says is true and the basing of every action on the unshakable assurance that we must take him at his word. When we do that, we stop existing and begin living. We know what *Life* with a capital L really means.

LIFE AND LIGHT

John 1:4 (*contd*)

> In him was life and the life was the light of men.

THE second of the great Johannine keywords which we meet here is the word *light*. This word occurs in the Fourth Gospel no fewer than twenty-one times. Jesus is the *light* of all people. The function of John the Baptist was to point men and women to that *light* which was in Christ. Twice Jesus calls himself the *light* of the world (8:12, 9:5). This *light* can be in men and women (11:10), so that they can become children of the *light* (12:36). 'I have come', said Jesus, 'as light into the world' (12:46). Let us see if we can understand something of this idea of the *light* which Jesus brings into the world. Three things stand out.

(1) The *light* Jesus brings is the *light* which puts chaos to flight. In the creation story, God moved upon the dark, formless chaos which was before the world began and said: 'Let there be light' (Genesis 1:3). The new-created light of God routed the empty chaos into which it came. So Jesus is *the light which shines in the darkness* (1:5). He is the one person who can save life from becoming a chaos. Left to ourselves, we are at the mercy of our passions and our fears.

When Jesus dawns upon life, light comes. One of the oldest fears in the world is the fear of the dark. There is a story of a child who was to sleep in a strange house. His hostess, thinking to be kind, offered to leave the light on when he went to bed. Politely he declined the offer. 'I thought', said his hostess, 'that you might be afraid of the dark.' 'Oh, no,' said the boy, 'you see, it's God's dark.' With Jesus, the night that surrounds us is as light as the day.

(2) The *light* which Jesus brings is a revealing *light*. It is their condemnation that people loved the darkness rather than the *light*; and they did so because their deeds were evil; and they hated the *light* lest their deeds should be exposed (3:19–20). The *light* which Jesus brings is something which shows things as they are. It strips away the disguises and the concealments; it shows things in all their nakedness; it shows them in their true character and their true values.

Long ago, the Cynics said that the truth is hated because it is like the light to sore eyes. In a poem written by the seventh-century English saint Caedmon, there is a strange picture. It is a picture of the last day, and in the centre of the scene there is the cross; and from the cross there flows a strange blood-red light, and the mysterious quality of that light is such that it shows things as they are. The externals, the disguises, the outer wrappings and trappings are stripped away; and everything stands revealed in the naked and awful loneliness of what it essentially is.

We never see ourselves until we see ourselves through the eyes of Jesus. We never see what our lives are like until we see them in the light of Jesus. Jesus often drives us to God by revealing us to ourselves.

(3) The *light* which Jesus brings is a guiding *light*. If people do not possess that *light*, they walk in darkness and do not know where they are going (12:36). When they receive that *light* and believe in it, they walk no more in darkness (12:46). One of the features of the gospel stories which no one can miss is the number of people who came running to Jesus asking: 'What am I to do?' When Jesus comes into life, the time of guessing and of groping is ended, the time of doubt and uncertainty and vacillation is gone. The path that was dark becomes light; the decision that was wrapped in a night of uncertainty is illumined. Without Jesus, we are like people on an unknown road in the pitch dark. With Jesus, the way is clear.

THE HOSTILE DARK

John 1:5

> And the light shines in the darkness, and the darkness
> did not put it out.

HERE we meet another of John's keywords – *darkness* (*skotos, skotia*). This word occurs seven times in the gospel. To John, there was a *darkness* in the world that was as real as the *light*.

(1) The *darkness* is hostile to the *light*. The light shines in the *darkness*, but, however hard the *darkness* tries, it cannot extinguish it. Those who sin love the *darkness* and hate the light, because the light shows up too many things.

It may well be that in John's mind there is a borrowed thought here. John, as we know, was prepared to go out and to take in new ideas, if by so doing he could present and commend the Christian message to others. The great Persian religion of Zoroastrianism had at this time a very great influence on people's thinking. It believed that there were two great opposing powers in the universe, the god of the light and the god of the dark, Ahriman and Ormuzd. This whole universe was a battleground in the eternal, cosmic conflict between the light and the dark; and all that mattered in life was the side that you chose.

So John is saying: 'Into this world there comes Jesus, the light of the world; there is a darkness which would seek to eliminate him, to banish him from life, to extinguish him. But there is a power in Jesus that is undefeatable. The darkness can hate him, but it can never get rid of him.' As has been truly said: 'Not all the darkness in the world can extinguish the littlest flame.' The unconquerable light will in the end defeat the hostile dark. John is saying: 'Choose your side in the eternal conflict and choose aright.'

(2) The *darkness* stands for the natural sphere of all those who hate the good. It is those whose deeds are evil who fear the light (3:19–20). The person who has something to hide loves the dark; but it is impossible to hide anything from God. His searchlight sweeps the shadows and illuminates the skulking evils of the world.

(3) There are certain passages where the *darkness* seems to stand for *ignorance*, especially for that wilful ignorance

which refuses the light of Jesus Christ. Jesus says: 'I am the light of the world. Whoever follows me will never walk in *darkness*' (8:12). He says to his disciples that the light will be with them only for so short a time; let them walk in it; if they do not, the *darkness* comes, and those who walk in *darkness* do not know where they are going (12:35). He says that he came with his light that men and women should not abide in *darkness* (12:46). Without Jesus Christ, we cannot find or see the way. It is like being blindfolded or even blind. Without Jesus Christ, life becomes lost. It was the German poet Goethe who in his dying words cried out for 'Light, more light!' It was one of the old Scots leaders who said to his friends towards the end: 'Light the candle that I may see to die.' Jesus is the light which shows us the road and which lights that road at every step of the way.

There are times when John uses this word *darkness* symbolically. He uses it at times to mean more than merely the dark of an earthly night. He tells of Jesus walking on the water. He tells how the disciples had embarked on their boat and were crossing the lake without Jesus; and then he says: '*It was now dark*, and Jesus had not yet come to them' (6:17). Without the presence of Jesus, there was nothing but the threatening dark. He tells of the resurrection morning and of the hours before those who had loved Jesus realized that he had risen from the dead. He begins the story: 'Early on the first day of the week, *while it was still dark*, Mary Magdalene came' (20:1). She was living at that moment in a world from which she thought Jesus had been eliminated, and a world like that was dark. He tells the story of the Last Supper. He tells how Judas received the piece of bread and then went out to do his terrible work and arrange for the betrayal of Jesus; and he says with a kind of sinister symbolism: 'So, after receiving the piece of bread, he immediately went out. *And it was night*' (13:30). Judas was going out into the night of a life which had betrayed Christ.

To John, the Christless life was life in the dark. The *darkness* stands for life without Christ, and especially for that which has turned its back on Christ.

Before we leave this passage, there is one other thing to note. The word which we have translated as *put out* is in Greek *katalambanein*. This word can have three meanings.

(a) It can mean that the darkness never *understood* the light. There is a sense in which the man or woman of the world simply cannot understand the demands of Christ and the way Christ offers. To such people, it seems sheer foolishness. You cannot understand Christ without first submitting to him.

(b) It can mean that the darkness never *overcame* the light. *Katalambanein* can mean *to pursue until one overtakes and so lays hold on and overcomes*. This could mean that the darkness of the world had done everything possible to eliminate Jesus Christ, even to crucifying him; but it could never destroy him. This could be a reference to the crucified and conquering Christ.

(c) It can be used of *extinguishing a fire or flame*. That is the sense in which we have taken it here. Although some people did all they could to obscure and extinguish the light of God in Christ, they could not quench it. In every generation, the light of Christ still shines in spite of such efforts to extinguish the flame.

THE WITNESS TO JESUS CHRIST

John 1:6–8

> There emerged a man sent from God whose name was
> John. He came as a witness, in order to bear witness to

the light, that through him all might believe. He himself
was not the light; his function was to bear witness to
the light.

IT is a strange fact that in the Fourth Gospel every reference
to John the Baptist is a reference of depreciation. There is an
explanation for that. John was a prophetic voice; for 400 years
the voice of prophecy had been silent, and in John it spoke
again. It seems that certain people were so fascinated by
John that they gave him a higher place than he ought to
have had. There are, in fact, indications that there was
actually a sect who put John the Baptist in the highest place.
We find an echo of them in Acts 19:3–4. In Ephesus, Paul
came upon certain people who knew nothing but the baptism
of John. It was not that the Fourth Gospel wished to criticize
John or that it underrated his importance. It was simply that
John knew that there were certain people who gave John the
Baptist a place that encroached upon the place of Jesus
himself.

So, all through the Fourth Gospel, John is careful to point
out that the place of John the Baptist in the scheme of things
was high, but that nonetheless it was still subordinate to
the place of Jesus Christ. Here he is careful to say that
John was not that light, but only a witness to the light (1:8).
He shows us John denying that he was the Christ, or even
that he was the great prophet whom Moses had promised
(1:20). When the Jews came to John and told him that Jesus
had begun his career as a teacher, they must have expected
John to resent this intrusion. But the Fourth Gospel shows
us John denying that the first place was his and declaring
that he must decrease while Jesus increased (3:25–30). It is
pointed out that Jesus was more successful in his appeal to
the people than John was (4:1). It is pointed out that even the

people said that John was not able to do the things that Jesus did (10:41).

Somewhere in the Church, there was a group who wished to give John the Baptist too high a place. John the Baptist himself gave no encouragement to that but rather did everything to discourage it. But the Fourth Gospel knew that that tendency was there and took steps to guard against it. It can still happen that a congregation may worship a preacher rather than Christ. It can still happen that people fix their attention upon the messenger rather than upon the king whose coming is announced. John the Baptist was not in the least to blame for what had happened; but John the evangelist was determined to see that no one should push Christ on to the sidelines.

It is more important to note that in this passage we come upon another of the great keywords of the Fourth Gospel. That is the word translated in the Revised Standard Version as *witness*. The Fourth Gospel presents us with witness after witness – eight, no less – to the supreme place of Jesus Christ.

(1) There is the witness of the *Father*. Jesus said: 'The Father who sent me has himself borne witness to me' (5:37). 'The Father who sent me bears witness to me' (8:18). What did Jesus mean by this? He meant two things.

He meant something which affected *himself*. In his heart the inner voice of God spoke, and that voice left him in no doubt as to who he was and what he was sent to do. Jesus did not regard himself as having himself chosen his task. His inner conviction was that God had sent him into the world to live and to die for all humanity.

He meant something which affected people. When people are confronted with Christ, there comes an inner conviction that this is none other than the Son of God. The nineteenth-century Roman Catholic theologian Father George Tyrrell has said that the world can never get away from that 'strange man upon the cross'. That inner power which always brings our eyes back to Christ even when we wish to forget him, that inner voice which tells us that this Jesus is none other than the Son of God and the Saviour of the world is the witness of God within our souls.

(2) There is the witness of *Jesus himself*. 'I bear witness', he said, 'to myself' (8:18). 'Even if I do bear witness to myself', he said, 'my testimony is true' (8:14). What does this mean? It means that it was what Jesus was that was his best witness. He claimed to be the light and the life and the truth and the way. He claimed to be the Son of God and one with the Father. He claimed to be the Saviour and the Master of all people. Unless his life and character had been what they were, such claims would have been merely shocking and blasphemous. What Jesus was in himself was the best witness that his claims were true.

(3) There is the witness of *his works*. He said: 'The works which the Father has granted me to accomplish . . . bear me witness' (5:36). 'The works that I do in my Father's name, they bear witness to me' (10:25). He tells Philip of his complete identity with the Father, and then goes on to say: 'Believe me because of the works themselves' (14:11). One of the condemnations levelled at the people is that they have seen his works and have not believed (15:24). We must note one thing – when John spoke of the works of Jesus, he was not speaking *only* of the miracles of Jesus; he was thinking of Jesus' whole life. He was thinking not only of the great outstanding moments, but of the life that Jesus lived every minute of the day. No other man could have done the mighty works that Jesus did unless he was closer to God than anyone else had ever been; but, equally, no other man could have lived that life of love and pity, compassion and

forgiveness, service and help in everyday life unless he had been in God and God had been in him. It is not by working miracles that we can prove that we belong to Christ, but by living a Christlike life every moment of every day. It is in the ordinary things of life that we show that we belong to him.

(4) There is the witness which *the Scriptures* bear to him. Jesus said: 'Search the scriptures, because you think that in them you have eternal life; and it is they that bear witness to me' (5:39). 'If you believed Moses, you would believe me; for he wrote about me' (5:46). It is Philip's conviction that he has found him of whom Moses and the law and the prophets wrote (1:45). All through the history of Israel, the people had dreamed of the day when God's Messiah would come. They had drawn their pictures and set down their ideas of him. And now in Jesus all these dreams and pictures and hopes were finally and fully realized. He for whom the world was waiting had come.

(5) There is the witness of *the last of the prophets*, John the Baptist. 'He came for testimony to bear witness to the light' (1:7–8). John bore witness that he saw the Spirit descending upon Jesus. The one in whom the prophetic witness culminated was the one who bore witness to Jesus to whom all the prophetic witness pointed.

(6) There is the witness of *those with whom Jesus came into contact*. The woman of Samaria bore witness to the insight and to the power of Jesus (4:39). The man born blind bore witness to his healing power (9:25, 38). The people who witnessed his miracles told of their wonder at the things he did (12:17). There is a legend which tells how the Sanhedrin sought for witnesses when Jesus was on trial. There came a crowd of people saying: 'I was a leper and he healed me'; 'I was blind and he opened my eyes'; 'I

was deaf and he made me able to hear.' That was precisely the kind of witness the Sanhedrin did *not* want. In every age and in every generation, there have always been a great crowd ready to bear witness to what Christ had done for them.

(7) There is the witness of *the disciples and especially of the writer of the gospel himself*. It was Jesus' commission to his disciples: 'You also are witnesses, because you have been with me from the beginning' (15:27). The writer of the gospel is a personal witness and guarantor of the things he relates. Of the crucifixion he writes: 'He who saw it has borne witness – his testimony is true' (19:35). 'This', he says, 'is the disciple who is bearing witness to these things, and who has written these things' (21:24). The story he tells is not something he has heard, no second-hand tale, but what he had seen and experienced himself. The best kind of witness of all is the one which can say: 'This is true, because I know it from my own experience.'

(8) There is the witness of *the Holy Spirit*. 'When the Counsellor comes . . . even the Spirit of truth . . . he will bear witness to me' (15:26). In the First Epistle, John writes: 'And the Spirit is the witness, because the Spirit is the truth' (1 John 5:7). To Jews, the Spirit had two functions. The Spirit brought God's truth to men and women, and the Spirit enabled them to recognize that truth when they saw it. It is the work of the Spirit within our hearts which enables us to recognize Jesus for what he is and to trust him for what he can do.

John wrote his gospel to present the unanswerable witness that Jesus Christ is the mind of God fully revealed to all people.

THE LIGHT OF ALL PEOPLE

John 1:9

> He was the real light, who, in his coming into the world,
> gives light to every man.

IN this verse, John uses a very significant word to describe
Jesus. He says that Jesus was the *real* light. In Greek, there
are two words which are very like each other. The Authorized
Version and the Revised Standard use the word *true* to
translate both of them; but they have different shades of
meaning. The first is *alēthēs. Alēthēs* means *true* as opposed
to *false*; it is the word that would be used of a statement
which is true. The other word is *alēthinos. Alēthinos* means
real or *genuine* as opposed to *unreal.*

So what John is saying is that Jesus is the real light that
has come to bring enlightenment. Before Jesus came, there
were other lights which were followed. Some were flickers
of the truth; some were faint glimpses of reality; some were
will o' the wisps which when followed led people out into
the dark and left them there. It is still the case. There are still
the partial lights; and there are still the false lights; and some
people still follow them. Jesus is the only genuine light, the
real light to guide us on our way.

John says that Jesus, by his coming into the world, brought
the real light to everyone. His coming was like a blaze of
light. It was like the coming of the dawn. A traveller tells
how once in Italy he was standing on a hill overlooking the
Bay of Naples. It was so dark that nothing could be seen;
then all of a sudden there came a lightning flash and everything, in every detail, was lit up. When Jesus came into this
world, he came like a light in the dark.

(1) His coming dissipated the shadows of *doubt*. Until he came, it was possible only to guess about God. 'It is difficult to find out about God,' said one of the Greeks, 'and when you have found out about him it is impossible to tell anyone else about him.' To pagans, God dwelt either in the shadows that no one can penetrate or in the light that no one can approach. But when Jesus came, people saw full-displayed what God is like. The shadows and the mists were gone; the days of guessing were at an end; there was no more need for a wistful agnosticism. The light had come.

(2) His coming dissipated the shadows of *despair*. Jesus came to a world that was in despair. People, as the philosopher Seneca said, are conscious of their helplessness in necessary things. They were longing for a hand let down to help them up. They hate their sins but cannot leave them. They despaired of ever making themselves or the world any better. But with the coming of Jesus a new power came into life. He came not only with knowledge but with power. He came not only to show people the right way but to enable them to walk in it. He gave them not only instruction but a presence in which all the impossible things had become possible. The darkness of pessimism and despair was gone forever.

(3) His coming dissipated the darkness of *death*. The ancient world feared death. At the best, death was annihilation and the human soul shuddered at the thought. At the worst, it was torture by the gods, and the human soul was afraid. But Jesus by his coming, by his life, his death, his resurrection showed that death was only the way to a larger life. The darkness was dispelled. Robert Louis Stevenson has a scene in one of his stories in which he draws the picture of a young man who has almost miraculously escaped in a duel in which he was certain he would be killed. As he walks away, his heart is singing: 'The bitterness of death is

past.' Because of Jesus, the bitterness of death is past for every one of us.

Further, Jesus is the light who lights *everyone* who comes into the world. The ancient world was exclusive. The Jews hated the Gentiles and held that they were created for no other purpose than to be fuel for the fires of hell. True, there was a lonely prophet who saw that Israel's destiny was to be a light to the Gentiles (Isaiah 42:6, 49:6), but that was a destiny which Israel had always definitely refused. The Greek world never dreamed that knowledge was for everyone. The Roman world looked down on the barbarians, the uncultured peoples without the law. But Jesus came to be a light to all people. Only the God and Father of our Lord Jesus Christ has a heart big enough to hold all the world.

UNRECOGNIZED

John I:IO–II

> He was in the world, and, although the world came into being through him, the world did not recognize him. It was into his own home that he came, and his own people did not welcome him.

WHEN John wrote this passage, two thoughts were in his mind.

(I) He was thinking of the time before Jesus Christ came into the world in the body. From the beginning of time, God's *Logos* has been active in the world. In the beginning, God's creating, dynamic *word* brought the world into being; and ever since it is the *word*, the *Logos*, the *reason* of God which has made the world an ordered whole and men and women thinking beings. If they had only had the sense to see him, the *Logos* was always recognizable in the universe.

65

The Westminster Confession of Faith begins by saying that 'the lights of nature, and the works of creation and providence do so far manifest the goodness, wisdom and power of God as to leave men inexcusable'. Long ago, Paul had said that the visible things of the world were so designed by God as to lead human thoughts to the invisible things, and that if people had looked with open eyes and an understanding heart at the world, their thoughts would have been inevitably led to the creator of the world (Romans 1:19–20). The world has always been such that, looked at in the right way, it would lead human minds to God.

Theology has always made a distinction between *natural* theology and *revealed* theology. Revealed theology deals with the truths that came to us directly from God in the words of the prophets, the pages of his book, and supremely in Jesus Christ. Natural theology deals with the truths that we can discover by the exercise of our own minds and intellects on the world in which we live. How, then, can we see God's *word*, God's *Logos*, God's *reason*, God's *mind* in the world in which we live?

(a) We must look *outwards*. It was always a basic Greek thought that where there is order there must be a mind. When we look at the world, we see an amazing order. The planets keep to their appointed courses. The tides observe their appointed times. Seed times and harvest, summer and winter, day and night come in their appointed order. Clearly there is order in nature, and, therefore, equally clearly there must be a mind behind it all. Further, that mind must be greater than any human mind because it achieves results that the human mind can never achieve. No one can make day into night, or night into day; no one can make a seed that will have in it the power of growth; no one can make a living thing. If in the world there is order, there must be intelligence; and if in that order there are things which are beyond the power of human thought, then the mind behind the order of nature must be a mind above and beyond human minds – and all at once we have reached God. To look outwards upon the world is to come face to face with the God who made it.

(b) We must look *upwards*. Nothing demonstrates the amazing order of the universe so much as the movement of the world. Astronomers tell us that there are many stars for every grain of sand upon the seashore. If we may put it in human terms, think of the traffic problem of the heavens; and yet the heavenly bodies keep their appointed courses and travel their appointed way. An astronomer is able to forecast to the minute and to the inch when and where a certain planet will appear. An astronomer can tell us when and where an eclipse of the sun will happen hundreds of years from now, and indicate to the second how long it will last. It has been said that 'no astronomer can be an atheist'. When we look upwards, we see God.

(c) We must look *inwards*. Where did we get the power to think, to reason and to know? Where did we get our knowledge of right and of wrong? Why do even the most evil-ridden people know deep in their hearts when they are doing a wrong thing? The philosopher Immanuel Kant said long ago that two things convinced him of the existence of God – the starry heavens above him and the moral law within him. We neither gave ourselves life, nor did we give ourselves the reason which guides and directs life. It must have come from some power outside ourselves. Where do remorse and regret and the sense of guilt come from? Why can we never do what we like and be at peace? When we look inwards, we find what the Roman emperor Marcus Aurelius called 'the god within', and what Seneca called 'the holy spirit which sits within our souls'. We cannot explain ourselves apart from God.

(d) We must look *backwards*. James Froude, the great historian, said that the whole of history is a demonstration of the moral law in action. Empires rise and empires collapse. As Rudyard Kipling wrote in 'Recessional':

> Lo, all our pomp of yesterday
> Is one with Nineveh and Tyre!

And it is a demonstrable fact of history that moral degeneration and national collapse go hand in hand. 'No nation', said George Bernard Shaw, 'has ever outlived the loss of its gods.' All history is the practical demonstration that there is a God.

So, then, even if Jesus Christ had never come into this world in bodily form, it would still have been possible for God's *word*, God's *Logos*, God's *reason* in action to be seen. But, although the action of the *word* was there for all to see, he went unrecognized.

UNRECOGNIZED

John 1:10–11 (*contd*)

> He was in the world, and, although the world came into being through him, the world did not recognize him. It was into his own home that he came, and his own people did not welcome him.

(2) In the end, God's creating and directing *word* did come into this world in the form of the man Jesus. John says that the *word* came to his own home and his own people gave him no welcome. What does he mean by that? He means that when God's *word* entered this world, he did not come to Rome

or to Greece or to Egypt or to the eastern empires. *He came to Palestine*; Palestine was specially God's land, and the Jews were specially God's people.

The very titles by which the Old Testament calls the land and the people show that. Palestine is repeatedly called *the holy land* (Zechariah 2:12; 2 Maccabees 1:7; Wisdom 12:3). It is called *the Lord's land*; God speaks of it as *his land* (Hosea 9:3; Jeremiah 2:7, 16:18; Leviticus 25:23). The Jewish nation is called *God's own treasured possession* (Exodus 19:5; Deuteronomy 7:6, 14:2; Psalm 135:4). The Jews are called *God's treasured people* (Deuteronomy 26:18). They are called *the Lord's own portion* (Deuteronomy 32:9).

Jesus came to a land which was peculiarly God's land and a people who were peculiarly God's people. He ought, there-fore, to have been coming to a nation that would welcome him with open arms; the door should have been wide open for him; he should have been welcomed like a traveller coming home; or, even more, like a king coming to his own – but *he was rejected*. He was received with hate and not with adoration.

Here is the tragedy of a people being prepared for a task and then refusing that task. It may be that parents plan and save and sacrifice to give a son or a daughter a chance in life, to prepare that son or daughter for some special task and opportunity – and then when the chance comes, the one for whom so much sacrifice was made refuses to grasp the opportunity, or fails miserably when confronted with the challenge. Therein is tragedy. And that is what happened to God.

It would be wrong to think that God prepared only the Jewish people. God is preparing every man and woman and child in this world for some task that he has in store for them. A novelist tells of a girl who refused to touch anything unpleasant or dirty. When she was asked why, she said: 'Some day something fine is going to come into my life, and I want to be ready for it.' The tragedy is that so many people refuse the task God has for them.

We may put it in another way – a way that strikes home – that there are so few people who become what they have it in them to be. It may be through lethargy and laziness, it may be through timidity and cowardice, it may be through lack of discipline and self-indulgence, it may be through involvement in second bests and byways; but the world is full of people who have never realized the possibilities which are in them. We need not think of the task God has in store for us in terms of some great act or achievement of which everyone will know. It may be to fit a child for life; it may be at some crucial moment to speak that word and exert that influence which will save a life from ruin; it may be to do some quite small job superlatively well; it may be to touch the lives of many by our hands, our voices or our minds. The fact remains that God is preparing us by all the experiences of life for *something*; and many refuse the task when it comes and never even realize that they are refusing it.

There is all the pathos in the world in the simple saying: 'He came to his own home – and his own people gave him no welcome.' It happened to Jesus long ago – and it is still happening.

CHILDREN OF GOD

John 1:12–13

> To all those who did receive him, to those who believe in his name, he gave the right to become the children of God. These were born not of blood, nor of any human

impulse, nor of any man's will, but their birth was of
God.

Not everyone rejected Jesus when he came; there were some
who did receive him and welcome him; and to them Jesus
gave the right to become children of God.

There is a sense in which we are not naturally children of
God. There is a sense in which we have to *become* children
of God. We may think of this in human terms, because human
terms are the only ones open to us.

Children fall into two categories. There are those who
never do anything else but make use of their home. All
through their youth, they take everything that the home has
to offer and give nothing in return. Their parents may work
and sacrifice to give them every chance in life, and they take
it as a right, never realizing what they are taking and making
no effort to deserve it or repay it. When they leave home,
they make no attempt to keep in touch. The home has served
its purpose and they have finished with it. They are aware of
no bond to be maintained and no debt to be paid. To their
parents they owe their existence; and to their parents they
owe what they are; but between children and parents there is
no bond of love and intimacy. The parents have given all in
love; but the children have given nothing in return.

On the other hand, there are children who are aware all
their lives of what their parents are doing and have done for
them. They take every opportunity to show their gratitude by
trying to live up to the aspirations their parents have for
them; as the years go on, they grow closer and closer to their
parents; the relationship becomes the relationship of fellowship and friendship. Even when they leave home, the bond is
still there and they are still conscious of a debt that can never
be repaid.

71

In the one case the children grow further and further away from the parents; in the other they grow nearer and nearer. In one sense the relationship is identical, but in another it is very different. In the second case there has been a growing together, absent in the first, which seals the relationship.

We may illustrate this kind of relationship from another, but a related, sphere. The name of a certain younger man was mentioned to a famous teacher, whose student the younger man claimed to be. The older man answered: 'He may have attended my lectures, but he was not one of my students.' There is a world of difference between sitting in a teacher's classroom and being that teacher's student. There can be contact without communion; there can be relationship without fellowship. We are all the children of God in the sense that we owe to him the creation and the preservation of our lives; but only some of us *become* children of God in the depth and intimacy of the true parent-and-child relationship.

It is the claim of John that we can enter into that true and real relationship only through Jesus Christ. When he says that it does not come from blood, he is using Jewish thought, for the Jews believed that a physical child was born from the union of the seed of the father with the blood of the mother. This relationship does not come from any human impulse or desire or from any act of the human will; it comes entirely from God. We cannot make ourselves children of God; we have to enter into a relationship which God offers us. We can never enter into friendship with God by our own will and power; there is a great gulf fixed between the human and the divine. We can only enter into friendship with God when God himself opens the way.

Again let us think in human terms. An ordinary citizen cannot approach a king with the offer of friendship; if there is ever to be such a friendship, it must depend entirely on the

approach of the king. It is so with us and God. We cannot by
will or achievement enter into fellowship with God, for we
are human and he is God. We can enter into it only when God
in his totally undeserved grace condescends to open the way
to himself.

But there is a human side to this. What God offers, we
have to appropriate. Human parents may offer their children
love, advice and friendship, and the children may refuse it
and prefer to take their own way. It is so with God; God offers
us *the right* to become his children, but we need not accept it.

We do accept it through believing in the name of Jesus
Christ. What does that mean? Hebrew thought and language
had a way of using *the name* which is strange to us. By that
expression, Jewish thought did not so much mean the name
by which individuals were called as their nature in so far as
it was revealed and known. For instance, in Psalm 9:10 the
psalmist says: 'Those who know *your name* put their trust in
you.' Clearly that does not mean that those who know that
God is called Yahweh will trust him; it means that those who
know God's character, God's nature, who know what God is
like, will be ready and willing to trust him for everything. In
Psalm 20:7 the psalmist says: 'Some take pride in chariots,
and some in horses, but our pride is in *the name* of the Lord
our God.' Clearly that does not mean that we will boast that
God is called Yahweh. It means that some people will put
their trust in human aids, but we will put our trust in God
because we know what he is like.

To trust in the name of Jesus therefore means to put our
trust in what he is. He was the embodiment of kindness and
love and gentleness and service. It is John's great central
doctrine that in Jesus we see the very mind of God, the attitude
of God to men and women. If we believe that, then we also
believe that God is like Jesus, as kind, as loving as Jesus was.

To believe in the name of Jesus is to believe that God is like
him; and it is only when we believe that, that we can submit
ourselves to God and become his children. Unless we had
seen in Jesus what God is like, we would never even have
dared to think of ourselves as being able to become the
children of God. It is what Jesus is that opens to us the possibility of becoming the children of God.

THE WORD BECAME FLESH

John 1:14

> So the Word of God became a person, and took up his
> abode in our being, full of grace and truth; and we
> looked with our own eyes upon his glory, glory like the
> glory which an only son receives from a father.

HERE we come to the sentence for the sake of which John
wrote his gospel. He has thought and talked about the word
of God, that powerful, creative, dynamic word which was
the agent of creation, that guiding, directing, controlling
word which puts order into the universe and intelligence into
human beings. These were ideas which were known and
familiar to both Jews and Greeks. Now he says the most
startling and incredible thing that he could have said. He says
quite simply: 'This word which created the world, this reason
which controls the order of the world, has become a person,
and with our own eyes we saw him.' The word that John uses
for *seeing* this word is *theasthai*; it is used in the New
Testament more than twenty times and is always used of
actual physical sight. This is no spiritual vision seen with the
eye of the soul or of the mind. John declares that the word
actually came to earth in the form of a man and was seen by

human eyes. He says: 'If you want to see what this creating word, this controlling reason, is like, look at Jesus of Nazareth.'

This is where John parted with all thought which had gone before him. This was the entirely new thing which John brought to the Greek world for which he was writing. Augustine afterwards said that in his pre-Christian days he had read and studied the great pagan philosophers and had read many things, but he had never read that the word became flesh.

To a Greek, this was the impossible thing. The one thing that no Greek would ever have dreamed of was that God could take a body. To a Greek, the body was an evil, a prison house in which the soul was shackled, a tomb in which the spirit was confined. Plutarch, the wise old Greek, did not even believe that God could control the happenings of this world directly; he had to do it by deputies and intermediaries, for, as Plutarch saw it, it was nothing less than blasphemy to involve God in the affairs of the world. Philo could never have said it. He said: 'The life of God has not descended to us; nor has it come as far as the necessities of the body.' The great Roman Stoic emperor, Marcus Aurelius, despised the body in comparison with the spirit. 'Therefore despise the flesh – blood and bones and a network, a twisted skein of nerves and veins and arteries . . . The composition of the whole body is under corruption.'

Here was the shatteringly new thing – that God could and would become a human person, that God could enter into this life that we live, that eternity could appear in time, that somehow the Creator could appear in creation in such a way that he could actually be seen.

So staggeringly new was this conception of God in a human form that it is not surprising that even in the Church there were some who could not believe it. What John says is that the word became *sarx*. Now *sarx* is the very word Paul uses over and over again to describe what he called *the flesh*, human nature in all its weakness and in all its liability to sin. The very thought of taking this word and applying it to God was something that their minds staggered at. So there arose in the Church a body of people called *Docetists*.

Dokein is the Greek word for *to seem to be*. These people held that Jesus in fact was only a phantom; that his human body was not a real body; that he could not really feel hunger and weariness, sorrow and pain; that he was in fact a disembodied spirit in the apparent form of a man. John dealt with these people much more directly in his First Letter. 'By this you know the Spirit of God: every spirit which confesses that Jesus Christ has come *in the flesh* is from God, and every spirit that does not confess Jesus is not from God. And this is the spirit of the antichrist' (1 John 4:2–3). It is true that this heresy was born of a kind of mistaken reverence which recoiled from saying that Jesus was really, fully and truly human. To John, it contradicted the whole Christian gospel.

It may well be that we are often so eager to conserve the fact that Jesus was fully God that we tend to forget the fact that he was fully human. *The word became flesh* – here, perhaps as nowhere else in the New Testament, we have the full humanity of Jesus gloriously proclaimed. In Jesus we see the creating word of God, the controlling reason of God, taking human nature upon himself. In Jesus we see God living life as he would have lived it if he had been a man. Supposing we said nothing else about Jesus, we could still say that he shows us how God would live this life that we have to live.

THE WORD BECAME FLESH

John 1:14 (*contd*)

> So the word of God became a person, and took up his
> abode in our being, full of grace and truth; and we
> looked with our own eyes upon his glory, glory like the
> glory which an only son receives from a father.

It might well be held that this is the greatest single verse in
the New Testament; we must therefore spend much time upon
it so that we may enter the more fully into its riches.

We have already seen how John has certain great words
which haunt his mind and dominate his thought and are the
themes out of which his whole message is elaborated. Here
we have three more of these words.

(1) The first is *grace*. This word always has two basic
ideas in it.

(a) It always has the idea of something completely undeserved. It always has the idea of something that we could
never have earned or achieved for ourselves. The fact that
God came to earth to live and to die for men and women is
not something which humanity deserved; it is an act of pure
love on the part of God. The word grace emphasizes at one
and the same time our own helpless poverty and God's
limitless kindness.

(b) It always has the idea of beauty in it. In modern Greek,
the word means *charm*. In Jesus we see the loveliness of
God. People had thought of God in terms of might and
majesty and power and judgment. They had thought of the
power of God which could crush all opposition and defeat all
rebellion; but in Jesus we are confronted with the sheer
loveliness of God.

(2) The second is *truth*. This word is one of the dominant notes of the Fourth Gospel. We meet it again and again. Here we can only briefly gather together what John has to say about Jesus and the truth.

(a) Jesus is the embodiment of the truth. He said: 'I am the truth' (cf. 14:6). To see truth, we must look at Jesus. Here is something infinitely precious for every mind and soul. It is difficult to grasp abstract ideas; most of us think in pictures. We could think and argue forever and we would very likely be no nearer arriving at a definition of beauty. But if we can point at a beautiful person and say that *is* beauty, the thing becomes clear. Ever since human beings began to think about God, they have been trying to define just who and what he is – and their puny minds get no nearer a definition. But we can cease our thinking and look at Jesus Christ and say: 'That is what God is like.' Jesus did not come to *talk* about God; he came to *show* people what God is like, so that the simplest mind might know him as intimately as the mind of the greatest philosopher.

(b) Jesus is the communicator of the truth. He told his disciples that if they continued with him they would know the truth (8:31). He told Pilate that his object in coming into this world was to witness to the truth (18:37). People will flock to a teacher or preacher who can really give them guidance for the tangled business of thinking and living. Jesus is the one who, amid the shadows, makes things clear; who, at the many crossroads of life, shows us the right way; who, in the baffling moments of decision, enables us to choose aright; who, amid the many voices which clamour for our allegiance, tells us what to believe.

(c) Even when Jesus left this earth in the body, he left us his Spirit to guide us into the truth. His Spirit is the Spirit of truth (14:17, 15:26, 16:13). He did not leave us only a book of instruction and a body of teaching. We do not need to search through some unintelligible textbook to find out what to do. Still, to this day, we can ask Jesus what to do, for his Spirit is with us every step of the way.

(d) The truth is what makes us free (8:32). There is always a certain liberating quality in the truth. Children often get strange, mistaken notions about things when they think about them for themselves; and often they become afraid. When they are told the truth, they are released from their fears. We may have fears of illness; we go to the doctor; even if the verdict is bad, at least we have been liberated from the vague fears which haunted our minds. The truth which Jesus brings liberates us from estrangement from God; it liberates us from frustration; it liberates us from our fears and weaknesses and defeats. Jesus Christ is the greatest liberator on earth.

(e) The truth can be resented. They sought to kill Jesus because he told them the truth (8:40). The truth may well condemn people; it may well show them how far wrong they were. 'Truth', said the Cynics, 'can be like the light to sore eyes.' The Cynics declared that the teacher who never annoyed anyone never did anyone any good. People may shut their ears and their minds to the truth; they may kill the person who tells them the truth – but the truth remains. No one ever destroyed the truth by refusing to listen to the voice that told it; and the truth will always catch up with us in the end.

(f) The truth can be disbelieved (8:45). There are two main reasons why people disbelieve the truth. They may disbelieve it because it seems too good to be true; or they may disbelieve it because they are so fastened to their half-truths that they will not let them go. In many instances, a half-truth is the worst enemy of the whole truth.

(g) The truth is not something abstract; it is something which must be done (3:21). It is something which must be known with the mind, accepted with the heart and acted out in the life.

THE WORD BECAME FLESH

John 1:14 (*contd*)

> So the word of God became a person, and took up his abode in our being, full of grace and truth; and we looked with our own eyes upon his glory, glory like the glory which an only son receives from a father.

A lifetime of study and thought could not exhaust the truth of this verse. We have already looked at two of the great theme words in it; now we look at the third – *glory*. Again and again John uses this word in connection with Jesus Christ. We shall first look at what John says about the glory of Christ, and then we shall go on to see if we can understand a little of what he means.

(1) The life of Jesus Christ was a manifestation of glory. When he performed the miracle of the water and the wine at Cana of Galilee, John says that he manifested forth his glory (2:11). To look at Jesus and to experience his power and love was to enter into a new glory.

(2) The glory which he manifests is the glory of God. It is not from human beings that he receives it (5:41). He seeks not his own glory but the glory of him who sent him (7:18). It is his Father who glorifies him (8:50, 54). It is the glory of God that Martha will see in the raising of Lazarus (11:4). The raising of Lazarus is for the glory of God, that the Son may be glorified thereby (11:4). The glory that was on Jesus,

that clung about him, that shone through him, that acted in him is the glory of God.

(3) Yet that glory was uniquely his own. At the end, he prays that God will glorify him with the glory that he had before the world began (17:5). He shines with no borrowed radiance; his glory is his and his by right.

(4) The glory which is his he has transmitted to his disciples. The glory which God gave him he has given to them (17:22). It is as if Jesus shared in the glory of God and the disciple shares in the glory of Christ. The coming of Jesus is the coming of God's glory among his people.

What does John mean by all this? To answer that, we must turn to the Old Testament. To the Jews, the idea of the *Shechinah* was very dear. The *Shechinah* means *that which dwells*; and it is the word used for the visible presence of God among men and women. Repeatedly in the Old Testament, we come across the idea that there were certain times when God's glory was visible among his people. In the desert, before the giving of the manna, the children of Israel 'looked towards the wilderness, and the glory of the Lord appeared in the cloud' (Exodus 16:10). Before the giving of the Ten Commandments, 'The glory of the Lord settled on Mount Sinai' (Exodus 24:16). When the Tabernacle had been erected and equipped, 'the glory of the Lord filled the tabernacle' (Exodus 40:34). When Solomon's Temple was dedicated, the priests could not enter in to minister, 'for the glory of the Lord filled the house of the Lord' (1 Kings 8:11). When Isaiah had his vision in the Temple, he heard the angelic choir singing that 'the whole earth is full of his glory' (Isaiah 6:3). Ezekiel in his ecstasy saw 'the likeness of the glory of the Lord' (Ezekiel 1:28). In the Old Testament, the glory of the Lord came at times when God was very close.

The glory of the Lord means quite simply the presence of God. John uses a homely illustration. A father gives to his eldest son his own authority, his own honour. The heir apparent to the throne, the king's heir, is invested with all the royal glory of his father. It was so with Jesus. When he came to this earth, the splendour of God was visible in him, and at the heart of that splendour was love. When Jesus came to this earth, the wonder of God was visible in him, and the wonder was love. People saw that God's glory and God's love were one and the same thing. The glory of God is not that of a despotic tyrant, but the splendour of love before which we fall not in abject terror but lost in wonder, love and praise.

THE INEXHAUSTIBLE FULLNESS

John 1:15–17

> John was his witness and his statement still sounds out: 'This is he of whom I said to you, he who comes after me has been advanced before me, because he was before me.' On his fullness we all of us have drawn, and from him we have received grace upon grace, for it was the law which was given by Moses, but grace and truth came through Jesus Christ.

WE have already seen that the Fourth Gospel was written in a situation where it was necessary to make sure that John the Baptist did not occupy an exaggerated position in anyone's thinking. So John begins this passage with a saying of John the Baptist which gives to Jesus the first place.

John the Baptist says of Jesus: 'He who comes after me was before me.' He may mean more than one thing by that. (a) Jesus was actually six months younger in age than John, and John may be saying quite simply: 'He who is my junior has been advanced beyond me.' (b) John may be saying: 'I was on the scene before Jesus; I occupied the centre of the stage before he did; my hand was laid to work before his was; but all that I was doing was to prepare the way for his coming; I was only the advance guard of the main force and the herald of the king.' (c) It may be that John is thinking in terms much deeper than that. He may be thinking in terms not of time but of eternity. He may be thinking of Jesus as the one who existed before the world began, and beside whom any human figure has no standing at all. It may be that all three ideas are in John's mind. It was not he who had exaggerated his own position; that was the mistake that some of his followers had made. To John, the highest place belonged to Jesus.

This passage then goes on to say three great things about Jesus.

(1) On his fullness we all have drawn. The word that John uses for *fullness* is a great word; it is *plērōma*, and it means the sum total of all that is in God. It is a word which Paul uses often. In Colossians 1:19, he says that all *plērōma* dwelt in Christ. In Colossians 2:9, he says that in Christ there dwelt the *plērōma* of deity in a bodily form. He meant that in Jesus there dwelt the totality of the wisdom, the power and the love of God. Just because of that, Jesus is inexhaustible. We can go to Jesus with any need and find that need supplied. We can go to Jesus with any ideal and find that ideal realized. In Jesus, the person who is in love with beauty will find the supreme beauty. In Jesus, the person to whom life is the search for knowledge will find the supreme revelation. In Jesus, the person who needs courage will find the pattern and the secret of being brave. In Jesus, the person who feels unable to cope with life will find the Master of life and the power to live. In Jesus, the person who is conscious of sin will find the

forgiveness for that sin and the strength to be good. In Jesus, the *plērōma*, the fullness of God, all that is in God, what the scholar B. F. Westcott called 'the spring of divine life', becomes available to everyone.

(2) From him we have received grace upon grace. Literally the Greek means *grace instead of grace*. What does that strange phrase mean?

(a) It may mean that in Christ we have found one wonder leading to another. When a missionary came to one of the ancient Scottish kings, the king asked him what he might expect if he became a Christian. The missionary answered: 'You will find wonder upon wonder and every one of them true.' Sometimes when we travel a very lovely road, vista after vista opens to us. At every view we think that nothing could be lovelier, and then we turn another corner and an even greater loveliness opens before us. When we embark on the study of some great subject, like music or poetry or art, we never get to the end of it. Always there are fresh experiences of beauty waiting for us. It is so with Christ. The more we know of him, the more wonderful he becomes. The longer we live with him, the more loveliness we discover. The more we think about him and with him, the wider the horizon of truth becomes. This phrase may be John's way of expressing the limitlessness of Christ. It may be his way of saying that those who keep company with Christ will find new wonders dawning upon their souls and enlightening their minds and capturing their hearts every day.

(b) It may be that we ought to take this expression quite literally. In Christ, we find *grace instead of grace*. The different ages and the different situations in life demand a different kind of grace. We need one grace in the days of prosperity and another in the days of adversity. We need one grace in the sunlit days of youth and another when the shadows of age begin to lengthen. The Church needs one grace in the days of persecution and another when the days of acceptance have come. We need one grace when we feel that we are on top of things and another when we are depressed and discouraged and near to despair. We need one grace to bear our own burdens and another to bear one another's burdens. We need one grace when we are sure of things and another when there seems nothing certain left in the world. The grace of God is never a static but always a dynamic thing. It never fails to meet the situation. One need invades life and one grace comes with it. That need passes and another need assaults us and with it another grace comes. All through life we are constantly receiving grace instead of grace, for the grace of Christ is triumphantly adequate to deal with any situation.

(3) The law was given by Moses, but grace and truth came through Jesus Christ. In the old way, life was governed by law. People had to do a thing whether they liked it or not, and whether they knew the reason for it or not; but with the coming of Jesus we no longer seek to obey the law of God like slaves; we seek to answer the love of God like sons and daughters. It is through Jesus Christ that God the law-giver has become God the Father, that God the judge has become God the lover of human souls.

THE REVELATION OF GOD

John 1:18

> No one has ever seen God. It is the unique one, he who is God, he who is in the bosom of the Father, who has told us all about God.

WHEN John said that no one has ever seen God, everyone in the ancient world would fully agree with him. People were fascinated and depressed and frustrated by what they regarded as the infinite distance and the utter unknowability of God. In the Old Testament, God is represented as saying to Moses: 'You cannot see my face; for no one shall see me and live' (Exodus 33:20). When God reminds the people of the giving of the law, he says: 'You heard the sound of words, but saw no form; there was only a voice' (Deuteronomy 4:12). No one in the Old Testament thought it possible to see God. The great Greek thinkers felt exactly the same. Xenophanes said: 'Guesswork is over all.' Plato said: 'Never man and God can meet.' Celsus laughed at the way that the Christians called God Father, because 'God is away beyond everything.' At the best, Apuleius said, men could catch a glimpse of God as a lightning flash lights up a dark night – one split second of illumination, and then the dark. As the New Testament scholar T. R. Glover said: 'Whatever God was, he was far from being within the reach of ordinary men.' There might be very rare moments of ecstasy when someone caught a glimpse of what might be called 'Absolute Being', but ordinary people were the prisoners of ignorance and fancy. There would be none to disagree with John when he said that no one has ever seen God.

But John does not stop there; he goes on to make the startling and tremendous statement that Jesus has fully revealed to us what God is like. What has come to us is what Archbishop J. H. Bernard of Dublin called 'the exhibition to the world of God in Christ'. Here again, the keynote of John's gospel sounds: 'If you want to see what God is like, look at Jesus.'

Why should it be that Jesus can do what no one else has ever done? Wherein lies his power to reveal God to men and women? John says three things about him.

(1) Jesus is *unique*. The Greek word is *monogenēs*, which
the Authorized Version translates as *only-begotten*. It is true
that that is what *monogenēs* literally means; but long before
this it had lost its purely physical sense, and had come to
have two special meanings. It had come to mean *unique*
and *specially beloved*. Obviously an only son has a unique
place and a unique love in his father's heart. So this word
came to express *uniqueness* more than anything else. It is
the conviction of the New Testament that there is no one
like Jesus. He alone can bring God to us and bring us to
God.

(2) Jesus is *God*. Here we have the very same form of
expression as we had in the first verse of the chapter. This
does not mean that Jesus is identical with God; it does
mean that in mind and character and being he is one with
God. In this case, it might be better if we thought of it as
meaning that Jesus is divine. To see him is to see what God
is.

(3) Jesus is *in the bosom of the Father*. To be in the bosom
of someone is the Hebrew phrase which expresses the
deepest intimacy possible in human life. It is used of mother
and child; it is used of husband and wife; a man speaks
of the wife of his bosom (Numbers 11:12; Deuteronomy
13:6); it is used of two friends who are in complete communion with one another. When John uses this phrase
about Jesus, he means that between Jesus and God there is
complete and uninterrupted intimacy. It is because Jesus is
so intimate with God that he is one with God and can reveal
him to us.

In Jesus Christ the distant, unknowable, invisible, un-
reachable God has come to men and women; and God can
never be a stranger to us again.

THE WITNESS OF JOHN

John 1:19–28

> This is the witness of John, when the Jews sent priests
> and Levites to him from Jerusalem to ask him: 'Who
> are you?' He quite definitely affirmed and stated: '*I* am
> not the Messiah.' So they asked him: 'What then are
> we to think? Are you Elijah?' He said: 'I am not.' 'Are
> you the promised prophet?' He answered: 'No.' So they
> said to him: 'Who are you? Tell us, so that we can give
> an answer to those who sent us. What claim do you
> make for yourself?' He said: 'I am the voice of one
> crying in the wilderness, "Make the Lord's road
> straight," as Isaiah the prophet said.' Now they had
> been sent by the Pharisees. So they asked him and said
> to him: 'If you are neither the Messiah, nor Elijah,
> nor the promised prophet, why then do you baptize?'
> John answered: '*I* baptize with water. But there is
> one standing among you, whom you do not know, I
> mean the one who is coming after me, the straps of
> whose sandals I am not worthy to unloose.' These things
> happened at Bethany, on the far side of Jordan, where
> John was baptizing.

WITH this passage John begins the narrative part of his gospel.
In the prologue he has shown what he intends to do; he is
writing his gospel to demonstrate that Jesus is the mind, the
reason, the word of God come into this world in the form of a
human person. Having set down his central thought, he now
begins the story of the life of Jesus.

No one is so careful of details of time as John is. Starting
from this passage and going on to 2:11, he tells step by step
the story of the first momentous week in the public life of
Jesus. The events of the first day are in 1:19–28; the story

of the second day is 1:29–34; the third day is unfolded in 1:35–9. The three verses 1:40–2 tell the story of the fourth day. The events of the fifth day are told in 1:43–51. The sixth day is left a blank. And the events of the last day of the week are told in 2:1–11.

In this same section from 1:19 to 2:11, the Fourth Gospel gives us three different kinds of witness to the greatness and the uniqueness of Jesus. (1) There is the witness of John the Baptist (1:19–34). (2) There is the witness of those who accepted Jesus as their Master, and who became his disciples (1:41–51). (3) There is the witness of Jesus' own wonderful powers (2:1–11). John is setting Jesus before us in three different contexts, and in each showing us his supreme wonder.

We have already seen that the Fourth Gospel had to take account of a situation in which John the Baptist was given a position far higher than he himself had claimed. As late as AD 250, the *Clementine Recognitions* tell us that 'there were some of John's disciples who preached about him as if their master was the Messiah'. In this passage, we see that that was a view that John the Baptist himself would have definitely repudiated.

Let us now turn to the passage itself. Right at the beginning, we come upon a characteristic of the Fourth Gospel. It is emissaries of the *Jews* who come to cross-question John. The word *Jews* (*Ioudaioi*) occurs in this gospel no fewer than seventy times; and always the Jews are the opposition. They are the people who have set themselves against Jesus. The mention of the Jews therefore brings the opposition on to the stage at an early point. The Fourth Gospel is two things. First, as we have seen, it is the exhibition of God in Jesus Christ. But, second, it is equally the story of the rejection of Jesus Christ by the Jews, the story of God's offer and their refusal, the story of God's love and human sin, the story of Jesus Christ's invitation and the Jews' rejection. The Fourth Gospel is the gospel in which love and warning are uniquely and vividly combined.

The deputation which came to interview John was composed of two kinds of people. First, there were the priests and the Levites. Their interest was very natural, for John was the son of Zacharias, and Zacharias was a priest (Luke 1:5). In Judaism, the only qualification for the priesthood was descent. If a man was not a descendant of Aaron, nothing could make him a priest; if he was a descendant of Aaron, nothing could stop him being one. Therefore, in the eyes of the authorities, John the Baptist was in fact a priest, and it was very natural that the priests should come to find out why he was behaving in such an unusual way. Second, there were emissaries of the Pharisees. It may well be that behind them was the Sanhedrin. One of the functions of the Sanhedrin was to deal with anyone who was suspected of being a false prophet. John was a preacher to whom the people were flocking in hordes. The Sanhedrin may well have felt it their duty to check up on this man in case he was a false prophet.

The whole thing shows how suspicious orthodoxy was of anything unusual. John did not conform to the normal idea of a priest; and he did not conform to the normal idea of a preacher; therefore the religious authorities of the day looked upon him askance. The Church always runs the danger of condemning a new way just because it is new. In one sense, there is hardly any institution in the world which resents change so much as the Church does. It has often rejected a great teacher and often refused some great adventure simply because it suspected all things new.

THE WITNESS OF JOHN

John 1:19–28 (*contd*)

THE emissaries of the orthodox could think of three things that John might claim to be.

(1) They asked him if he was the Messiah. The Jews were waiting, and are waiting to this day, for the Messiah. There was no one idea of the Messiah. Some people expected one who would bring peace over all the earth. Some expected one who would bring in the reign of righteousness. Most expected one who would be a great national champion to lead the armies of the Jews as conquerors over all the world. Some expected a supernatural figure straight from God. Still more expected a prince to rise from David's line. Frequently, messianic pretenders arose and caused rebellions. The time of Jesus was an excited age. It was natural to ask John if he claimed to be the Messiah. John completely rejected that claim; but he rejected it with a certain hint. In the Greek, the word *I* is stressed by its position. It is as if John said: '*I* am not the Messiah; but, if you only knew, the Messiah is here.'

(2) They asked him if he was Elijah. It was the Jewish belief that, before the Messiah came, Elijah would return to herald his coming and to prepare the world to receive him. Particularly, Elijah was to come to arrange all disputes. He would settle what things and what people were clean and unclean; he would settle who were Jews and who were not Jews; he would bring together again families which were estranged. So much did the Jews believe this that the traditional law said that money and property whose owners were disputed, or anything found whose owner was unknown, must wait 'until Elijah comes'. This belief, that Elijah would come

before the Messiah, goes back to Malachi 4:5. It was even believed that Elijah would anoint the Messiah to his kingly office, as all kings were anointed, and that he would raise the dead to share in the new kingdom; but John denied that any such honour was his.

(3) They asked him if he was the expected and promised prophet. It was sometimes believed that Isaiah and, especially, Jeremiah would return at the coming of the Messiah. But this is really a reference to the assurance which Moses gave to the people in Deuteronomy 18:15: 'The Lord your God will raise up for you a prophet like me from among your own people; you shall heed such a prophet.' That was a promise that no Jew ever forgot. They waited and longed for the emergence of the prophet who would be the greatest of all prophets, *the Prophet par excellence*. But once again John denied that this honour was his.

So they asked him who he was; his answer was that he was nothing but a voice bidding men and women prepare the way for the King. The quotation is from Isaiah 40:3. All the gospels cite it (Mark 1:3; Matthew 3:3; Luke 3:4). The idea behind it is this. The roads of Palestine were not surfaced and metalled. They were mere tracks. When a king was about to visit a province, when a conqueror was about to travel through his domains, the roads were smoothed and straightened out and put in order. What John was saying was: 'I am nobody; I am only a voice telling you to get ready for the coming of the King, for he is on the way.'

John was what every true preacher and teacher ought to be – only a voice, a pointer to the King. The last thing that he wanted anyone to do was to look at him; he wanted people to forget him and see only the King.

But the Pharisees were puzzled about one thing – what right had John to baptize? If he had been the Messiah, or even Elijah or the prophet, he might have baptized. Ezekiel had said: 'I will sprinkle clean water upon you, and you shall be clean' (Ezekiel 36:25). Zechariah had said: 'On that day a fountain shall be opened for the house of David and the inhabitants of Jerusalem, to cleanse them from sin and impurity' (Zechariah 13:1). But why should John baptize?

What made the matter still more strange was this. This kind of baptism was not for Israelites at all. It was *proselytes*, incomers from other faiths, who were baptized. Israelites were never baptized; they were God's already and did not need to be washed. But *Gentiles* had to be washed in baptism. John was making Israelites do what only Gentiles had to do. He was suggesting that *the chosen people had to be cleansed.* That was indeed precisely what John believed. But he did not answer directly.

He said: 'I am baptizing only with water; but there is one among you – you don't recognize him – and I am not worthy to untie the straps of his shoes.' John could not have cited a more menial office. To untie the straps of sandals was slaves' work. There was a Rabbinic saying which said that a disciple might do for his master anything that a servant did, *except* only to untie his sandals. That was too menial a service for even a disciple to render. So John said: 'One is coming whose slave I am not fit to be.' We are to understand that by this time the baptism of Jesus had taken place at which John had recognized Jesus. So here John is saying again: 'The King is coming. And, for his coming, you need to be cleansed as much as any Gentile. Prepare yourself for the entry into history of the King.'

John's function was to be only the preparer of the way. Any greatness he had came from the greatness of the one whose coming he foretold. He is the great example of a man prepared to obliterate himself in order that Jesus Christ may be seen. He was only, as he saw it, a signpost pointing to Christ. God give *us* grace to forget ourselves and to remember only Christ.

THE LAMB OF GOD

John 1:29–31

> On the next day, John saw Jesus as he was coming towards him, and said: 'See! The Lamb of God who is taking away the sin of the world! This is he of whom I said to you: "There is a man who is coming after me, who has been advanced before me, because he was before me." Even I did not know him. All the same, the reason that I came baptizing with water is that he might be shown forth to Israel.'

HERE we come to the second day of this momentous week in the life of Jesus. By this time, his baptism and his temptations were past and he was about to set his hand to the work which he came into the world to do. Once again, the Fourth Gospel shows us John paying spontaneous tribute to Jesus. He calls him by that tremendous title which has become woven into the very language of devotion – *The Lamb of God*. What was in John's mind when he used that title? There are at least four pictures which may well contribute something to it.

(1) It may well have been that John was thinking of the Passover lamb. The Passover Feast was not very far away (John 2:13). The old story of the Passover was that it was the blood of the slain lamb which protected the houses of the Israelites on the night when they left Egypt (Exodus 12:11–13). On that night when the Angel of Death walked abroad

and slew the first-born of the Egyptians, the Israelites were to smear their doorposts with the blood of the slain lamb, and the angel, seeing it, would pass over that house. The blood of the lamb delivered them from destruction. It has been suggested that even as John the Baptist saw Jesus, there passed by flocks of lambs, being driven up to Jerusalem from the country districts to serve as sacrifices for the Passover Feast. The blood of the Passover lamb delivered the Israelites in Egypt from death; and it may be that John was saying: 'There is the one true sacrifice who can deliver you from death.' Paul too thought of Jesus as the Passover lamb (1 Corinthians 5:7). There is a deliverance that only Jesus Christ can win for us.

(2) John was the son of a priest. He would know all the ritual of the Temple and its sacrifices. Every morning and every evening, a lamb was sacrificed in the Temple for the sins of the people (Exodus 29:38–42). So long as the Temple stood, this daily sacrifice was made. Even when the people were starving in war and in siege, they never omitted to offer the lamb until in AD 70 the Temple was destroyed. It may be that John is saying: 'In the Temple, a lamb is offered every night and every morning for the sins of the people; but in this Jesus is the only sacrifice that can deliver men and women from sin.'

(3) There are two great pictures of the lamb in the prophets. Jeremiah writes: 'But I was like a gentle lamb led to the slaughter' (Jeremiah 11:19). And Isaiah has the great picture of the one who was brought 'like a lamb to the slaughter' (cf. Isaiah 53:7). Both these great prophets had the vision of one who by his sufferings and his sacrifice, meekly and lovingly borne, would redeem his people. Maybe John is saying: 'Your prophets dreamed of the one who was to love and suffer and die for the people; that one has come.' It is

certainly true that in later times the picture of Isaiah 53 became to the Church one of the most precious forecasts of Jesus in all the Old Testament. It may be that John the Baptist was the first to see it in this way.

(4) There is a fourth picture which would be very familiar to the Jews, although very strange to us. Between the Old and New Testaments there were the days of the great struggles of the Maccabees. In those days the lamb, and especially the horned lamb, was the symbol of a great conqueror. Judas Maccabaeus is so described, as are Samuel and David and Solomon. The lamb – strange as it may sound to us – stood for the conquering champion of God. It may well be that this is no picture of gentle and helpless weakness, but rather a picture of conquering majesty and power. Jesus was the champion of God who fought against sin and mastered it in single contest.

There is sheer wonder in this phrase, the Lamb of God. It haunted the writer of the Revelation. Twenty-nine times he used it. It becomes one of the most precious titles of Christ. In one word it sums up the love, the sacrifice, the suffering and the triumph of Christ.

John says that he did not know Jesus. Now John was a relative of Jesus (Luke 1:36), and he must have been acquainted with him. What John is saying is not that he did not know *who* Jesus was, but that he did not know *what* Jesus was. It had suddenly been revealed to him that Jesus was none other than the Son of God.

Once again, John makes clear what his only function was. It was to point others to Christ. He was nothing and Christ was everything. He claimed no greatness and no place for himself; he was only the man who, as it were, drew back the curtain and left Jesus occupying the lonely centre of the stage.

THE COMING OF THE SPIRIT

John 1:32-4

> So John bore his witness. 'With my own eyes,' he said,
> 'I saw the Spirit coming down from heaven, as it might
> have been a dove, and the Spirit remained upon him.
> And I did not know him. But it was he who sent me to
> baptize with water who said to me: "The one on whom
> you see the Spirit coming down and remaining is the one
> who baptizes with the Holy Spirit." And I saw it happen;
> and my witness stands that this is the Son of God.'

SOMETHING had happened at the baptism of Jesus which had
convinced John beyond all doubt that Jesus was the Son of
God. As the fathers of the Church saw centuries ago, it was
something which only the eye of the mind and soul could
see. But John saw it and was convinced.

In Palestine, the dove was a sacred bird. It was not hunted
and it was not eaten. The Jewish scholar Philo noticed the
number of doves at Ascalon, because it was not permitted to
catch and kill them, and they were tame. In Genesis 1:2, we
read of the creative Spirit of God moving upon the face of
the waters. The Rabbis used to say that the Spirit of God
moved and fluttered like a dove over the ancient chaos,
breathing order and beauty into it. The picture of the dove
was one which the Jews knew and loved.

It was at his baptism that the Spirit came down upon Jesus
with power. We must remember that at this time the *Christian*
doctrine of the Spirit had not yet come into being. We have to
wait for the last chapters of John's gospel and for Pentecost
for that to emerge. When John the Baptist spoke of the Spirit
coming upon Jesus, he must have been thinking in *Jewish*
terms. What then was the Jewish idea of the Spirit?

The Jewish word for Spirit is *ruach*, the word which means *wind*. In Judaism, there were always three basic ideas of the Spirit. The Spirit was *power*, power like a mighty rushing wind; the Spirit was *life*, the very dynamic of human existence; the Spirit was *God*; the power and the life of the Spirit were beyond mere human achievement and attainment; the coming of the Spirit into a person's life was the coming of God. Above all, it was the Spirit who controlled and inspired the prophets. 'I am filled with power, with the spirit of the Lord, and with justice and might, to declare to Jacob his transgression and to Israel his sin' (Micah 3:8). God speaks to Isaiah of 'my spirit that is upon you, and my words that I have put in your mouth' (Isaiah 59:21). 'The spirit of the Lord God is upon me, because the Lord has anointed me; he has sent me to bring good news' (Isaiah 61:1). 'A new heart I will give you, and a new spirit I will put within you . . . I will put my spirit within you' (Ezekiel 36:26–7). We may say that the Spirit of God did three things for those on whom he came. First, he brought to them the truth of God. Second, he gave them the power to recognize that truth when they saw it. Third, he gave them the ability and the courage to preach that truth to others. To a Jew, the Spirit was God coming into a person's life.

At his baptism, the Spirit came upon Jesus in a different way from that in which he ever came on any other person. Most people have what might be called spasmodic experiences of the Spirit. They have their moments of dazzling illumination, of extraordinary power, of superhuman courage. But these moments come and go. Twice (verses 32–3), John goes out of his way to point out that the Spirit *remained* on Jesus. Here was no momentary inspiration. In Jesus, the Spirit took up his permanent abode. That is still another way of saying that the mind and the power of God were uniquely in Jesus.

Here we can learn a great deal of what the word *baptism* means. The Greek verb *baptizein* means *to dip* or *to submerge*. It can be used of clothes being *dipped* in dye; it can be used of a ship *submerged* beneath the waves; it can be used of a person who is so drunk that he is *soaked* in drink. When John says that Jesus will baptize with the Holy Spirit, he means that Jesus can bring God's Spirit to us in such a way that we are saturated and our life and being are flooded with that Spirit.

Now what did this baptism mean for John? His own baptism meant two things. (1) It meant *cleansing*. It meant being washed from the impurities that cling to us. (2) It meant *dedication*. It meant going out to a new and a different and a better life. But Jesus' baptism was *a baptism of the Spirit*. If we remember the Jewish conception of the Spirit, we can say that when the Spirit takes possession of us certain things happen.

(1) Our lives are *enlightened*. There comes to us the knowledge of God and God's will. We know what God's purpose is, what life means, where duty lies. Some of God's wisdom and light has come into us.

(2) Our lives are *strengthened*. Knowledge without power is a haunting and frustrating thing. But the Spirit gives us not only knowledge to know the right, but also strength and power to do it. The Spirit gives us a triumphant adequacy to cope with life.

(3) Our lives are *purified*. Christ's baptism with the Spirit was to be a baptism of *fire* (Matthew 3:11; Luke 3:16). The dross of evil things, the alloy of the lower things, the base admixture is burned away until we become clean and pure.

Often our prayers for the Spirit are a kind of theological and liturgical formality; but when we know that for which we are praying, these prayers become a desperate cry from the heart.

THE FIRST DISCIPLES

John 1:35–9

> On the next day John was again standing with two of his disciples. John looked at Jesus as he walked. 'See!' he said, 'The Lamb of God!' And the two disciples heard him speaking and followed Jesus. Jesus turned and saw them following him. 'What are you looking for?' he said to them. 'Rabbi' (the word means Teacher), they said to him, 'where are you staying?' He said to them: 'Come and see!' They came and saw where he was staying, and they stayed with him throughout that day. And it was about 4 pm.

NEVER was a passage of Scripture fuller of little revealing touches than this.

Once again, we see John the Baptist pointing beyond himself. He must have known very well that to speak to his disciples about Jesus like that was to invite them to leave him and transfer their loyalty to this new and greater teacher; and yet he did it. There was no jealousy in John. He had come to attach people not to himself but to Christ. There is no harder task than to take the second place when once the first place was enjoyed. But as soon as Jesus emerged on the scene, John never had any other thought than to send people to him.

So the two disciples of John followed Jesus. It may well be that they were too shy to approach him directly and followed respectfully some distance behind. Then Jesus did something entirely characteristic. He turned and spoke to them. That is to say, he met them half-way. He made things easier for them. He opened the door that they might come in.

Here we have the symbol of the divine initiative. It is always God who takes the first step. When the human mind begins to seek and the human heart begins to long, God comes to meet us far more than half-way. God does not leave us to search and search until we come to him; God comes out to meet us. As Augustine said, we could not even have begun to seek for God unless he had already found us. When we go to God, we do not go to one who hides himself and keeps us at a distance; we go to one who stands waiting for us, and who even takes the initiative by coming to meet us on the road.

Jesus began by asking these two men the most fundamental question in life. 'What are you looking for?' he asked them. It was very relevant to ask that question in Palestine in the time of Jesus. Were they legalists, looking only for subtle and recondite conversations about the little details of the law, like the scribes and Pharisees? Were they ambitious time-servers looking for position and power, like the Sadducees? Were they nationalists looking for a political demagogue and a military commander who would smash the occupying power of Rome, like the Zealots? Were they humble men of prayer looking for God and for his will, like the Quiet in the Land? Or were they simply puzzled, bewildered, sinful men looking for light on the road of life and forgiveness from God?

It would be well if every now and again we were to ask ourselves: 'What am I looking for? What's my aim and goal? What am I really trying to get out of life?'

Some are searching for *security*. They would like a position which is safe, money enough to meet the needs of life and to put some past for the time when work is done, a material security which will take away the essential worry about material things. This is not a wrong aim, but it is a low aim, and an inadequate thing to which to direct all life; for, in the last analysis, there is no safe security in the chances and the changes of this life.

Some are searching for what they would call a *career*, for power, prominence, prestige, for a place to fit the talents and the abilities they believe themselves to have, for an opportunity to do the work they believe themselves capable of doing. If this is directed by motives of personal ambition it can be a bad aim; if it is directed by motives of the service of our neighbours it can be a high aim. But it is not enough, for its horizon is limited by time and by the world.

Some are searching for some kind of *peace*, for something to enable them to live at peace with themselves, and at peace with God, and at peace with others. This is the search for God; this aim only Jesus Christ can meet and supply.

The answer of John's disciples was that they wished to know where Jesus stayed. They called him *Rabbi*; that is a Hebrew word which literally means *My great one*. It was the title of respect given by students and seekers after knowledge to their teachers and to wise men. John, the evangelist, was writing for Greeks. He knew they would not recognize that Hebrew word, so he translated it for them by the Greek word *didaskalos*, *teacher*. It was not mere curiosity which made these two ask this question. What they meant was that they did not wish to speak to Jesus only on the road, in passing, as chance acquaintances might stop and exchange a few words. They wished to linger long with him and talk out their problems and their troubles. Those who would be Jesus' disciples can never be satisfied with a passing word. They want to meet Jesus, not as an acquaintance in passing, but as a friend in their own homes.

Jesus' answer was: 'Come and see!' The Jewish Rabbis had a way of using that phrase in their teaching. They would say: 'Do you want to know the answer to this question? Do you want to know the solution to this problem? Come and see, and we will think about it together.' When Jesus said: 'Come and see!' he was inviting them, not only to come and talk, but to come and find the things that he alone could open out to them.

John, who wrote the gospel, finishes the paragraph – 'It was about 4 pm.' It may very well be that he finishes that way because he was one of the two himself. He could tell you the very hour of the day and no doubt the very stone of the road he was standing on when he met Jesus. At 4 pm on a spring afternoon in Galilee, life became a new thing for him.

SHARING THE GLORY

John 1:40–2

> Andrew, Simon Peter's brother, was one of the two who had heard John speaking about Jesus, and who had followed him. First thing in the morning, he went and found his own brother Simon. 'We have found the Messiah,' he said to him. (The word *Messiah* means the same as the word *Christ*.) He brought him to Jesus. Jesus looked intently at him. 'You are Simon, Jona's son,' he said. 'You will be called Cephas.' *Cephas* is the same name as *Peter* and means a *rock*.

THE Revised Standard Version has it that Andrew '*first* found his brother Simon'. In the Greek manuscripts, there are two readings. Some manuscripts have the word *prōton*, which means *first*, and that is the reading that the Revised Standard Version has translated. Other manuscripts have *prōi*, which means *early in the morning*. In our translation, we have taken the second reading because it suits better the story of the first momentous week in Jesus' life to regard this event as taking place on the next day.

Again John explains a Hebrew word in order to help his Greek readers to understand better. *Messiah* and *Christ* are the same word. *Messiah* is Hebrew and *Christ* is Greek; both mean *anointed*. In the ancient world, as is still the case with the British monarchy, kings were anointed with oil at their coronation. *Messiah* and *Christos* both mean *God's anointed king*.

We do not possess a great deal of information about Andrew, but even the little that we know perfectly paints his character. He is one of the most attractive men in the apostolic band. He has two outstanding characteristics.

(1) Andrew was characteristically the man who was prepared to take second place. Again and again he is identified as *Simon Peter's brother*. It is clear that he lived under the shadow of Peter. People might not know who Andrew was, but everyone knew Peter; and when people spoke of Andrew they described him as Peter's brother. Andrew was not one of the inner circle of the disciples. When Jesus healed Jairus' daughter, when he went up to the Mount of Transfiguration, when he underwent his temptation in Gethsemane, it was Peter, James and John whom he took with him. It would have been so easy for Andrew to resent this. Was he not one of the first two disciples who ever followed Jesus? Did Peter not owe his meeting with Jesus to him? Might he not reasonably have expected a foremost place in the apostolic band? But all that never even occurred to Andrew. He was quite content to stand back and let his

brother have the limelight; he was quite content to play a humble part in the company of the Twelve. To Andrew, matters of precedence and place and honour mattered nothing at all. All that mattered was to be with Jesus and to serve him as well as he could. Andrew is the patron saint of all who humbly and loyally and ungrudgingly take the second place.

(2) Andrew is characteristically the man who was always introducing others to Jesus. There are only three times in the gospel story when Andrew is brought into the centre of the stage. There is this incident here, in which he brings Peter to Jesus. There is the incident in John 6:8-9 when he brings to Jesus the boy with the five loaves and two small fishes. And there is the incident in John 12:22 when he brings the inquiring Greeks into the presence of Jesus. It was Andrew's great joy to bring others to Jesus. He stands out as the man whose one desire was to share the glory. He is the man with the missionary heart. Having himself found the friendship of Jesus, he spent all his life in introducing others to that friendship. Andrew is our great example in that he could not keep Jesus to himself.

When Andrew brought Peter to Jesus, Jesus looked at Peter. The word used of that look is *emblepein*. It describes a concentrated, intent gaze, the gaze which does not see only the superficial things that lie on the surface, but which reads a person's heart. When Jesus saw Simon, as he was then called, he said to him: 'Your name is Simon; but you are going to be called Cephas, which means a rock.'

In the ancient world, most people had two names. Greek was the universal language, and most people had a name in their own native tongue by which they were known to their friends and their family circle, and also a name in the

Greek tongue by which they were known in the business and the commercial and the wider world. Sometimes one name was a translation of the other. *Peter* was the *Greek* and *Cephas* the *Aramaic* for a *rock*; *Thomas* was the Aramaic and *Didymus* the Greek for a *twin*; *Tabitha* was the Aramaic and *Dorcas* the Greek for a *gazelle*. Sometimes the Greek name was chosen because it sounded like the Aramaic name. A Jew who was called *Eliakim* or *Abel* in his own tongue might become *Alcimus* or *Apelles* to his Greek circle of acquaintances. So then *Peter* and *Cephas* are not different names; they are the same name in different languages.

In the Old Testament, a change of name often denoted a new relationship with God. For instance, *Jacob* became *Israel* (Genesis 32:28), and *Abram* became *Abraham* (Genesis 17:5) when they entered into a new relationship with God. When a person entered into a new relationship with God, it was as if life began all over again and that person became new, so that a new name was needed.

But the great thing about this story is that it tells us *how Jesus looks at us*. He does not only see what we are; he also sees what we *can become*. He sees not only the *actualities* in us; he also sees the *possibilities*. Jesus looked at Peter and saw in him not only a Galilaean fisherman but one who had it in him to become the rock on which his Church would be built. Jesus sees us not only as we are, but as we can be; and he says: 'Give your life to me, and I will make you what you have it in you to be.' Once someone came on Michelangelo chipping away with his chisel at a huge, shapeless piece of rock. He asked the sculptor what he was doing. 'I am releasing the angel imprisoned in this marble,' he answered. Jesus is the one who sees and can release the hidden potential in each of us.

THE SURRENDER OF NATHANAEL

John 1:43–51

> On the next day Jesus determined to go away to Galilee;
> and there he found Philip. Jesus said to him: 'Follow
> me!' Now Philip came from Bethsaida, which was the
> town from which Andrew and Peter came. Philip went
> and found Nathanael and said to him: 'We have found
> the One about whom Moses wrote in the law, and about
> whom the prophets spoke – I mean Jesus, the son of
> Joseph, the man from Nazareth.' Nathanael said to him:
> 'Can anything good come out of Nazareth?' Philip said
> to him: 'Come and see!' When Jesus saw Nathanael
> coming towards him, he said: 'See! A man who is really
> an Israelite! A man in whom there is no guile!'
> Nathanael said to him: 'How do you know me?' 'Before
> Philip called you,' said Jesus, 'I saw you when you were
> under the fig tree.' 'Rabbi,' answered Nathanael, 'you
> are the Son of God; you are the King of Israel.' Jesus
> answered: 'Do you believe because I said to you, "I
> saw you under the fig-tree"? You will see greater things
> than these.' He said to him: 'This is the truth I tell you
> – you will see the heavens opened, and the angels of
> God ascending and descending on the Son of Man.'

AT this point in the story, Jesus left the south and went north
to Galilee. There, perhaps in Cana, he found and called Philip.
Philip, like Andrew, could not keep the good news to himself.
As the Swiss theologian F. L. Godet said: 'One lighted torch
serves to light another.' So Philip went and found his friend
Nathanael. He told him that he believed that he had discovered
the long-promised Messiah in Jesus, the man from Nazareth.
Nathanael was contemptuous. There was nothing in the Old
Testament which foretold that God's chosen one should come

from Nazareth. Nazareth was a quite undistinguished place. Nathanael himself came from Cana, another Galilaean town, and, in country places, jealousy between town and town, and rivalry between village and village, is notorious. Nathanael's reaction was to declare that Nazareth was not the kind of place that anything good was likely to come out of. Philip was wise. He did not argue. He said simply: 'Come and see!'

Not very many people have ever been argued into Christianity. Often our arguments do more harm than good. The only way to convince people of the supremacy of Christ is to confront them with Christ. On the whole, it is true to say that it is not argumentative and philosophical preaching and teaching which have won men and women for Christ; it is the presentation of the story of the cross.

There is a story which tells how, towards the end of the nineteenth century, Thomas Huxley, the great agnostic, was a member of a house party at a country house. Sunday came round, and most of the members prepared to go to church; but, very naturally, Huxley did not propose to go. Huxley approached a man known to have a simple and radiant Christian faith. He said to him: 'Suppose you don't go to church today. Suppose you stay at home and you tell me quite simply what your Christian faith means to you and why you are a Christian.' 'But', said the man, 'you could demolish my arguments in an instant. I'm not clever enough to argue with you.' Huxley said gently: 'I don't want to argue with you; I just want you to tell me simply what this Christ means to you.' The man stayed at home and told Huxley most simply of his faith. When he had finished there were tears in the great agnostic's eyes. 'I would give my right hand,' he said, 'if only I could believe that.'

It was not clever argument that touched Huxley's heart. He could have dealt efficiently and devastatingly with any

argument that that simple, uncomplicated Christian was likely
to have produced; but the simple presentation of Christ went
straight to his heart. The best argument is to say to people:
'Come and see!' Of course, we have to know Christ ourselves
before we can invite others to come to him. The true
evangelist must personally have met Christ first.

So Nathanael came; and Jesus could see into his heart.
'Here', said Jesus, 'is a genuine Israelite, a man in whose
heart there is no guile.' That was a tribute that any devout
Israelite would recognize. 'Happy are those', said the
psalmist, 'to whom the Lord imputes no iniquity, and in whose
spirit there is no deceit' (Psalm 32:2). 'He had done no
violence,' said the prophet of the Servant of the Lord, 'and
there was no deceit in his mouth' (Isaiah 53:9).

Nathanael was surprised that anyone could give a verdict
like that on so short an acquaintance, and he demanded how
Jesus could possibly know him. Jesus told him that he had
already seen him under the fig tree. What is the significance
of that? To the Jews, the fig tree always stood for peace.
Their idea of peace was when they could be undisturbed
under their own vines and their own fig trees (cf. 1 Kings
4:25; Micah 4:4). Further, the fig tree was leafy and shady
and it was the custom to sit and meditate under the roof of
its branches. No doubt that was what Nathanael had been
doing; and no doubt as he sat under the fig tree he had
prayed for the day when God's chosen one should come. No
doubt he had been meditating on the promises of God. And
now he felt that Jesus had seen into the very depths of his
heart.

It was not so much that Jesus had seen him under the fig
tree that surprised Nathanael; it was the fact that Jesus had
read the thoughts of his inmost heart. Nathanael said to
himself: 'Here is the man who understands my dreams! Here

is the man who knows my prayers! Here is the man who has
seen into my most intimate and secret longings, longings
which I have never even dared put into words! Here is
the man who can translate the inarticulate sigh of my soul!
This must be God's promised Anointed One and no other.'
Nathanael capitulated forever to the man who read and
understood and satisfied his heart.

It may be that Jesus smiled. He quoted the old story of
Jacob at Bethel who had seen the golden ladder leading up
to heaven (Genesis 28:12–13). It was as if Jesus said:
'Nathanael, I can do far more than read your heart. I can be
for you and for everyone the way, the ladder that leads to
heaven.' It is through Jesus and Jesus alone that human souls
can mount the ladder which leads to heaven.

This passage presents us with a problem. Who was
Nathanael? In the Fourth Gospel, he is one of the first group
of disciples; in the other three gospels, he never appears at
all. More than one explanation has been given.

(1) It has been suggested that Nathanael is not a real figure
at all, but an ideal figure standing for all the true Israelites
who burst the bonds of national pride and prejudice and gave
themselves to Jesus Christ.

(2) On the same basis, it has been suggested that he stands
either for Paul or for the beloved disciple. Paul was the great
example of the Israelite who had accepted Christ; the beloved
disciple was the ideal disciple. Again the supposition is that
Nathanael stands for an ideal; that he is a type and not a
person. If this were the only mention of Nathanael, that might
be true; but Nathanael appears again in John 21:2, and there
is no thought of him as an ideal there.

(3) He has been identified with Matthew, because both
Matthew and *Nathanael* mean *the gift of God*. We saw that in
those days most people had two names; but then one name

was Greek and the other Jewish. In this case, both *Matthew* and *Nathanael* are Jewish names.

(4) There is a simpler explanation. *Nathanael* was brought to Jesus by *Philip*. *Nathanael's* name is never mentioned in the other three gospels; and in the Fourth Gospel *Bartholomew's* name is never mentioned. Now, in the list of the disciples in Matthew 10:3 and Mark 3:18, *Philip* and *Bartholomew* come together, as if it was natural and inevitable to connect them. Moreover, *Bartholomew* is really a *second* name. It means *Son of Tholmai* or *Ptolemy. Bartholomew* must have had another name, a first name; and it is at least possible that *Bartholomew* and *Nathanael* are the same person under different names. That certainly fits the facts.

Whatever else, it is true that Nathanael stands for the Israelite whose heart was cleansed of pride and prejudice and who saw in Jesus the one who satisfied the longing of his waiting, seeking heart.

THE NEW EXHILARATION

John 2:1–11

> Two days after this there was a wedding in Cana of Galilee; and Jesus' mother was there. And Jesus was invited to the wedding and so were his disciples. When the wine had run short, Jesus' mother said to him: 'They have no wine.' Jesus said to her: 'Lady, let me handle this in my own way. My hour has not yet come.' His mother said to the servants: 'Do whatever he tells you to do.' There were six stone water pots standing there – they were needed for the Jewish purifying customs – and each of them held about twenty or thirty gallons. Jesus said to them: 'Fill the water pots with water.' They filled them up to the very brim. He said to them: 'Draw

from them now, and take what you draw to the steward
in charge.' They did so. When the steward had tasted
the water which had become wine – he did not know
where it came from, but the servants who had drawn
the water knew – the steward called the bridegroom
and said to him: 'Everyone first sets before the guests
the good wine, and then, when they have drunk their
fill, he sets before them the inferior wine. You have
kept the good wine until now.'

Jesus did the first of his signs in Cana of Galilee, and
displayed his glory; and his disciples believed on him.

THE very richness of the Fourth Gospel presents those who
would study it and anyone who would expound it with a
problem. Always there are two things. There is a simple
surface story that anyone can understand and retell; but there
is also a wealth of deeper meaning for those who have the
eagerness to search and the eyes to see and the minds to
understand. There is so much in a passage like this that we
must study it in stages. We shall look at it first of all quite
simply to set it within its background and to see it come alive.
We shall then look at certain of the things it tells us about
Jesus and his work. And finally we shall look at the permanent
truth which John is seeking to tell us in it.

Cana of Galilee is so called to distinguish it from Cana in
Coelo-Syria. It was a village quite near to Nazareth. Jerome,
who stayed in Palestine, says that he saw it from Nazareth. In
Cana, there was a wedding feast to which Mary went and at
which she held a special place. She had something to do with
the arrangements, for she was worried when the wine ran
out; and she had authority enough to order the servants to do
whatever Jesus told them to do. Some of the later gospels
which never got into the New Testament add certain details
to this story. One of the Coptic gospels tells us that Mary was

a sister of the bridegroom's mother. There is an early set of Prefaces to the books of the New Testament called the Monarchian Prefaces which tell us that the bridegroom was none other than John himself, and that his mother was Salome, the sister of Mary. We do not know whether these extra details are true or not, but the story is so vividly told that it is clearly an eyewitness account.

There is no mention of Joseph. The explanation most probably is that by this time Joseph was dead. It would seem that Joseph died quite soon, and that the reason why Jesus spent eighteen long years in Nazareth was that he had to take upon himself the support of his mother and his family. It was only when his younger brothers and sisters were able to look after themselves that he left home.

The scene is a village wedding feast. In Palestine a wedding was a really notable occasion. It was the Jewish law that the wedding of a virgin should take place on a Wednesday. This is interesting because it gives us a date from which to work back; and if this wedding took place on a Wednesday it must have been the Sabbath day when Jesus first met Andrew and John and they stayed the whole day with him. The wedding festivities lasted for far more than one day. The wedding ceremony itself took place late in the evening, after a feast. After the ceremony, the young couple were conducted to their new home. By that time it was dark and they were conducted through the village streets by the light of flaming torches and with a canopy over their heads. They were taken by as long a route as possible so that as many people as possible would have the opportunity to wish them well. But a newly married couple did not go away for their honeymoon; they stayed at home; and for a week they kept open house. They wore crowns and dressed in their bridal robes. They were treated like a king and queen, were actually addressed as king and queen, and their word was law. In a life where there was much poverty and constant hard work, this week of festivity and joy was one of the supreme occasions.

It was in a happy time like this that Jesus gladly shared. But something went wrong. It is likely that the coming of Jesus caused something of a problem. He had been invited to the feast, but he had arrived not alone but with five disciples. Five extra people may well have caused complications. Five unexpected guests might provide any festival with a problem, and the wine ran out.

For a Jewish feast, wine was essential. 'Without wine,' said the Rabbis, 'there is no joy.' It was not that people were drunk, but in this part of the world wine was an essential. Drunkenness was in fact a great disgrace, and they actually drank their wine in a mixture composed of two parts of wine to three parts of water. At any time, the failure of provisions would have been a problem, for hospitality in the middle east is a sacred duty; but for the provisions to fail at a wedding would be a terrible humiliation for the bride and the bridegroom.

So Mary came to Jesus to tell him that it was so. The Authorized Version translation of Jesus' reply makes it sound very discourteous. It makes him say: 'Woman, what have I to do with thee?' That is indeed a translation of the *words*, but it does not in any way give the *tone*.

The phrase, 'What have I to do with you?' was a common conversational phrase. When it was uttered angrily and sharply it did indicate complete disagreement and reproach, but when it was spoken gently it indicated not so much reproach but misunderstanding. It means: 'Don't worry; you don't quite understand what is going on; leave things to me, and I will settle them in my own way.' Jesus was simply telling Mary to leave things to him, that he would have his own way of dealing with the situation.

The word *woman* (*gunai*) is also misleading. It sounds to us very rough and abrupt. But it is the same word that Jesus used on the cross to address Mary as he left her to the care of John (John 19:26). In Homer, it is the title by which Odysseus addresses Penelope, his well-loved wife. It is the title by which Augustus, the Roman emperor, addressed Cleopatra, the famous Egyptian queen. So far from being a rough and discourteous way of address, it was a title of respect. We have no way of speaking in English which exactly renders it; but it is better to translate it *lady*, which gives at least the courtesy in it.

However Jesus spoke, Mary was confident of him. She told the servants to do as Jesus told them to do. At the door, there were six great water jars. The word that the Authorized Version translates as *firkin* represents the Hebrew measure called the *bath*, which was a measure equivalent to between eight and nine gallons. The jars were very large; they would each hold between twenty and thirty gallons.

John was writing his gospel for Greeks, and so he explains that these jars were there to provide water for the purifying ceremonies of the Jews. Water was required for two purposes. First, it was required for cleansing the feet on entry to the house. The roads were not surfaced. Sandals were merely a sole attached to the foot by straps. On a dry day the feet were covered by dust and on a wet day they were soiled with mud; and the water was used for cleansing them. Second, it was required for the handwashing. Strict Jews washed their hands before a meal and between each course. First the hand was held upright and the water was poured over it in such a way that it ran right to the wrist; then the hand was held pointing down and the water was poured in such a way that it ran from the wrist to the fingertips. This was done with each hand in turn; and then each palm was cleansed by rubbing it with the fist of the other hand. The Jewish ceremonial law insisted that this should be done not only at the beginning of a meal but also between courses. If it was not done, the hands were technically *unclean*. It was for this footwashing and hand-washing that these great stone jars of water stood there.

Jesus commanded that the jars should be filled to the brim. John mentions that point to make it clear that nothing else but water was put into them. He then told them to draw out the water and to take it to the *architriklinos*, the steward in charge. At their banquets, the Romans had a toastmaster called the *arbiter bibendi*, the arranger of the drinking. Sometimes one of the guests acted as a kind of master of ceremonies at a Jewish wedding. But our equivalent of the *architriklinos* is really the head waiter. He was responsible for the seating of the guests and the correct running of the feast. When he tasted the water which had become wine, he was astonished. He called the bridegroom – it was the bridegroom's parents who were responsible for the feast – and spoke jestingly. 'Most people', he said, 'serve the good wine first; and then, when the guests have drunk a good deal, and their palates are dulled and they are not in much of a condition to appreciate what they are drinking, they serve the inferior wine; but you have kept the best until now.'

So it was at a village girl's wedding in a Galilaean village that Jesus first showed his glory; and it was there that his disciples caught another dazzling glimpse of what he was.

THE NEW EXHILARATION

John 2:1–11 (*contd*)

WE note three general things about this wonderful deed which Jesus did.

(1) We note *when* it happened. It happened at a wedding feast. Jesus was perfectly at home at such an occasion. He was no severe, austere killjoy. He loved to share in the happy rejoicing of a wedding feast.

There are certain religious people who shed a gloom wherever they go. They are suspicious of all joy and happiness. To them, religion is a thing of black clothes, the lowered voice, the expulsion of social fellowship. It was said of Alice Freeman Palmer by one of her students: 'She made me feel as if I was bathed in sunshine.' Jesus was like that. The Baptist scholar C. H. Spurgeon in his book *Lectures to my Students* has some wise, if caustic, advice. 'Sepulchral tones may fit a man to be an undertaker, but Lazarus is not called out of his grave by hollow moans.' 'I know brethren who from head to foot, in garb, tone, manner, necktie and boots are so utterly *parsonic* that no particle of manhood is visible . . . Some men appear to have a white cravat twisted round their souls, their manhood is throttled with that starched rag.' 'An individual who has no geniality about him had better be an undertaker, and bury the dead, for he will never succeed in influencing the living.' 'I commend cheerfulness to all who would win souls; not levity and frothiness, but a genial, happy spirit. There are more flies caught with honey than with vinegar, and there will be more souls led to heaven by a man who wears heaven in his face than by one who bears Tartarus [bears a fierce expression] in his looks.'

Jesus never counted it a crime to be happy. Why should his followers do so?

(2) We note *where* it happened. It happened in a humble home in a village in Galilee. This miracle was not performed against the background of some great occasion and in the presence of vast crowds. It was performed in a home. A. H. N. Green Armytage in his book, *A Portrait of St Luke*,

speaks of how Luke delighted to show Jesus against a background of simple, homely things and people. In a vivid phrase, he says that St Luke's gospel 'domesticated God'; it brought God right into the home circle and into the ordinary things of life. Jesus' action at Cana of Galilee shows what he thought of a home. As the Revised Standard Version has it, he 'manifested forth his glory', and that manifestation took place within a home.

There is a strange paradox in the attitude of many people to the place they call home. They would admit at once that there is no more precious place in all the world; and yet, at the same time, they would also have to admit that in it they claim the right to be far more discourteous, far more boorish, far more selfish, far more impolite than they would dare to be in any society of strangers. Many of us treat the ones we love most in a way that we would never dare to treat a chance acquaintance. So often it is strangers who see us at our best and those who live with us who see us at our worst. We ought always to remember that it was in a humble home that Jesus manifested forth his glory. To him, home was a place for which nothing but his best was good enough.

(3) We note *why* it happened. We have already seen that in the middle east hospitality was always a sacred duty. It would have brought embarrassed shame to that home that day if the wine had run out. It was to save a humble Galilaean family from hurt that Jesus put forth his power. It was in sympathy, in kindness, in understanding for ordinary people that Jesus acted.

Nearly everyone can do the big thing on the big occasion; but it takes Jesus to do the big thing on a simple, homely occasion like this. There is a kind of natural human maliciousness which rather enjoys the misfortunes of others and which delights to make a good story of them in idle gossip. But

Jesus, the Lord of all life, and the King of glory, used his power to save a Galilaean wedding couple from humiliation. It is just by such deeds of understanding, simple kindliness that we too can show that we are followers of Jesus Christ.

Further, this story shows us very beautifully two things about Mary's faith in Jesus.

(1) Instinctively Mary turned to Jesus whenever something went wrong. She knew her son. It was not till he was thirty years old that Jesus left home; and all these years Mary lived with him. There is an old legend which tells of the days when Jesus was a little baby in the home in Nazareth. It tells how in those days, when people felt tired and worried and hot and bothered and upset, they would say: 'Let us go and look at Mary's child,' and they would go and look at Jesus, and somehow all their troubles rolled away. It is still true that those who know Jesus intimately turn instinctively to him when things go wrong – and they never find him wanting.

(2) Even when Mary did not understand what Jesus was going to do, even when it seemed that he had refused her request, Mary still believed in him so much that she turned to the serving folk and told them to do whatever Jesus told them to do. Mary had the faith which could trust even when it did not understand. She did not know what Jesus was going to do, but she was quite sure that he would do the right thing. In every life come periods of darkness when we do not see the way. In every life come things which are such that we do not see why they came or any meaning in them. Happy are those who in such a case still trust even when they cannot understand.

Still further, this story tells us something about Jesus. In answer to Mary, he said: 'My hour has not yet come.' All through the gospel story, Jesus talks about *his hour*. In John 7:6, 8 it is the hour of his emergence as the Messiah. In John

12:23 and 17:1, and in Matthew 26:18, 45 and in Mark 14:41 it is the hour of his crucifixion and his death. All through his life, Jesus knew that he had come into this world for a definite purpose and a definite task. He saw his life not in terms of his wishes, but in terms of God's purpose for himself. He saw his life not against the shifting background of time, but against the steady background of eternity. All through his life, he went steadily towards that hour for which he knew that he had come into the world. It is not only Jesus who came into this world to fulfil the purpose of God. It has been said that each one of us is 'a dream and an idea of God'. We, too, must think not of our own wishes and our own desires, but of the purpose for which God sent us into his world.

THE NEW EXHILARATION

John 2:1–11 (*contd*)

Now we must think of the deep and permanent truth which John is seeking to teach when he tells this story.

We must remember that John was writing out of a double background. He was a Jew and he was writing for Jews; but his great object was to write the story of Jesus in such a way that it would come home also to the Greeks.

Let us look at it first of all from the *Jewish* point of view. We must always remember that beneath John's simple stories there is a deeper meaning which is open only to those who have eyes to see. In all his gospel, John never wrote an unnecessary or an insignificant detail. Everything means something, and everything points beyond.

There were six stone water pots; and at the command of Jesus, the water in them turned to wine. According to the Jews, *seven* is the number which is complete and perfect;

and *six* is the number which is unfinished and imperfect. The six stone water pots stand for all the imperfections of the Jewish law. Jesus came to do away with the imperfections of the law and to put in their place the new wine of the gospel of his grace. Jesus turned the imperfection of the law into the perfection of grace.

There is another thing to note in this connection. There were six water pots; each held between twenty and thirty gallons of water; Jesus turned the water into wine. That would give anything up to 180 gallons of wine. Simply to state that fact is to show that John did not mean the story to be taken with crude literalness. What John did mean to say is that when the grace of Jesus comes to men and women there is enough and to spare for all. No wedding party on earth could drink 180 gallons of wine. No need on earth can exhaust the grace of Christ; there is a glorious superabundance in it.

John is telling us that in Jesus the imperfections have become perfection, and the grace has become illimitable, sufficient and more than sufficient for every need.

Let us look at it now from the Greek point of view. It so happens that the Greeks actually possessed stories like this. Dionysos was the Greek god of wine. Pausanias was a Greek who wrote a description of his country and of its ancient ceremonies. In his description of Elis, he describes an old ceremony and belief: 'Between the market place and the Menius is an old theatre and a sanctuary of Dionysos; the image is by Praxiteles. No god is more revered by the Eleans than Dionysos is, and they say that he attends their festival of the Thyia. The place where they hold the festival called the Thyia is about a mile from the city. Three empty kettles are taken into the building and deposited there by the priests in the presence of the citizens and of any strangers who may happen to be staying in the country. On the doors of the buildings the priests, and all who choose to do so, put their seals. Next day they are free to examine the seals, and on entering the building they find the kettles full of wine. I was not there myself at the time of the festival, but the most respectable men of Elis, and strangers too, swore that the facts were as I have said.'

So the Greeks, too, had their stories like this; and it is as if John said to them: 'You have your stories and your legends about your gods. They are only stories and you know that they are not really true. But Jesus has come to do what you have always dreamed that your gods could do. He has come to make the things you longed for come true.'

To the Jews, John said: 'Jesus has come to turn the imperfection of the law into the perfection of grace.' To the Greeks, he said: 'Jesus has come really and truly to do the things you only dreamed the gods could do.'

Now we can see what John is teaching us. Every story tells us not of something Jesus did once and never again, but of something which he is forever doing. John tells us not of things that Jesus once did in Palestine, but of things that he still does today. And what John wants us to see here is not that Jesus once on a day turned some water pots of water into wine; he wants us to see that whenever Jesus comes into a person's life, there comes a new quality which is like turning water into wine. Without Jesus, life is dull and stale and flat; when Jesus comes into it, life becomes vivid and sparkling and exciting. Without Jesus, life is drab and uninteresting; with him it is thrilling and exhilarating.

When the missionary doctor Sir Wilfred Grenfell was appealing for volunteers for his work in Labrador, he said that he could not promise them much money, but he could promise them the time of their lives. That is what Jesus promises us. Remember that John was writing seventy years after Jesus was crucified. For seventy years he had thought and meditated and remembered, until he saw meanings and significances that he had not seen at the time. When John told this story, he was remembering what life with Jesus was like; and he said, 'Wherever Jesus went and whenever he came into life, it was like water turning into wine.' This story is John saying to *us*: 'If you want the new exhilaration, become a follower of Jesus Christ, and there will come a change in your life which will be like water turning into wine.'

THE ANGER OF JESUS

John 2:12–16

> After this Jesus went down to Capernaum with his mother and his brothers and his disciples; and they stayed there for a short time.
>
> The Passover Feast of the Jews was near, and Jesus went up to Jerusalem. In the Temple he found those who were selling oxen and sheep and doves, and the money-changers sitting at their tables. He made a scourge of cords and drove them all out of the Temple, and the sheep and the oxen as well. He scattered the coins of the exchangers and overturned their tables. He said to those who were selling doves: 'Take these away and stop making my Father's house a house of trade.'

AFTER the wedding feast at Cana of Galilee, Jesus and his friends returned for a short visit to Capernaum, on the north shore of the Sea of Galilee and about twenty miles distant.

Shortly after this, Jesus set out to observe the Passover Feast in Jerusalem. The Passover fell on 15th Nisan, which is about the middle of April; and, according to the law, it was obligatory for every adult male Jew who lived within fifteen miles of Jerusalem to attend the feast.

Here we have a very interesting thing. At first sight, John has a quite different chronology of the life of Jesus from that of the other three gospels. In them, Jesus is depicted as going to Jerusalem only once. The Passover Feast at which he was crucified is the only one they mention, and his only visit to Jerusalem except the visit to the Temple when he was a boy. But in John we find Jesus making frequent visits to Jerusalem. John tells us of no fewer than three Passovers – this present one, the one in 6:4 and the one in 11:55. In addition, according to John's story, Jesus was in Jerusalem for an unnamed feast in 5:1; for the Feast of Tabernacles in 7:2, 10; and for the Feast of the Dedication in 10:22. In point of fact, in the other three gospels the main ministry of Jesus is in Galilee; in John, Jesus is in Galilee only for brief periods (2:1–12, 4:43–5:1, 6:1–7:14), and his main ministry is in Jerusalem.

The truth is that there is no real contradiction here. John and the others are telling the story from different points of view. They do not contradict but complement each other. Matthew, Mark and Luke concentrate on the ministry in Galilee; John concentrates on the ministry in Jerusalem. Although the other three tell us of only one visit to Jerusalem and one Passover there, they imply that there must have been many others. At his last visit, they show us Jesus mourning over Jerusalem: 'Jerusalem, Jerusalem, the city that kills the prophets and stones those who are sent to it! How often have I desired to gather your children together as a hen gathers her brood under her wings, and you were not willing!' (Matthew 23:37). Jesus could never have spoken like that if he had not made repeated appeals to Jerusalem and if the visit at which he was crucified was his first. We ought not to talk about the contradictions between the Fourth Gospel and the other three, but to use them all to get as complete a picture of the life of Jesus as possible.

But there is a real difficulty we must face. This passage tells of the incident known as the cleansing of the Temple. John sets it right at the *beginning* of the ministry of Jesus, while the other three gospel writers set it right at the *end* (Matthew 21:12–13; Mark 11:15–17; Luke 19:45–6). This definitely needs explanation; and various explanations have been put forward.

(1) It is suggested that Jesus cleansed the Temple twice, once at the beginning and once at the end of his ministry. That is not very likely, because if he had done this staggering thing once, it is very unlikely that he would ever have had the chance to do it again. His reappearance in the Temple would have been a sign for such precautions to be taken that a repetition of it would not have been possible.

(2) It is suggested that John is right and that the other three are wrong. But the incident fits in much better at the end of Jesus' ministry. It is the natural succession to the blazing courage of the triumphal entry and the inevitable prelude to the crucifixion. If we have to choose between John's dating and the dating of the other three, we must choose the dating of the three.

(3) It is suggested that when John died he left his gospel not completely finished; that he left the various incidents written out on separate sheets of papyrus and not bound together. It is then suggested that the sheet containing the account of this incident got out of place and was inserted near the beginning of the manuscript instead of near the end. That is quite possible, but it involves assuming that the person who arranged the manuscript did not know the correct order, which is difficult to believe when he must have known at least some of the other gospels.

(4) We must always remember that John, as someone has said, is more interested in the truth than in the facts. He is not

interested in writing a chronological biography of Jesus but supremely interested in showing Jesus as the Son of God and the Messiah. It is probable that John was thinking back to the great prophecies of the coming of the Messiah. 'And the Lord whom you seek will suddenly come to his temple. The messenger of the covenant in whom you delight – indeed, he is coming, says the Lord of hosts. But who can endure the day of his coming, and who can stand when he appears? For he is like a refiner's fire and like fullers' soap . . . he will purify the descendants of Levi . . . until they present offerings to the Lord in righteousness. Then the offering of Judah and Jerusalem will be pleasing to the Lord as in the days of old and as in former years' (Malachi 3:1–4). John had these tremendous prophecies ringing in his mind. He was not interested in *when* Jesus cleansed the Temple; he was supremely interested in the fact that Jesus *did* cleanse the Temple, because that cleansing was the act of the promised Messiah of God. All the likelihood is that John put this tremendous incident here to set in the very forefront of his story the great fact that Jesus was the Messiah of God who had come to cleanse the worship of men and women and to open the door to God. It is not the date that John is interested in; the date does not matter; his great concern is to show that Jesus' actions prove him to be the promised one of God. Right at the beginning, he shows us Jesus acting as God's Messiah must act.

THE ANGER OF JESUS

John 2:12–16 (*contd*)

Now let us see why Jesus acted as he did. His anger is a terrifying thing; the picture of Jesus with the whip is an awe-inspiring sight. We must see what moved Jesus to this white-hot anger in the Temple courts.

The Passover was the greatest of all the Jewish feasts. As
we have already seen, the law laid it down that every adult
male Jew who lived within fifteen miles of Jerusalem was
bound to attend it. But it was not only the Jews in Palestine
who came to the Passover. By this time Jews were scattered
all over the world, but they never forgot their ancestral faith
and their ancestral land; and it was the dream and aim of all
Jews, no matter in what land they stayed, to celebrate at least
one Passover in Jerusalem. Astonishing as it may sound, it is
likely that as many as 2,250,000 Jews sometimes assembled
in the holy city to keep the Passover.

There was a tax that every Jew over nineteen years of age
must pay. That was the Temple tax. It was necessary that all
should pay that tax so that the Temple sacrifices and the
Temple ritual might be carried out day by day. The tax was
one half-shekel. It was equivalent to almost two days'
wages. For all ordinary purposes in Palestine, all kinds of
currency were valid. Silver coins from Rome and Greece and
Egypt and Tyre and Sidon and Palestine itself all were in
circulation and all were valid. But the Temple tax had to be
paid either in Galilaean shekels or in shekels of the sanctuary.
These were Jewish coins, and so could be used as a gift to the
Temple; the other currencies were foreign and so were
unclean; they might be used to pay ordinary debts, but not a
debt to God.

Pilgrims arrived from all over the world with all kinds of
coins. So in the Temple courts there sat the *money-changers*.
If their trade had been straightforward they would have been
fulfilling an honest and a necessary purpose. But what they
did was to charge a commission for every half-shekel they
changed, and to make a second charge on every half-shekel
of change they had to give if a larger coin was tendered. So,
if a man came with a coin the value of which was two shekels,

he had to pay to get it changed, and again to get his change of three half-shekels. In other words, the money-changers made considerable capital out of him – on such a transaction the equivalent of one day's wage.

The wealth which accrued from the Temple tax and from this method of money-changing was fantastic. The annual revenue of the Temple from the Temple tax has been estimated to run to the equivalent of £100,000. The money-changers themselves made a tidy profit running into thousands. When Crassus captured Jerusalem and raided the Temple treasury in 54 BC, he took from it the equivalent of several millions without coming near to exhausting it.

The fact that the money-changers received some commission when they changed the coins of the pilgrims was not in itself wrong. The *Talmud* laid it down: 'It is necessary that everyone should have half a shekel to pay for himself. Therefore when he comes to the exchange to change a shekel for two half-shekels he is obliged to allow the money-changer some gain.' The word for this commission was *kollubos*, and the money-changers are called *kollubistai*. This word *kollubos* produced the comedy character name Kollybos in Greek and Collybus in Latin, which meant much the same as Shylock in English.

What enraged Jesus was that pilgrims to the Passover, who could ill afford it, were being fleeced at an exorbitant rate by the money-changers. It was a rampant and shameless social injustice – and what was worse, it was being done in the name of religion.

Besides the money-changers there were also the sellers of oxen and sheep and doves. Frequently a visit to the Temple meant a sacrifice. Many a pilgrim would wish to make thank-offering for a favourable journey to the holy city; and most acts and events in life had their appropriate sacrifice. It might therefore seem to be a natural and helpful thing that the victims for the sacrifices could be bought in the Temple court. It might well have been so. But the law was that any animal offered in sacrifice must be perfect and unblemished. The Temple authorities had appointed inspectors (*mumcheh*) to examine the victims which were to be offered, and a fee was charged for this inspection. If a worshipper bought a victim outside the Temple, it was to all intents and purposes certain that it would be rejected after examination. Again that might not have mattered much, but a pair of doves could cost as much as fifteen times more inside the Temple than if it had been purchased outside. Here again was bare-faced extortion at the expense of poor and humble pilgrims, who were practically blackmailed into buying their victims from the Temple booths if they wished to sacrifice at all – once more a glaring social injustice aggravated by the fact that it was perpetrated in the name of pure religion.

It was that which moved Jesus to flaming anger. We are told that he took cords and made a whip. The early Christian biblical scholar Jerome thinks that the very sight of Jesus made the whip unnecessary. 'A certain fiery and starry light shone from his eyes, and the majesty of the Godhead gleamed in his face.' Just because Jesus loved God, he loved God's children, and it was impossible for him to stand passively by while the worshippers of Jerusalem were treated in this way.

THE ANGER OF JESUS

John 2:12–16 (*contd*)

WE have seen that it was the deliberate and shameless exploitation of the pilgrims which moved Jesus to immediate wrath; but there were deep things behind the cleansing of the

Temple. Let us see if we can penetrate to the even deeper reasons why Jesus took this drastic step.

No two of the evangelists give Jesus' words in precisely the same way. They all remembered their own version. It is only by putting all the accounts together that we get a true picture of what Jesus said. So then let us set down the different ways in which the writers report the words of Jesus. Matthew gives them as: '"My house shall be called a house of prayer"; but you are making it a den of robbers' (Matthew 21:13). Mark has it: '"My house shall be called a house of prayer for all the nations" . . . But you have made it a den of robbers' (Mark 11:17). Luke has it: '"My house shall be a house of prayer"; but you have made it a den of robbers' (Luke 19:46). John has it: 'Take these things out of here! Stop making my Father's house a market-place!' (John 2:16).

There were at least three reasons why Jesus acted as he did, and why anger was in his heart.

(1) He acted as he did because God's house was being desecrated. In the Temple, there was worship without reverence. Reverence is an instinctive thing. Edward Seago, the artist, tells how he took the children of some travellers on a visit to a cathedral in England. They were wild enough children at ordinary times. But from the moment they came into the cathedral they were strangely quiet; all the way home they were unusually solemn; and it was not until the evening that they returned to their normal boisterousness. Instinctive reverence was in their uninstructed hearts.

Worship without reverence can be a terrible thing. It may be worship which is formalized and pushed through anyhow; the most dignified prayers on earth can be read like a passage from an auctioneer's catalogue. It may be worship which does not realize the holiness of God, and which sounds as if, in the New Testament scholar H. H. Farmer's phrase, the worshipper was 'pally with the Deity'. It may be worship in which leader or congregation are completely unprepared. It may be the use of the house of God for purposes and in a way where reverence and the true function of God's house are forgotten. In that court of God's house at Jerusalem, there would be arguments about prices, disputes about coins that were worn and thin, the clatter of the market place. That particular form of irreverence may not be common now, but there are other ways of offering an irreverent worship to God.

(2) Jesus acted as he did in order to show that the whole paraphernalia of animal sacrifice was completely irrelevant. For centuries the prophets had been saying exactly that. 'What to me is the multitude of your sacrifices? says the Lord; I have had enough of burnt-offerings of rams and the fat of fed beasts; I do not delight in the blood of bulls, or of lambs, or of goats . . . bringing offerings is futile' (Isaiah 1:11–13). 'For on the day that I brought your ancestors out of the land of Egypt, I did not speak to them or command them concerning burnt-offerings and sacrifices' (Jeremiah 7:22). 'With their flocks and herds they shall go to seek the Lord, but they will not find him' (Hosea 5:6). 'Though they offer choice sacrifices, though they eat flesh, the Lord does not accept them' (Hosea 8:13). 'For you have no delight in sacrifice; if I were to give a burnt-offering, you would not be pleased' (Psalm 51:16). There was a chorus of prophetic voices telling of the sheer irrelevance of the burnt offerings and the animal sacrifices which smoked continuously upon the altar at Jerusalem. Jesus acted as he did to show that no sacrifice of any animal can ever put a person right with God.

We are not totally free from this very tendency today. True, we will not offer animal sacrifice to God. But we can identify his service with the installation of stained-glass windows, the obtaining of a more sonorous organ, the lavishing of

money on stone and lime and carved wood, while real worship
is far away. It is not that these things are to be condemned –
far from it. They are often – thank God – the lovely offerings
of the loving heart. When they are aids to true devotion they
are God-blessed things; but when they are substitutes for true
devotion they make God sick at heart.

(3) There is still another reason why Jesus acted as he
did. Mark has a curious little addition which none of the other
gospels has: 'My house shall be called the house of prayer
for all the nations' (Mark 11:17). The Temple consisted of a
series of courts leading into the Temple proper and to the
Holy Place. There was first the Court of the Gentiles, then
the Court of the Women, then the Court of the Israelites, then
the Court of the Priests. All this buying and selling was going
on in the Court of the Gentiles, which was the only place into
which a Gentile might come. Beyond that point, access to
him was barred. So then if there was a Gentile whose heart
God had touched, he might come into the Court of the
Gentiles to meditate and pray and distantly touch God. The
Court of the Gentiles was the only place of prayer he knew.

The Temple authorities and the Jewish traders were making
the Court of the Gentiles into an uproar and a rabble where
no man could pray. The lowing of the oxen, the bleating of
the sheep, the cooing of the doves, the shouts of the traders,
the rattle of the coins, the voices raised in bargaining disputes
– all these combined to make the Court of the Gentiles a
place where worship became impossible. The conduct in the
Temple court shut out the seeking Gentile from the presence
of God. It may well be that this was uppermost in Jesus'
mind; it may well be that Mark alone preserved the little
phrase which means so much. Jesus was moved to the depths
of his heart because those who were seeking God were being
shut out from his presence.

Is there anything in our church life – a snobbishness, an exclusiveness, a coldness, a lack of welcome, a tendency to make the congregation into a closed club, an arrogance, a fastidiousness – which keeps the seeking stranger out? Let us remember the wrath of Jesus against those who made it difficult and even impossible for the seeking stranger to make contact with God.

THE NEW TEMPLE

John 2:17-22

> His disciples remembered that there is a Scripture which stands written: 'For zeal for your house has consumed me.' Then the Jews demanded of him: 'What sign do you show us to justify your acting in this way?' Jesus answered: 'Destroy this Temple and in three days I will raise it up.' Then the Jews said: 'It has taken forty-six years to build the Temple so far, and are you going to raise it up in three days?' But he was speaking about the temple of his body. So when he was raised from the dead, his disciples remembered that he had said this, and they believed on the Scripture and on the word which Jesus spoke.

IT was quite certain that an act like the cleansing of the Temple would produce an immediate reaction in those who saw it happening. It was not the kind of thing that anyone could look at with complete indifference. It was much too staggering for that.

Here we have two reactions. First, there is the reaction of the disciples, which was to remember the words of Psalm 69:9. The point is that this Psalm was taken to refer to the Messiah. When the Messiah came, he would be burned up with a zeal for the house of God. When this verse leapt into their minds, it meant the conviction that Jesus was the Messiah seized the minds of the disciples even more deeply and more definitely. This action befitted none but the Messiah, and they were surer than ever that Jesus was in fact the Anointed One of God.

Second, there is the reaction of the Jews, a very natural one. They asked what right Jesus had to act like that and demanded that he should at once prove his credentials by some sign. The point is this. They acknowledged the act of Jesus to be that of one who thereby claimed to be the Messiah. It was always expected that when the Messiah came he would confirm his claims by doing amazing things. False Messiahs did in fact arise and promise to cleave the waters of Jordan in two or make the walls of the city collapse at a word. The popular idea of the Messiah was connected with wonders. So the Jews said: 'By this act of yours you have publicly claimed to be the Messiah. Now show us some wonder which will prove your claim.'

Jesus' reply constitutes the great problem of this passage. What did he really say? And what did he really mean? It is always to be remembered that verses 21 and 22 are John's interpretation written long afterwards. He was inevitably reading into the passage ideas which were the product of seventy years of thinking about and experience of the risen Christ. As Irenaeus said long ago: 'No prophecy is fully understood until after the fulfilment of it.' But what did Jesus originally say and what did he originally mean?

There is no possible doubt that Jesus spoke words which were very like these, words which could be maliciously twisted into a destructive claim. When Jesus was on trial, the false witness borne against him was: 'This fellow said, "I am able to destroy the temple of God and to build it in three days"' (Matthew 26:61). The charge levelled against Stephen was: 'We have heard him say that this Jesus of Nazareth will destroy this place and will change the customs that Moses handed on to us' (Acts 6:14).

We must remember two things and we must put them together. First, Jesus certainly never said he would destroy the material Temple and then rebuild it. Jesus in fact looked for the end of the Temple. He said to the woman of Samaria that the day was coming when God would be worshipped neither in Mount Gerizim, nor in Jerusalem, but in spirit and in truth (John 4:21). Second, the cleansing of the Temple, as we have seen, was a dramatic way of showing that the whole Temple worship with its ritual and its sacrifice was irrelevant and could do nothing to lead people to God. It is clear that Jesus did expect that the Temple would pass away; that he had come to render its worship unnecessary and obsolete; and that therefore he would never suggest that he would rebuild it.

We must now turn to Mark. As so often, we find the little extra suggestive and illuminating phrase there. As Mark relates the charge against Jesus, it ran: 'I will destroy this temple that is made with hands, and in three days I will build another, *not made with hands*' (Mark 14:58). What Jesus really meant was that his coming had put an end to this way of worshipping God that was made and arranged according to human design and had put in its place a spiritual worship; that he put an end to all this business of animal sacrifice and priestly ritual and put in its place a direct approach to the Spirit of God which did not need an elaborately built Temple and a ritual of incense and sacrifice offered by human hands. The threat of Jesus was: 'Your Temple worship, your elaborate ritual and your lavish animal sacrifices are at an end, because I have come.' The promise of Jesus was: 'I will give you a way to come to God without all this human elaboration and human ritual. I have come to destroy this Temple in Jerusalem and to make the whole earth the Temple where it is possible to know the presence of the living God.'

The Jews saw that. It was in 19 BC that Herod had begun to build that wondrous Temple; it was not until AD 64 that the building was finally finished. It was forty-six years since it had been started; it was to be nearly another forty years before it was ended. Jesus shattered the Jews by telling them that all its magnificence and splendour and all the money and skill that had been lavished on it were completely irrelevant; that he had come to show people a way to come to God without any Temple at all.

That must be what Jesus actually said; but in the years to come John saw far more than that in Jesus' saying. He saw in it nothing less than a prophecy of the resurrection; *and John was right*. He was right for this basic reason, that the whole round earth could never become the temple of the living God until Jesus was released from the body and was everywhere present; and until he was with men and women everywhere, even to the end of the world.

It is the presence of the living, risen Christ which makes the whole world into the Temple of God. So John says that when they remembered, they saw in this a promise of the resurrection. They did not see that at the time; they could not; it was only their own experience of the living Christ which one day showed them the true depth of what Jesus said.

Finally, John says that 'they believed the Scripture'. What Scripture? John means that Scripture which haunted the early Church – 'or let your faithful one see the Pit' (Psalm 16:10). Peter quoted it at Pentecost (Acts 2:31); Paul quoted it at Antioch (Acts 13:35). It expressed the confidence of the

Church in the power of God and in the resurrection of Jesus Christ.

We have here the tremendous truth that our contact with God, our entry into his presence and our approach to him are not dependent on anything that human hands can build or human minds devise. In the street, in the home, at business, on the hills, on the open road or in church, we have our inner temple, the presence of the risen Christ forever with us throughout all the world.

THE SEARCHER OF HUMAN HEARTS

John 2:23–5

> When he was in Jerusalem, at the Passover, at the Feast, many believed in his name, as they saw the signs which he did; but Jesus himself would not entrust himself to them, because he knew them all, and because he had no need that anyone should testify to him what man is like, for he well knew what was in human nature.

JOHN does not relate the story of any wonder that Jesus did in Jerusalem at the Passover season; but Jesus did do wonders there; and there were many who, when they saw his powers, believed in him. The question John is answering here is – if there were many who believed in Jerusalem right at the beginning, why did Jesus not there and then set up his standard and openly declare himself?

The answer is that Jesus knew human nature only too well. He knew that there were many whose interest in him would be short-lived. He knew that there were many who were attracted only by the sensational things he did. He knew that there were none who understood the way that he had chosen. He knew that there were many who would have followed him while he continued to produce miracles and wonders and signs, but who, if he had begun to talk to them about service and self-denial, if he had begun to talk to them about self-surrender to the will of God, if he had begun to talk to them about a cross and about carrying a cross, would have stared at him with blank incomprehension and left him on the spot.

It is a great characteristic of Jesus that he did not want followers unless they clearly knew and definitely accepted what was involved in following him. He refused to cash in on a moment's popularity. If he had entrusted himself to the mob in Jerusalem, they would have declared him Messiah there and then and would have waited for the kind of material action they expected the Messiah to take. But Jesus was a leader who refused to ask anyone ever to accept him until the full implications of that acceptance were understood. He insisted that people should know what they were doing.

Jesus knew human nature. He knew the fickleness and instability of human hearts. He knew that people can be swept away in a moment of emotion, and then back out when they discover what decision really means. He knew how human nature hungers for the spectacular. He wanted not a crowd cheering they knew not what, but a small company who knew what they were doing and who were prepared to follow to the end.

There is one thing we must note in this passage, for we shall have occasion to mark it again and again. When John speaks of Jesus' miracles, he calls them *signs*. The New Testament uses three different words for the wonderful works of God and of Jesus, and each has something to tell us about what a miracle really is.

(1) It uses the word *teras*. *Teras* simply means a marvellous thing. It is a word with no moral significance at all. A

conjuring trick might be a *teras*. A *teras* was simply an astonishing happening which left people gasping with surprise. The New Testament never uses this word alone of the works of God or of Jesus.

(2) It uses the word *dunamis*. *Dunamis* literally means *power*; it is the word from which *dynamite* comes. It can be used of any kind of extraordinary power. It can be used of the power of growth, of the powers of nature, of the power of a drug, of the power of a human genius. It always has the meaning of an effective power which does things and which anyone can recognize.

(3) It uses the word *sēmeion*. *Sēmeion* means a *sign*. This is John's favourite word. To him, a miracle was not simply an astonishing happening; it was not simply a deed of power; it was a sign. That is to say, it told people something about the person who did it; it revealed something of his character; it laid bare something of his nature; it was an action through which it was possible to understand better and more fully the character of the person who did it. To John, the supreme thing about the miracles of Jesus was that *they told people something about the nature and the character of God*. The power of Jesus was used to heal the sick, to feed the hungry, to comfort the sorrowing; and the fact that Jesus used his power in that way was proof that God cared for the sorrows and the needs and the pains of men and women. To John, the miracles were signs of the love of God.

In any miracle, then, there are three things. There is the wonder which leaves people dazzled, astonished and aghast. There is the power which is effective, which can deal with and mend a broken body, an unhinged mind or a bruised heart, which can do things. There is the sign which tells us of the love in the heart of the God who does such things for us.

THE MAN WHO CAME BY NIGHT

John 3:1–6

> There was a man who was one of the Pharisees who
> was called Nicodemus, a ruler of the Jews. He came to
> Jesus by night and said to him: 'Rabbi, we know that
> you are a teacher who has come from God, for no one
> can do the signs which you do unless God is with him.'
> Jesus answered him: 'This is the truth I tell you – unless
> a man is reborn from above, he cannot see the kingdom
> of God.' Nicodemus said to him: 'How can a man be
> born when he is old? Surely he cannot enter into his
> mother's womb a second time and be born?' Jesus
> answered: 'This is the truth I tell you – unless a man is
> born of water and the Spirit, he cannot enter into the
> kingdom of God. That which is born from the flesh is
> flesh, and that which is born of the Spirit is spirit.'

FOR the most part, we see Jesus surrounded by the ordinary
people; but here we see him in contact with one of the
aristocracy of Jerusalem. There are certain things that we
know about Nicodemus.

(1) Nicodemus must have been wealthy. When Jesus died,
Nicodemus brought for his body 'a mixture of myrrh and
aloes, weighing about a hundred pounds' (John 19:39) – and
only a wealthy man could have brought that.

(2) Nicodemus was a Pharisee. In many ways, the
Pharisees were the best people in the whole country. There
were never more than 6,000 of them; they were what was
known as a *chaburah*, or brotherhood. They entered into this
brotherhood by taking a pledge in front of three witnesses
that they would spend all their lives observing every detail of
the scribal law.

What exactly did that mean? To the Jews, the law was the
most sacred thing in all the world. The law was the first five
books of the Old Testament. They believed it to be the perfect
word of God. To add one word to it or to take one word away
from it was a deadly sin. Now if the law is the perfect and
complete word of God, that must mean that it contained
everything that anyone needed to know for the living of a
good life, if not explicitly, then implicitly. If it was not there
in so many words, it must be possible to deduce it. The law
as it stood consisted of great, wide, noble principles which
people had to work out for themselves. But, for the later Jews,
that was not enough. They said: 'The law is complete; it
contains everything necessary for the living of a good life;
therefore in the law there must be a regulation to govern every
possible incident in every possible moment for every possible
individual.' So they set out to extract from the great principles
of the law an infinite number of rules and regulations to
govern every conceivable situation in life. In other words,
they changed the law of the great principles into the legalism
of by-laws and regulations.

The best example of what they did is to be seen in the
Sabbath law. In the Bible itself, we are simply told that we
must remember the Sabbath day to keep it holy and that on
that day no work must be done, either by a man or by his
servants or his animals. Not content with that, the later Jews
spent hour after hour and generation after generation defining
what work is and listing the things that may and may not be
done on the Sabbath day. The *Mishnah* is the codified scribal
law. The scribes spent their lives working out these rules
and regulations. In the Mishnah, the section on the Sabbath
extends to no fewer than twenty-four chapters. The *Talmud*
is the explanatory commentary on the Mishnah, and in the
Jerusalem Talmud the section explaining the Sabbath law runs

to sixty-four and a half columns; and in the Babylonian Talmud it runs to 156 double folio pages. And we are told about a Rabbi who spent two and a half years in studying one of the twenty-four chapters of the Mishnah.

The kind of thing they did was this. To tie a knot on the Sabbath was to work; but a knot had to be defined. 'The following are the knots the making of which renders a man guilty; the knot of camel drivers and that of sailors; and as one is guilty by reason of tying them, so also of untying them.' On the other hand, knots which could be tied or untied with one hand were quite legal. Further, 'a woman may tie up a slit in her shift and the strings of her cap and those of her girdle, the straps of shoes or sandals, of skins of wine and oil'. Now see what happened. Suppose a man wished to let down a bucket into a well to draw water on the Sabbath day. He could not tie a rope to it, for a knot on a rope was illegal on the Sabbath; but he could tie it to a woman's girdle and let it down, for a knot in a girdle was quite legal. That was the kind of thing which to the scribes and Pharisees was a matter of life and death; that was religion; that to them was pleasing and serving God.

Take the case of making a journey on the Sabbath. Exodus 16:29 says: 'Each of you stay where you are; do not leave your place on the seventh day.' A Sabbath day's journey was therefore limited to 2,000 cubits, that is, 1,000 yards. But, if a rope was tied across the end of a street, the whole street became one house and a man could go 1,000 yards beyond the end of the street. Or, if a man deposited enough food for one meal on Friday evening at any given place, that place technically became his house and he could go 1,000 yards beyond it on the Sabbath day. The rules and regulations and the evasions piled up by the hundred and the thousand.

Take the case of carrying a burden. Jeremiah 17:21–4 said: 'For the sake of your lives, take care that you do not bear a burden on the sabbath day.' So a burden had to be defined. It was defined as 'food equal in weight to a dried fig, enough wine for mixing in a goblet, milk enough for one swallow, honey enough to put upon a wound, oil enough to anoint a small member, water enough to moisten an eye-salve', and so on and on. It had then to be settled whether or not on the Sabbath a woman could wear a brooch, a man could wear an artificial leg or dentures; or would it be carrying a burden to do so? Could a chair or even a child be lifted? And so on and on the discussions and the regulations went.

It was the *scribes* who worked out these regulations; it was the *Pharisees* who dedicated their lives to keeping them. Obviously, however misguided a man might be, he must be desperately in earnest if he proposed to undertake obedience to every one of the thousands of rules. That is precisely what the Pharisees did. The name *Pharisee* means *the separated one*; and the Pharisees were those who had separated themselves from all ordinary life in order to keep every detail of the law of the scribes.

Nicodemus was a Pharisee, and it is astonishing that a man who regarded goodness in that light and who had given himself to that kind of life in the conviction that he was pleasing God should wish to talk to Jesus at all.

(3) Nicodemus was a ruler of the Jews. The word is *archōn*. This is to say that he was a member of the Sanhedrin. The Sanhedrin was a court of seventy members and was the supreme court of the Jews. Of course under the Romans its powers were more limited than once they had been; but they were still extensive. In particular the Sanhedrin had religious jurisdiction over every Jew in the world; and one of its duties was to examine and deal with anyone suspected of being a

false prophet. Again it is amazing that Nicodemus should come to Jesus at all.

(4) It may well be that Nicodemus belonged to a distinguished Jewish family. Way back in 63 BC when the Romans and the Jews had been at war, Aristobulus, the Jewish leader, sent a certain Nicodemus as his ambassador to Pompey, the Roman emperor. Much later in the terrible last days of Jerusalem, the man who negotiated the surrender of the garrison was a certain Gorion, who was the son of either Nicomedes or Nicodemus. It may well be that both these men belonged to the same family as our Nicodemus, and that it was one of the most distinguished families in Jerusalem. If that is true, it is amazing that this Jewish aristocrat should come to this homeless prophet who had been the carpenter of Nazareth, that he might talk to him about his soul.

It was by night that Nicodemus came to Jesus. There were probably two reasons for that.

(1) It may have been a sign of caution. Nicodemus quite frankly may not have wished to commit himself by coming to Jesus by day. We must not condemn him. The wonder is that with his background, he came to Jesus at all. It was infinitely better to come at night than not at all. It is a miracle of grace that Nicodemus overcame his prejudices and his upbringing and his whole view of life enough to come to Jesus.

(2) But there may be another reason. The Rabbis declared that the best time to study the law was at night when it could be done undisturbed. Throughout the day, Jesus was surrounded by crowds of people all the time. It may well be that Nicodemus came to Jesus by night because he wanted an absolutely private and completely undisturbed time with Jesus.

Nicodemus was a puzzled man, a man with many honours and yet with something lacking in his life. He came to Jesus for a talk so that somehow in the darkness of the night he might find light.

THE MAN WHO CAME BY NIGHT

John 3:1–6 (*contd*)

WHEN John relates conversations that Jesus had with inquirers, he has a way of following a certain scheme. We see that scheme very clearly here. The inquirer says something (verse 2). Jesus answers in a saying that is hard to understand (verse 3). That saying is misunderstood by the inquirer (verse 4). Jesus answers with a saying that is even more difficult to understand (verse 5). And then there follows a discourse and an explanation. John uses this method in order that we may see people thinking things out for themselves and so that we may do the same.

When Nicodemus came to Jesus, he said that no one could help being impressed with the signs and wonders that he did. Jesus' answer was that it was not the signs and the wonders that were really important; the important thing was such a change in a person's inner life that it could only be described as a new birth.

When Jesus said that it was necessary to be *born anew*, Nicodemus misunderstood him, and the misunderstanding came from the fact that the word which the Revised Standard Version translates *anew*, the Greek word *anōthen*, has three different meanings. (1) It can mean *from the beginning, completely radically*. (2) It can mean *again*, in the sense of *for the second time*. (3) It can mean *from above*, and, therefore, *from God* (as in the New Revised Standard

Version). It is not possible for us to get all these meanings into any English word; and yet all three of them are in the phrase *born anew*. To be born anew is to undergo such a radical change that it is like a new birth; it is to have something happen to the soul which can only be described as being born all over again; and the whole process is not a human achievement, because it comes from the grace and power of God.

When we read the story, it looks at first sight as if Nicodemus took the word *anew* in only the second sense, and with a crude literalism. How can anyone, he said, enter again into his mother's womb and be born a second time when he is already an old man? But there is more to Nicodemus' answer than that. In his heart, there was a great unsatisfied longing. It is as if he said with infinite, wistful yearning: 'You talk about being born anew; you talk about this radical, fundamental change which is so necessary. I know that it is *necessary*; but in my experience it is *impossible*. There is nothing I would like more; but you might as well tell me, a fully grown man, to enter into my mother's womb and be born all over again.' It is not the *desirability* of this change that Nicodemus questioned; that he knew only too well; it is the *possibility*. Nicodemus is up against the eternal problem, the problem of someone who wants to be changed and who cannot change himself.

This phrase *born anew*, this idea of *rebirth*, runs all through the New Testament. Peter speaks of being born anew by God's great mercy (1 Peter 1:3); he talks about being *born anew* not of perishable seed, but of imperishable (1 Peter 1:23). James speaks of God giving us birth by the word of truth (James 1:18). The Letter to Titus speaks of *the water of rebirth* (Titus 3:5). Sometimes this same idea is spoken of as a death followed by a resurrection or a re-creation. Paul speaks of

the Christian as dying with Christ and then rising to life anew
(Romans 6:1–11). He speaks of those who have lately come
into the Christian faith as *infants in Christ* (1 Corinthians
3:1–2). If any are in Christ, it is as if they had been *created*
all over again (2 Corinthians 5:17). In Christ, there is a new
creation (Galatians 6:15). The new self is *created* after God
in righteousness (Ephesians 4:22–4). The person who is at
the first beginnings of the Christian faith is a child (Hebrews
5:12–14). All over the New Testament, this idea of *rebirth*
and *re-creation* occurs.

Now this was not an idea which was in the least strange to
the people who heard it in New Testament times. Jews knew
all about rebirth. When a man from another faith became a
Jew and had been accepted into Judaism by prayer and
sacrifice and baptism, he was regarded as being *reborn.* 'A
proselyte who embraces Judaism', said the Rabbis, 'is like a
new-born child.' So radical was the change that the sins he
had committed before his reception were all done away with,
for now he was a different person. It was even theoretically
argued that such a man could marry his own mother or his
own sister, because he was a completely new man, and all the
old connections were broken and destroyed. The Jews knew
the idea of rebirth.

Greeks also knew the idea of rebirth and knew it well. By
far the most real religion of the Greeks at this time was the
faith of the mystery religions. The mystery religions were all
founded on the story of some suffering and dying and rising
god. This story was played out as a passion play. The initiate
had a long course of preparation, instruction, asceticism and
fasting. The drama was then played out with gorgeous music,
marvellous ritual, incense and everything to play upon the
emotions. As it was played out, the worshipper's aim was to
become one with the god in such a way that he passed through

the god's sufferings and shared the god's triumph and the god's divine life. The mystery religions offered mystic union with some god. When that union was achieved, the initiate was, in the language of the mysteries, *a twice-born*. The Hermetic Mysteries had as part of their basic belief: 'There can be no salvation without regeneration.' Apuleius, who went through initiation, said that he underwent 'a voluntary death', and that thereby he attained 'his spiritual birthday', and was 'as it were reborn'. Many of the mystery initiations took place at midnight when the day dies and is reborn. In the Phrygian, the initiate, after his initiation, was fed with milk as if he was a new-born babe.

The ancient world knew all about rebirth and regeneration. It longed for it and searched for it everywhere. The most famous of all mystery ceremonies was the *taurobolium*. The candidate was put into a pit. On the top of the pit there was a lattice-work cover. On the cover a bull was slain by having its throat cut. The blood poured down and the initiate lifted up his head and bathed himself in the blood; and when he came out of the pit he was *renatus in aeternum*, reborn for all eternity. When Christianity came to the world with a message of rebirth, it came with precisely that for which all the world was seeking.

What, then, does this rebirth mean for us? In the New Testament, and especially in the Fourth Gospel, there are four closely interrelated ideas. There is the idea of rebirth; there is the idea of the kingdom of heaven, into which people cannot enter unless they are reborn; there is the idea of being children of God; and there is the idea of eternal life. This idea of being reborn is not something which is peculiar to the thought of the Fourth Gospel. In Matthew, we have the same great truth put more simply and more vividly: 'Unless you change and become like children, you will never enter the kingdom of heaven' (Matthew 18:3). All these ideas have a common thought behind them.

BORN AGAIN

John 3:1-6 (*contd*)

LET us start with the *kingdom of heaven*. What does it mean? We get our best definition of it from the Lord's Prayer. There are two petitions side by side:

> Your kingdom come:
> Your will be done in earth as it is in heaven.

It is characteristic of Jewish style to say things twice, the second way explaining and amplifying the first. Any verse of the Psalms will show us this Jewish habit of what is technically known as parallelism:

> The Lord of hosts is with us;
> the God of Jacob is our refuge. (Psalm 46:7)

> For I know my transgressions,
> and my sin is ever before me. (Psalm 51:3)

> He makes me lie down in green pastures;
> he leads me beside still waters. (Psalm 23:2)

Let us apply that principle to these two petitions in the Lord's Prayer. The second petition amplifies and explains the first; we then arrive at the definition: *the kingdom of heaven is a society where God's will is as perfectly done on earth as it is in heaven.* To be in the kingdom of heaven is therefore to lead a life in which we have willingly submitted everything to the will of God; it is to have arrived at a stage when we perfectly and completely accept the will of God.

Now let us take the idea of being a child of God. In one sense, this is a tremendous *privilege*. To those who believe, there is given the power to become God's children (John 1:12). But the very essence of being a child of God is necessarily *obedience*. 'They who have my commandments *and keep them* are those who love me' (John 14:21). The essence of this relationship is love; and the essence of love is obedience. We cannot with any reality say that we love a person and then do things which hurt and grieve that person's heart. This relationship is a privilege, but a privilege which is entered into only when full obedience is given. So then to be children of God and to be in the kingdom are one and the same thing. The children of God and the citizens of the kingdom are both people who have completely and willingly accepted the will of God.

Now let us take *eternal life*. It is far better to speak of *eternal* life than to speak of *everlasting* life. The main idea behind eternal life is not simply that of duration. It is quite clear that a life which went on forever could just as easily be hell as heaven. The idea behind eternal life is the idea of a certain quality of life. What kind? There is only one person who can properly be described by this adjective *eternal* (*aiōnios*), and that one person is God. Eternal life is the kind of life that God lives; it is God's life. To enter into eternal life is to enter into possession of that kind of life which is the life of God. It is to be lifted up above merely human, transient things into that joy and peace which belong only to God. Clearly we can enter into this close fellowship with God only when we render to him that love, that reverence, that devotion and that obedience which truly bring us into fellowship with him.

Here, then, we have three great related conceptions – entry into the kingdom of heaven, becoming children of God and eternal life – and all are dependent on and are the products of perfect obedience to the will of God. It is just here that the idea of being *reborn* comes in. It is what links all these three conceptions together. It is quite clear that, as we are and in our own strength, we are quite unable to render to God this perfect obedience; it is only when God's grace enters into us and takes possession of us and changes us that we can give to him the reverence and the devotion we ought to give. It is through Jesus Christ that we are reborn; it is when he enters into possession of our hearts and lives that the change comes.

When that happens, we are born of *water and the Spirit*. There are two thoughts there. *Water* is the symbol of cleansing. When Jesus takes possession of our lives, when we love him with all our heart, the sins of the past are forgiven and forgotten. *The Spirit* is the symbol of *power*. When Jesus takes possession of our lives, it is not only that the past is forgotten and forgiven; if that were all, we might well proceed to make the same mess of life all over again; but into life there enters a new power which enables us to be what by ourselves we could never be and to do what by ourselves we could never do. Water and the Spirit stand for the cleansing and the strengthening power of Christ, which wipes out the past and gives victory in the future.

Finally, in this passage, John lays down a great law. That which is born of the flesh is flesh, and that which is born of the Spirit is spirit. Human beings by themselves are flesh, and their power is limited to what the flesh can do. By themselves, they cannot be other than defeated and frustrated; that we know only too well; it is the universal fact of human experience. But the very essence of the Spirit is power and life which are beyond human power and human life; and when the Spirit takes possession of us, the defeated life of human nature becomes the victorious life of God.

To be born again is to be changed in such a way that it can be described only as rebirth and re-creation. The change comes when we love Jesus and allow him into our hearts. Then we are forgiven for the past and armed by the Spirit for the future; then we can truly accept the will of God. And then we become citizens of the kingdom; then we become children of God; then we enter into eternal life, which is the very life of God.

THE DUTY TO KNOW AND THE RIGHT TO SPEAK

John 3:7–13

> 'Do not be surprised that I said to you: "You must be reborn from above." The wind blows where it will, and you hear the sound of it, but you do not know whence it comes and whither it goes. So is everyone that is born of the Spirit.' Nicodemus answered: 'How can these things happen?' Jesus answered: 'Are you the man whom everyone regards as the teacher of Israel, and you do not understand these things? This is the truth I tell you – we speak what we know, and we bear witness to what we have seen; but you do not receive our witness. If I have spoken to you of earthly things and you do not believe me, how will you believe me if I speak to you about heavenly things? No one has gone up to heaven, except he who came down from heaven, I mean, the Son of Man, who is in heaven.'

THERE are two kinds of misunderstanding. There is the misunderstanding of those who misunderstand because they have not yet reached a stage of knowledge and of experience at which they are able to grasp the truth. When people are in that state, our duty is to do all that we can to explain things to them so that they will be able to grasp the knowledge which is being offered to them. There is also the misunderstanding of those who are unwilling to understand; there is a failure to see which comes from the refusal to see. Some people can deliberately shut their minds to truth which they do not wish to accept.

Nicodemus was like that. The teaching about a new birth from God should not have been strange to him. Ezekiel, for instance, had spoken repeatedly about the new heart that must be created in an individual. 'Cast away from you all the transgressions that you have committed against me, and get yourselves a new heart and a new spirit! Why will you die, O house of Israel?' (Ezekiel 18:31). 'A new heart I will give you, and a new spirit I will put within you' (Ezekiel 36:26). Nicodemus was an expert in Scripture, and again and again the prophets had spoken of that very experience of which Jesus was speaking. If people do not wish to be reborn, they will deliberately misunderstand what rebirth means. If people do not wish to be changed, they will deliberately shut their eyes and their minds and their hearts to the power which can change them. In the last analysis, what is the matter with so many of us is simply the fact that, when Jesus Christ comes with his offer to change us and re-create us, we more or less say: 'No thank you: I am quite satisfied with myself as I am, and I don't want to be changed.'

Nicodemus was driven back on another defence. In effect he said: 'This rebirth about which you talk may be possible; but I can't understand how it works.' The answer of Jesus depends for its point on the fact that the Greek word for *spirit*, *pneuma*, has two meanings. It is the word for *spirit*, but it is also the regular word for *wind*. The same is true of the Hebrew word *ruach*; it too means both *spirit* and *wind*. So Jesus said to Nicodemus: 'You can hear and see and feel the *wind* [*pneuma*]; *but you do not know where it comes from or where it is going to*. You may not understand how and why the wind blows; but you can see what it does. You may not understand where a gale came from or where it is going to, but you can see the trail of flattened fields and uprooted trees that it leaves behind it. There are many things about the wind you may not understand; but its effect is plain for all to see.' He went on: 'The *Spirit* [*pneuma*] is exactly the same. You may not know how the Spirit works; but you can see the effect of the Spirit in human lives.'

Jesus said: 'This is no theoretical situation of which we are speaking. We are talking of what we have actually seen. We can point to many people who have been reborn by the power of the Spirit.' The story is told of a workman who had been a drunken reprobate and was converted. His workmates did their best to make him feel a fool. 'Surely,' they said to him, 'you can't believe in miracles and things like that. Surely, for instance, you don't believe that Jesus turned water into wine.' 'I don't know', the man answered, 'whether he turned water into wine when he was in Palestine, but I do know that in my own house and home he has turned beer into furniture!'

There are any number of things in this world which we use every day without knowing how they work. Comparatively few of us know how electricity or radio or television works; but we do not deny that they exist because of that. Many of us drive a car with only the haziest notion of what goes on inside its engine; but our lack of understanding does not prevent us using and enjoying the benefits which a car confers. We may not understand how the Spirit works; but the effect of the Spirit on the lives of men and women is there for all to see. The unanswerable argument for Christianity is the Christian life. No one can disregard a faith which is able to make bad people good.

Jesus said to Nicodemus: 'I have tried to make things simple for you; I have used simple human pictures taken from everyday life; and you have not understood. How can you ever expect to understand the deep things if even the simple things are beyond you?' There is a warning here for every one of us. It is easy to sit in discussion groups, to sit in a study and to read books; it is easy to discuss the intellectual truth of Christianity; but the essential thing is to experience the power of Christianity. And it is fatally easy to start at the wrong end and to think of Christianity as something to be discussed, not as something to be experienced. It is certainly important to have an intellectual grasp of every aspect of Christian truth; but it is still more important to have a vital experience of the power of Jesus Christ. When we undergo treatment from a doctor, when we have to have surgery, when we are given some medicine to take, we do not need to know the anatomy of the human body, the scientific effect of the anaesthetic, the way in which the drugs work on our bodies, in order to be cured. Ninety-nine out of every 100 accept the cure without being able to say how it was brought about. There is a sense in which Christianity is like that. At its heart there is a mystery, but it is not the mystery of intellectual appreciation; it is the mystery of redemption.

In reading the Fourth Gospel, there is the difficulty of knowing when the words of Jesus stop and the words of the writer of the gospel begin. John has thought so long about the words of Jesus that he glides quite naturally and easily from them to his own thoughts about them. Almost certainly the last words of this passage are the words of John. It is as if someone asked: 'What right has Jesus to say these things? What guarantee do we have that they are true?' John's answer is simple and profound. 'Jesus', he says, 'came down from heaven to tell us the truth of God. And, when he had lived among men and women and died for them, he returned to his glory.' It was John's contention that Jesus' right to speak came from the fact that he knew God personally, that he had come direct from the secrets of heaven to earth, that what he said to men and women was most literally God's own truth – for Jesus was and is the embodied mind of God.

THE UPLIFTED CHRIST

John 3:14–15

> 'And as Moses lifted up the serpent in the wilderness, so the Son of Man must be lifted up, that everyone who believes in him may have eternal life.'

JOHN goes back to a strange Old Testament story which is told in Numbers 21:4–9. On their journey through the wilderness, the people of Israel murmured and complained and regretted that they had ever left Egypt. To punish them, God sent a plague of deadly, fiery serpents; the people repented and cried for mercy. God instructed Moses to make an image of a serpent and to hold it up in the centre of the camp; and those who looked upon the serpent were healed. That story much impressed the Israelites. They told how in later times that bronze serpent became an idol and in the days of Hezekiah had to be destroyed because people were worshipping it (2 Kings 18:4). The Jews themselves were always a little puzzled by this incident in view of the fact that they were absolutely forbidden to make graven images. The Rabbis explained it this way: 'It was not the serpent that gave life. So long as Moses lifted up the serpent, they believed on him who had commanded Moses to act thus. It was God who healed them.' The healing power lay not in the bronze serpent;

it was only a symbol to turn their thoughts to God; and when they did that, they were healed.

John took that old story and used it as a kind of parable of Jesus. He says: 'The serpent was lifted up; the people looked at it; their thoughts were turned to God; and by the power of that God in whom they trusted they were healed. Even so Jesus must be lifted up; and when people turn their thoughts to him, and believe in him, they too will find eternal life.'

There is a wonderfully suggestive thing here. The verb *to lift up* is *hupsoun*. The strange thing is that it is used of Jesus in two senses. It is used of his being *lifted up upon the cross*; and it is used of his being *lifted up into glory* at the time of his ascension into heaven. It is used of the cross in John 8:28, 12:32. It is used of Jesus' ascension into glory in Acts 2:33, 5:31; Philippians 2:9. There was a double lifting up in Jesus' life – the lifting on the cross and the lifting into glory. And the two are inextricably connected. The one could not have happened without the other. For Jesus, the cross was the way to glory; had he refused it, had he evaded it, had he taken steps to escape it, as he might so easily have done, there would have been no glory for him. It is the same for us. We can, if we like, choose the easy way; we can, if we like, refuse the cross that every Christian is called to bear; but if we do, we lose the glory. It is an unalterable law of life that if there is no cross, there is no crown.

In this passage, we have two expressions whose meaning we must face. It will not be possible to extract all their meaning, because they both mean more than we can ever discover; but we must try to grasp at least something of it.

(1) There is the phrase which speaks of *believing in Jesus.* It means at least three things.

(a) It means believing with all our hearts that God is as Jesus declared him to be. It means believing that God loves us, that God cares for us, that God wants nothing more than to forgive us. It was not easy for a Jew to believe that. The Jews looked on God as one who imposed his laws upon his people and punished them if they broke them. They looked on God as a judge and on men and women as criminals at his judgment seat. They looked on God as one who demanded sacrifices and offerings; to get into his presence, it was necessary to pay the price laid down. It was hard to think of God not as a judge waiting to exact penalty, not as a task-master waiting to pounce, but as a Father who longed for nothing so much as to have his erring children come back home. It cost the life and the death of Jesus to communicate that message. And we cannot begin to be Christians until with all our hearts we believe it.

(b) How can we be sure that Jesus knew what he was talking about? What guarantee is there that his wonderful good news is true? Here we come upon the second article in belief. We must believe that Jesus is the Son of God, that in him is the mind of God, that he knew God so well, was so close to God, was so one with God, that he could tell us the absolute truth about him.

(c) But belief has a third element. We believe that God is a loving Father because we believe that Jesus is the Son of God and that therefore what he says about God is true. Then comes this third element. We must stake everything on the fact that what Jesus says is true. Whatever he says, we must do; whenever he commands, we must obey. When he tells us to cast ourselves unreservedly on the mercy of God, we must do so. We must take Jesus at his word. Every smallest action in life must be done in unquestioning obedience to him.

So, belief in Jesus has these three elements – belief that God is our loving Father, belief that Jesus is the son of God

and therefore tells us the truth about God and life, and un-
swerving and unquestioning obedience to Jesus.

(2) The second great phrase is *eternal life*. We have already
seen that eternal life is the very life of God himself. But let
us ask this: if we possess eternal life, what do we have? If we
enter into eternal life, what is it like? To have eternal life
envelops every relationship in life with peace.

(a) It gives us peace with God. We are no longer cringing
before a tyrannical king or seeking to hide from an austere
judge. We are at home with our Father.

(b) It gives us peace with one another. If we have been
forgiven, we must be forgiving. It enables us to see other
people as God sees them. It makes us and all people into one
great family joined in love.

(c) It gives us peace with life. If God is Father, God is
working all things together for good. The eighteenth-century
German dramatist G. E. Lessing used to say that if he had
one question to ask the Sphinx, who knew everything, it
would be: 'Is this a friendly universe?' When we believe
that God is Father, we also believe that such a father's hand
will never cause his child a needless tear. We may not
understand life any better, but we will not resent life any
longer.

(d) It gives us peace with ourselves. In the last analysis,
we are more afraid of ourselves than of anything else. We
know our own weaknesses; we know the force of our own
temptations; we know our own tasks and the demands of our
own lives. But now we know that we are facing it all with
God. It is not we who live but Christ who lives in us. There is
a peace founded on strength in his life.

(e) It makes us certain that the deepest peace on earth is
only a shadow of the ultimate peace which is to come. It
gives us a hope and a goal to which we may travel. It gives us

a life of glorious wonder here and yet, at the same time, a life in which the best is yet to be.

THE LOVE OF GOD

John 3:16

> 'For God so loved the world that he gave his only Son
> so that everyone who believes in him should not perish
> but have everlasting life.'

ALL great men and women have had their favourite texts, but this has been called 'everybody's text'. Herein for every one of us is the very essence of the gospel. This text tells us certain great things.

(1) It tells us that the initiative in all salvation lies with God. Sometimes Christianity is presented in such a way that it sounds as if God had to be pacified, as if he had to be persuaded to forgive. Sometimes the picture is drawn of a stern, angry, unforgiving God and a gentle, loving, forgiving Jesus. Sometimes the Christian message is presented in such a way that it sounds as if Jesus did something which changed the attitude of God to men and women from condemnation to forgiveness. But this text tells us that it was with God that it all started. It was God who sent his Son, and he sent him because he loved the world he had created. At the back of everything is the love of God.

(2) It tells us that the mainspring of God's being is love. It is easy to think of God as looking at human beings in their heedlessness and their disobedience and their rebellion and saying: 'I'll break them: I'll discipline them and punish them and scourge them until they come back.' It is easy to think of God as seeking human allegiance in order to satisfy his own

desire for power and for what we might call a completely
subject universe. The tremendous thing about this text is that
it shows us God acting not for his own sake but for ours; not
to satisfy his desire for power, not to bring a universe to heel,
but to satisfy his love. God is not like an absolute monarch
who treats each individual as a subject to be reduced to abject
obedience. God is the Father who cannot be happy until his
wandering children have come home. God does not smash
people into submission; he yearns over them and woos them
into love.

(3) It tells us of the width of the love of God. It was *the
world* that God so loved. It was not a nation; it was not the
good people; it was not only the people who loved him; it
was the world. The unlovable and the unlovely, the lonely
who have no one else to love them, those who love God and
those who never think of him, those who rest in the love of
God and those who spurn it – all are included in this vast
inclusive love of God. As St Augustine had it: 'God loves
each one of us as if there was only one of us to love.'

LOVE AND JUDGMENT

John 3:17–21

> 'For God did not send his Son into the world to condemn
> the world, but that the world might be saved through
> him. He who believes in him is not condemned; but he
> who does not believe already stands condemned. And
> this is the reason of this condemnation – the light came
> into the world and men loved the darkness rather than
> the light, for their deeds were evil. Everyone whose
> deeds are depraved hates the light, and does not come
> to the light, but his deeds stand convicted. But he who

> puts the truth into action comes to the light, that his
> deeds may be made plain for all to see, because they
> are done in God.'

HERE we are faced with one of the apparent paradoxes of the
Fourth Gospel – the paradox of love and judgment. We have
just been thinking of the love of God, and now suddenly we
are confronted with judgment and condemnation and
conviction. John has just said that it was because God so
loved the world that he sent his Son into the world. Later he
will go on to show us Jesus saying: 'I came into this world
for judgement' (9:39). How can both things be true?

It is quite possible to offer someone an experience in
nothing but love and for that experience to turn out a judgment. It is quite possible to offer someone an experience
which is meant to do nothing but bring joy and bliss and yet
for that experience to turn out a judgment. Suppose we love
great music and get nearer to God immersed in the surge and
thunder of a great symphony than anywhere else. Suppose
we have friends who do not know anything about such music
and we wish to introduce them to this great experience, to
share it with them, and give them this contact with the
invisible beauty which we ourselves enjoy. We have no aim
other than to give our friends the happiness of a great new
experience. We take them to a symphony concert; and in a
very short time they are fidgeting and gazing around the hall,
extremely bored. Those friends have passed judgment on
themselves that they have no music in their souls. The
experience designed to bring them new happiness has become
only a judgment.

This always happens when people are confronted with
greatness. We may take our friends to see some great master-
piece of art; we may take them to listen to the most eloquent

of preachers; we may give them a great book to read; we may take them to gaze upon some beauty. Their reactions are a judgment; if they find no beauty and no thrill, we know that there is a blind spot in their souls. A visitor was being shown round an art gallery by one of the attendants. In that gallery there were certain masterpieces beyond all price, possessions of eternal beauty and unquestioned genius. At the end of the tour, the visitor said: 'Well, I don't think much of your old pictures.' The attendant answered quietly: 'Sir, I would remind you that these pictures are no longer on trial, but those who look at them are.' All that the man's reaction had done was to show his own pitiable blindness.

This is so with regard to Jesus. If when people are confronted with Jesus their souls respond to that wonder and beauty, they are on the way to salvation. But if when they are confronted with Jesus they see nothing lovely, they stand condemned. Their reaction has condemned them. God sent Jesus in love. He sent him for the salvation of those people; but that which was sent in love has become a condemnation. It is not God who has condemned them; God only loved them; the people have condemned themselves.

Those who react in hostility to Jesus have loved the darkness rather than the light. The terrible thing about really good people is that they always have a certain unconscious element of condemnation in them. It is when we compare ourselves with them that we see ourselves as we are. Alcibiades, the spoilt Athenian man of genius, was a companion of Socrates, and every now and again he used to break out: 'Socrates, I hate you, for every time I meet you, you let me see what I am.' Those who are engaged on evil tasks do not want a flood of light on themselves or on what they are doing; but those engaged on an honourable task do not fear the light.

Once an architect came to Plato and offered for a certain sum of money to build him a house into none of whose rooms it would be possible to see. Plato said: 'I will give you double the money to build a house into whose every room everyone can see.' It is only evildoers who do not wish to see themselves and who do not wish anyone else to see them. Such people will inevitably hate Jesus Christ, for Christ will show them what they are, and that is the last thing that they want to see. It is the concealing darkness that they love and not the revealing light.

By our reaction to Jesus Christ, we stand revealed and our souls laid bare. If we regard Christ with love, even with wistful yearning, there is hope for us; but if in Christ we see nothing attractive, we have condemned ourselves. The one who was sent in love has become our judge.

A MAN WITHOUT ENVY

John 3:22–30

> After these things Jesus and his disciples went to the district of Judaea. He spent some time there with them, and he was baptizing; and John was baptizing at Ainon, near Salem, because there was much water there. The people kept coming to him and being baptized, for John had not yet been thrown into prison. A discussion arose between some of John's disciples and a Jew about the matter of cleansing. So they came to John and said to him: 'Rabbi, look now! The man who was with you on the other side of Jordan, the man to whom you bore your witness, is baptizing and they are all going to him.' John answered: 'A man can receive only what is given to him from heaven. You yourselves can testify that I said, "I am not the Anointed One of God," but, "I have

been sent before him." He who has the bride is the bridegroom. But the friend of the bridegroom who stands and listens for him rejoices at the sound of the voice of the bridegroom. So, then, my joy is complete. He must increase, but I must decrease.'

WE have already seen that part of the aim of the writer of the Fourth Gospel is to ensure that John the Baptist received his proper place as the forerunner of Jesus, but no higher place than that. There were those who were still ready to call John master and lord; the writer of the Fourth Gospel wishes to show that John had a high place, but that the highest place was reserved for Jesus alone; and he also wishes to show that John himself never had any other idea than that Jesus was supreme. To that end, he shows us the ministry of John and the ministry of Jesus overlapping. The synoptic gospels are different: Mark 1:14 tells us that it was *after* John was put into prison that Jesus began his ministry. We need not argue which account is historically correct; but the likelihood is that the Fourth Gospel makes the two ministries overlap so that by contrast the supremacy of Jesus may be clearly shown.

One thing is certain – this passage shows us the loveliness of the humility of John the Baptist. It was clear that people were leaving John for Jesus. John's disciples were worried. They did not like to see their master take second place. They did not like to see him abandoned while the crowds flocked out to hear and see this new teacher.

In answer to their complaints, it would have been very easy for John to feel injured, neglected and unjustifiably forgotten. Sometimes a friend's sympathy can be the worst possible thing for us. It can make us feel sorry for ourselves and encourage us to think that we have not had a fair deal. But John had a mind above that. He told his disciples three things.

(1) He told them that he had never expected anything else. He told them that in point of fact he had assured them that his was not the leading place, but that he was merely sent as the herald, the forerunner and the preparer for the greater one to come. It would ease life a great deal if more people were prepared to play the subordinate role. So many people look for great things to do. John was not like that. He knew well that God had given him a subordinate task. It would save us a lot of resentment and heartbreak if we realized that there are certain things which are not for us, and if we accepted with all our hearts and did with all our might the work that God has given us to do. To do a secondary task *for God* makes it a great task. As Robert Browning put it in 'Pippa Passes': 'All service ranks the same with God.' Any task done for God is necessarily great.

(2) He told them that they could not receive more than God gave them. If the new teacher was winning more followers, it was not because he was stealing them from John but because God was giving them to him. There was a certain American minister called Dr Spence; once he was popular and his church was full; but as the years passed his people drifted away. To the church across the road came a new young minister who was attracting the crowds. One evening in Dr Spence's church there was a very small gathering. The doctor looked at the little flock. 'Where have all the people gone?' he asked. There was an embarrassed silence; then one of his office-bearers said: 'I think they have gone to the church across the street to hear the new minister.' Dr Spence was silent for a moment; then he smiled. 'Well, then,' he said, 'I think we ought to follow them.' And he descended from his pulpit and led his people across the road. What jealousies, what heartburnings, what resentfulness we might escape, if we would only remember that the success of others is given

to them by God, and we were prepared to accept God's verdict and God's choice.

(3) Finally, John used a very vivid picture which every Jew would recognize, for it was part of the heritage of Jewish thought. He called Jesus the bridegroom and himself the friend of the bridegroom. One of the great pictures of the Old Testament is of Israel as the bride of God and God as the bridegroom of Israel. The union between God and Israel was so close that it could be likened only to a wedding. When Israel went after strange gods, it was as if she were guilty of infidelity to the marriage bond (Exodus 34:15; cf. Deuteronomy 31:16; Psalm 73:27; Isaiah 54:5). The New Testament took this picture over and spoke of the Church as the bride of Christ (2 Corinthians 11:2; Ephesians 5:22–32). It was this picture that was in John's mind. Jesus had come from God; he was the Son of God, Israel was his rightful bride and he was Israel's bridegroom. But one place John did claim for himself, that of the friend of the bridegroom.

The friend of the bridegroom, the *shoshben*, had a unique place at a Jewish wedding. He acted as the liaison between the bride and the bridegroom; he arranged the wedding; he sent out the invitations; he presided at the wedding feast. He brought the bride and the bridegroom together. And he had one special duty. It was his duty to guard the bridal chamber and to let no false lover in. He would open the door only when in the dark he heard the bridegroom's voice and recognized it. When he heard the bridegroom's voice, he let him in and went away rejoicing, for his task was completed and the lovers were together. He did not grudge the bridegroom the bride. He knew that his only task had been to bring bride and bridegroom together. And when that task was done, he willingly and gladly faded out of the centre of the picture.

John's task had been to bring Israel and Jesus together, to arrange the marriage between Christ the bridegroom and Israel the bride. That task completed, he was happy to fade into obscurity, for his work was done. It was not with envy that he said that Jesus must increase and he must decrease; it was with joy. It may be that sometimes we would do well to remember that it is not to ourselves we must try to attach people; it is to Jesus Christ. It is not for ourselves we seek the loyalty of others; it is for him.

THE ONE FROM HEAVEN

John 3:31–6

> He who comes from above is above all. He who is from the earth is from the earth and speaks from the earth. He who comes from heaven is above all. It is to what he has seen and heard that he bears witness; and no one receives his witness. He who has received his witness sets his seal on the fact that God is true. He whom God sent speaks the words of God, for he does not partially measure out the Spirit upon him. The Father loves the Son and has given all things into his hand. He who believes in the Son has eternal life. He who does not believe in the Son will not see life, but the wrath of God rests upon him.

As we have seen before, one of the difficulties in the Fourth Gospel is to know when the characters are speaking and when John is adding his own commentary. These verses may be the words of John the Baptist; but more likely they are the witness and the comment of John the evangelist.

John begins by asserting the supremacy of Jesus. If we want information, we have to go to the person who possesses that information. If we want information about a family, we will get it at first hand only from a member of that family. If we want information about a town, we will get it at first hand only from someone who comes from that town. So, if we want information about God, we will get it only from the Son of God; and if we want information about heaven and heaven's life, we will get it only from him who comes from heaven. When Jesus speaks about God and about the heavenly things, says John, it is not something overheard, no second-hand tale, no information from a secondary source; he tells us that which he himself has seen and heard. To put it very simply, because Jesus alone knows God, he alone can give us the facts about God, and these facts are the gospel.

It is John's grief that so few accept the message that Jesus brought; but when people do accept it, they attest the fact that in their belief the word of God is true. In the ancient world, if a man wished to give his full approval to a document, such as a will or an agreement or a constitution, he affixed his seal to the foot of it. The seal was the sign that he agreed with this and regarded it as binding and true. So when people accept the message of Jesus, they affirm and attest that they believe what God says is true.

John goes on: we can believe what Jesus says, because on him God poured out the Spirit in full measure, keeping nothing back. Even the Jews themselves said that the prophets received from God *a certain measure of the Spirit*. The full measure of the Spirit was reserved for God's own chosen one. Now, in Hebrew thought the Spirit of God had two functions – first, the Spirit revealed God's truth to men and women; and, second, the Spirit enabled them to recognize and understand that truth when it came to them. So to say that the Spirit was on Jesus in the completest possible way is to say that he perfectly knew and perfectly understood the truth of God. To put that in another way – to listen to Jesus is to listen to the very voice of God.

Finally, John again sets before us the eternal choice – life or death. All through history, this choice had been set before Israel. Deuteronomy records the words of Moses: 'See, I have set before you today life and prosperity, death and adversity . . . I call heaven and earth to witness against you today that I have set before you life and death, blessings and curses. Choose life so that you and your descendants may live' (Deuteronomy 30:15–20). The challenge was reiterated by Joshua: 'Choose this day whom you will serve' (Joshua 24:15). It has been said that all life concentrates upon a man or woman at the crossroads. Once again, John returns to his favourite thought. What matters is the reaction people have to Christ. If that reaction is love and longing, they will know life. If it is indifference or hostility, they will know death. It is not that God sends his wrath upon them; it is that they bring that wrath upon themselves.

BREAKING DOWN THE BARRIERS

John 4:1–9

> So when Jesus learned that the Pharisees had heard that he was making and baptizing more disciples than John (although it was not Jesus himself who was in the habit of baptizing but his disciples), he quitted Judaea and went away again to Galilee. Now he had to pass through Samaria. He came to a town of Samaria, called Sychar, which is near the piece of ground which Jacob gave to Joseph, his son, and Jacob's well was there. So Jesus, tired from the journey, was sitting by the well just as he was. It was about 12 noon. There came a woman of Samaria to draw water. Jesus said to her: 'Give me to

drink.' For his disciples had gone away into the town to buy provisions. So the Samaritan woman said to him: 'How is it that you who are a Jew ask a drink from me, a Samaritan woman?' (For there is no familiarity between Jews and Samaritans.)

FIRST of all, let us set the scene of this incident. Palestine is only 120 miles long from north to south. But within that 120 miles there were in the time of Jesus three definite divisions of territory. In the extreme north lay Galilee; in the extreme south lay Judaea; and in between lay Samaria. Jesus did not wish at this stage in his ministry to be involved in a controversy about baptism; so he decided to quit Judaea for the time being and transfer his operations to Galilee. There was a centuries-old feud between the Jews and the Samaritans, the cause of which we will shortly see. But the quickest way from Judaea to Galilee lay through Samaria. Using that route, the journey could be done in three days. The alternative route was to cross the Jordan, go up the eastern side of the river to avoid Samaria, recross the Jordan north of Samaria and then enter Galilee. This was a route which took twice as long. So, Jesus had to pass through Samaria if he wished to take the shortest route to Galilee.

On the way, they came to the town of Sychar. Just short of Sychar, the road to Samaria forks. One branch goes north-east to Scythopolis; the other goes west to Nablus and then north to Engannim. At the fork of the road, there stands to this day the well known as Jacob's well.

This was an area which had many Jewish memories attached to it. There was a piece of ground there which had been bought by Jacob (Genesis 33:18–19). Jacob, on his deathbed, had bequeathed that ground to Joseph (Genesis 48:22). And, on Joseph's death in Egypt, his body had been taken back to Palestine and buried there (Joshua

24:32). So around this area there gathered many Jewish memories.

The well itself was more than 100 feet deep. It is not a springing well of water; it is a well into which the water percolates and gathers. But clearly it was a well so deep that no one could gain water from it unless he had something with which to draw the water.

When Jesus and his little band came to the fork in the road Jesus sat down to rest, for he was tired from the journey. It was 12 noon. The Jewish day runs from 6 am to 6 pm, and the sixth hour is 12 noon. So the heat was at its greatest, and Jesus was weary and thirsty from travelling. His disciples went on ahead to buy some food in the Samaritan town. Something must have been beginning to happen to them. Before they had met Jesus it is entirely unlikely that they would have even thought of buying food in any Samaritan town. Little by little, perhaps even unconsciously, the barriers were going down.

As Jesus sat there, there came to the well a Samaritan woman. Why she should come to that well is something of a mystery, for it was more than half a mile from Sychar where she must have lived, and there was water there. Might it be that she was so much of a moral outcast that the women even drove her away from the village well and she had to come here to draw water? Jesus asked her to give him a drink. She turned in astonishment. 'I am a Samaritan,' she said. 'You are a Jew. How is it that you ask a drink from me?' And then John explains to the Greeks for whom he is writing that there was no kind of come-and-go at all between the Jews and the Samaritans.

Now it is certain that all we have here is the briefest possible report of what must have been a long conversation. Clearly there was much more to this meeting than is recorded here. If we may use an analogy, this is like the minutes of a committee meeting where we have only the salient points of the discussion recorded. I think that the Samaritan woman must have unburdened her soul to this stranger. How else could Jesus have known of her tangled domestic affairs? For one of the very few times in her life, she had found one with kindness in his eyes instead of critical superiority; and she opened her heart.

Few stories in the gospel record show us so much about the character of Jesus.

(1) It shows us the reality of his humanity. Jesus was weary from the journey, and he sat by the side of the well exhausted. It is very significant that John, who stresses the sheer deity of Jesus Christ more than any other of the gospel writers, also stresses his humanity to the full. John does not show us a figure freed from the tiredness and the struggle of our humanity. He shows us one for whom life was an effort as it is for us; he shows us one who also was tired and had to go on.

(2) It shows us the warmth of his sympathy. From an ordinary religious teacher, from one of the orthodox religious leaders of the day, the Samaritan woman would have fled in embarrassment. She would have avoided such an individual. If by any unlikely chance he had spoken to her, she would have met him with an ashamed and even a hostile silence. But it seemed the most natural thing in the world to talk to Jesus. She had at last met someone who was not a critic but a friend, one who did not condemn but who understood.

(3) It shows us Jesus as the breaker-down of barriers. The quarrel between the Jews and the Samaritans was an old, old story. Way back about 720 BC, the Assyrians had invaded the northern kingdom of Samaria and had captured and subjugated it. They did what conquerors often did in those days – they transported practically the whole population to

Media (2 Kings 17:6). Into the district the Assyrians brought other people – from Babylon, from Cuthah, from Ava, from Hamath and from Sepharvaim (2 Kings 17:24). Now it is not possible to transport a whole people. Some of the people of the northern kingdom were left. Almost inevitably they began to intermarry with the incoming foreigners; and thereby they committed what to the Jews was an unforgivable crime. They lost their racial purity. In a strict Jewish household even to this day, if a son or a daughter marries a Gentile, his or her funeral service is carried out. Such a person is dead in the eyes of orthodox Judaism. So, the great majority of the inhabitants of Samaria were carried away to Media. They never came back but were assimilated into the country into which they were taken. They are the lost ten tribes. Those who remained in the country intermarried with the incoming strangers and lost their right to be called Jews at all.

In course of time, a similar invasion and a similar defeat happened to the southern kingdom, whose capital was Jerusalem. Its inhabitants also were carried off to Babylon; but they did not lose their identity; they remained stubbornly and unalterably Jewish. In time there came the days of Ezra and Nehemiah, and the exiles returned to Jerusalem by the grace of the Persian king. Their immediate task was to repair and rebuild the shattered Temple. The Samaritans came and offered their help in this sacred task. They were contemptuously told that their help was not wanted. They had lost their Jewish heritage and they had no right to share in the rebuilding of the house of God. Smarting under this repulse, they turned bitterly against the Jews of Jerusalem. It was about 450 BC when that quarrel took place, and it was as bitter as ever in the days of Jesus.

It had been further embittered when the renegade Jew Manasseh married a daughter of the Samaritan Sanballat

(Nehemiah 13:28) and proceeded to found a rival Temple on Mount Gerizim, which was in the centre of the Samaritan territory. Still later in the Maccabaean days, in 129 BC, John Hyrcanus, the Jewish general and leader, led an attack against Samaria and sacked and destroyed the Temple on Mount Gerizim. Between Jews and Samaritans, there was an embittered hatred. The Jews contemptuously called them Chuthites or Cuthaeans after one of the peoples whom the Assyrians had settled there. The Jewish Rabbis said: 'Let no man eat of the bread of the Cuthaeans, for he who eats their bread is as he who eats swine's flesh.' Ecclesiasticus depicts God as saying: 'Two nations my soul detests, and the third is not even a people: those who live [on the mountain of Samaria], and the Philistines, and that foolish people that live in Shechem' (Ecclesiasticus 50:25–6). Shechem was one of the most famous of Samaritan cities. The hatred was returned with interest. It is told that Rabbi Jochanan was passing through Samaria on his way to Jerusalem to pray. He passed by Mount Gerizim. A Samaritan saw him, and asked him: 'Where are you going?' 'I am going to Jerusalem,' he said, 'to pray.' The Samaritan answered: 'Would it not be better for you to pray in this holy mountain [Mount Gerizim] than in that accursed house?' Pilgrims from Galilee to Jerusalem had to pass through Samaria, if, as we have seen, they travelled by the quickest way; and the Samaritans delighted to hinder them.

The Jewish–Samaritan quarrel was more than 400 years old. But it smouldered as resentfully and as bitterly as ever. It was small wonder that the Samaritan woman was astonished that Jesus, a Jew, should speak to her, a Samaritan.

(4) But there was still another way in which Jesus was taking down the barriers. The Samaritan was a woman. The strict Rabbis forbade a Rabbi to greet a woman in public. A

Rabbi might not even speak to his own wife or daughter or
sister in public. There were even Pharisees who were called
'the bruised and bleeding Pharisees' because they shut their
eyes when they saw a woman on the street and so walked
into walls and houses! For a Rabbi to be seen speaking to a
woman in public was the end of his reputation – and yet Jesus
spoke to this woman. Not only was she a woman; she was
also a woman of notorious character. No decent man, let alone
a Rabbi, would have been seen in her company, or even
exchanging a word with her – and yet Jesus spoke to her.

To a Jew, this was an amazing story. Here was the Son of
God, tired and weary and thirsty. Here was the holiest of
men, listening with understanding to a sorry story. Here was
Jesus breaking through the barriers of nationality and
orthodox Jewish custom. Here is the beginning of the
universality of the gospel; here is God so loving the world,
not in theory, but in action.

THE LIVING WATER

John 4:10–15

> Jesus answered her: 'If you knew the free gift that God
> is offering you, and if you knew who is speaking to
> you, and if you knew who was saying to you: "Give me
> to drink," you would have asked him, and he would
> have given you living water.' The woman said to him:
> 'Sir, you have no bucket to draw with and the well is
> deep. Where does this living water that you have come
> from? Are you greater than our father Jacob who gave
> us the well, and who himself drank from it with his
> children and his cattle?' Jesus answered her: 'Everyone
> who drinks of this water will thirst again; but whoever
> drinks of the water that I will give him will never thirst

again for ever. But the water that I will give him will
become a well of water within him, springing up to give
him life eternal.' The woman said to him: 'Sir, give me
this water, so that I will not thirst, and so that I will not
have to come here to draw water.'

WE have to note that this conversation with the Samaritan
woman follows exactly the same pattern as the conversation
with Nicodemus. Jesus makes a statement. The statement is
taken in the wrong sense. Jesus remakes the statement in an
even more vivid way. It is still misunderstood; and then Jesus
compels the person with whom he is speaking to discover
and to face the truth for herself. That was Jesus' usual way of
teaching; and it was a most effective way, for, as someone
has said: 'There are certain truths which a man cannot *accept*;
he must *discover* them for himself.'

Just as Nicodemus did, the woman took the words of Jesus
quite literally when she was meant to understand them spiritually. It was *living* water of which Jesus spoke. In ordinary language, to a Jew, *living* water was *running* water. It was the
water of the running stream as against the water of the stagnant
cistern or pool. This well, as we have seen, was not a springing
well, but a well into which the water percolated from the
subsoil. To a Jew, *running, living* water from the stream was
always better. So the woman is saying: 'You are offering me
pure stream water. Where are you going to get it?'

She goes on to speak of 'our father Jacob'. The Jews would,
of course, have strenuously denied that Jacob was the father
of the Samaritans, but it was part of the Samaritan claim that
they were descended from Joseph, the son of Jacob, by way
of Ephraim and Manasseh. The woman is in effect saying to
Jesus: 'This is blasphemous talk. Jacob, our great ancestor,
when he came here, had to dig this well to gain water for his
family and his cattle. Are you claiming to be able to get fresh,

running stream water? If you are, you are claiming to be wiser and more powerful than Jacob. That is a claim that no one has any right to make.'

When people were on a journey, they usually carried with them a bucket made from the skin of some animal so that they could draw water from any well at which they halted. No doubt Jesus' band had such a bucket; and no doubt the disciples had taken it into the town with them. The woman saw that Jesus did not possess such a traveller's bucket, and so again she says in effect: 'You need not talk about drawing water and giving it to me. I can see for myself that you do not have a bucket with which to draw water.' H. B. Tristram begins his book entitled *Eastern Customs in Bible Lands* with this personal experience. He was sitting beside a well in Palestine beside the scene of the inn which figures in the story of the Good Samaritan. 'An Arab woman came down from the hills above to draw water; she unfolded and opened her goatskin bottle, and then untwined a cord, and attached it to a very small leathern bucket which she carried, by means of which she slowly filled her skin, fastened its mouth, placed it on her shoulder, and bucket in hand, climbed the mountain. I thought of the woman of Samaria at Jacob's well, when an Arab footman, toiling up the steep path from Jericho, heated and wearied with his journey, turned aside to the well, knelt and peered wistfully down. But he had "nothing to draw with and the well was deep". He lapped a little moisture from the water spilt by the woman who had preceded him, and, disappointed, passed on.' It was just that that the woman was thinking of when she said that Jesus had nothing with which to draw water from the depths of the well.

But the Jews had another way of using the word *water*. They often spoke of the *thirst* of the soul for God; and they often spoke of quenching that thirst with *living water*. Jesus was not using terms that were bound to be misunderstood; he was using terms that anyone with spiritual insight should have understood. In the Book of Revelation, that promise is: 'To the thirsty I will give water as a gift from the spring of the water of life' (Revelation 21:6). The Lamb is to lead them to springs of living waters (Revelation 7:17). The promise was that the chosen people would draw water with joy from the wells of salvation (Isaiah 12:3). The psalmist spoke of his soul being thirsty for the living God (Psalm 42:1). God's promise was: 'I will pour water on the thirsty land' (Isaiah 44:3). The summons was that everyone who was thirsty should come to the waters and freely drink (Isaiah 55:1). Jeremiah's complaint was that the people had forsaken God who was the fountain of living waters and had dug out broken cisterns which could hold no water (Jeremiah 2:13). Ezekiel had had his vision of the river of life (Ezekiel 47:1–12). In the new world, there would be a cleansing fountain opened (Zechariah 13:1). The waters would go forth from Jerusalem (Zechariah 14:8).

Sometimes the Rabbis identified this living water with the wisdom of the law; sometimes they identified it with nothing less than the Holy Spirit of God. All Jewish pictorial religious language was full of this idea of the thirst of the soul which could be quenched only with the living water which was the gift of God. But the woman chose to understand this with an almost crude literalism. She was blind because she would not see.

Jesus went on to make a still more startling statement that he could give her living water which would banish her thirst forever. The point is that again the woman took this literally; but in point of fact it was nothing less than a messianic claim. In the prophetic vision of the age to come, the age of God, the promise was: 'They shall not hunger or thirst' (Isaiah

49:10). It was with God and none other that the living fountain of the all-quenching water existed. 'With you is the fountain of life,' the psalmist had cried (Psalm 36:9). It is from the very throne of God that the river of life is to flow (Revelation 22:1). It is the Lord who is the fountain of living water (Jeremiah 17:13). It is in the messianic age that the parched ground is to become a pool and the thirsty ground springs of water (Isaiah 35:7). When Jesus spoke about bringing to men and women the water which quenches thirst forever, he was doing no less than stating that he was the Anointed One of God who was to bring in the new age.

Again the woman did not see it. And I think that this time she spoke with a jest, as if humouring one who was a little mad. 'Give me this water,' she said, 'so that I will never be thirsty again and will not have to walk to the well day after day.' She was jesting with a kind of humouring contempt about eternal things.

At the heart of all this, there is the fundamental truth that in the human heart there is a thirst for something that only Jesus Christ can satisfy. In one of his books, the American novelist Sinclair Lewis draws a picture of a respectable little businessman who kicked over the traces. He is talking to the girl he loves. She says to him: 'On the surface we seem quite different; but deep down we are fundamentally the same. We are both desperately unhappy about something – and we don't know what it is.' In each of us, there is this nameless unsatisfied longing, this vague discontent, this something lacking, this frustration.

In his novel, *Sorrell and Son*, Warwick Deeping tells of a conversation between Sorrell and his son. The boy is talking about life. He says that it is like groping in an enchanted fog. The fog breaks for a moment; you see the moon or a girl's face; you think you want the moon or the face; and then the fog comes down again and leaves you groping for something, you don't quite know what. William Wordsworth, in the 'Ode on the Intimations of Immortality', speaks of

> Those obstinate questionings
> Of sense and outward things,
> Fallings from us, vanishings;
> Blank misgivings of a creature
> Moving about in worlds not realized.

Augustine talks about 'our hearts being restless till they find rest in thee'.

Part of the human situation is that we cannot find happiness out of the things that the human situation has to offer. As Robert Browning expressed it in 'Bishop Blougram's Apology':

> Just when we're safest, there's a sunset touch,
> A fancy from a flower-bell, someone's death,
> A chorus ending from Euripides –
> And that's enough for fifty hopes and fears
> As old and new at once as Nature's self
> To rap and knock and enter in our soul.

We are never safe from the longing for eternity which God has put into the human soul. There is a thirst which only Jesus Christ can satisfy.

FACING THE TRUTH

John 4:15–21

> The woman said to him: 'Sir, give me this water, so that I will not thirst, and so that I will not have to come here to draw water.' Jesus said to her: 'Go, call your husband, and come back here.' The woman answered:

'I have not got a husband.' Jesus said to her: 'You spoke well when you said, "I have not got a husband." For you have had five husbands, and the one you now have is not your husband. This is the truth that you have told.' The woman said to him: 'Sir, I see that you are a prophet. Our fathers worshipped in this mountain and you say Jerusalem is the place where we ought to worship.' Jesus said: 'Woman, believe me, the hour is coming when you will worship the Father neither in this mountain nor in Jerusalem.'

WE have seen how the woman jestingly asked Jesus to give her the living water in order that she should not thirst again and might be spared the tiring journey to the well. Suddenly and stabbingly, Jesus brought her to her senses. The time for verbal byplay was past; the time for jesting was over. 'Go,' said Jesus, 'and fetch your husband and come back with him.' The woman stiffened as if a sudden pain had caught her; she recoiled as if hit by a sudden shock; she grew white as one who had seen a sudden apparition; and so indeed she had, *for she had suddenly caught sight of herself.*

She was suddenly compelled to face herself and the looseness and immorality and total inadequacy of her life. There are two revelations in Christianity: the revelation of God and the revelation of ourselves. We never really see ourselves until we see ourselves in the presence of Christ; and then we are appalled at the sight. There is another way of putting it – Christianity begins with a sense of sin. It begins with the sudden realization that life as we are living it will not do. We awake to ourselves and we awake to our need of God.

Some people have held, because of this mention of the five husbands, that this story is not an actual incident but an allegory. We have seen that when the original people of

Samaria were exiled and transported to Media, people from
five other places were brought in. These five different people
brought in their own gods (2 Kings 17:29); and it has been
held that the woman stands for Samaria and the five husbands
for the five false gods to whom the Samaritans, as it were,
married themselves. The sixth husband stands for the true
God, but they worship him not truly but in ignorance; and
therefore they are not married to him at all. It may be that
there is a reminder of this Samaritan infidelity to God in the
story; but it is far too vivid to be a manufactured allegory. It
reads too much like life.

Someone has said that prophecy is criticism based on hope.
A prophet points out to an individual or a nation what is
wrong; but this is done not to push them into despair but to
point the way to cure and to amendment and to rightness of
life. So Jesus began by revealing to this woman her own sinful
state, but goes on to tell her of the true worship in which our
souls can meet God.

The woman's question sounds strange to us. She says, and
she is obviously troubled when she says it: 'Our fathers say
that we ought to worship here on Mount Gerizim; you say
that we ought to worship in Jerusalem; what am I to do?'
The Samaritans adjusted history to suit themselves. They
taught that it was on Mount Gerizim that Abraham had been
willing to sacrifice Isaac; they taught that it was there that
Melchizedek had appeared to Abraham; they declared that it
was on Mount Gerizim that Moses had first erected an altar
and sacrificed to God when the people entered the promised
land, although in fact it was on Mount Ebal that that was
done (Deuteronomy 27:4). They tampered with the text of
Scripture and with history to glorify Mount Gerizim. The
woman had been brought up to regard Mount Gerizim as the
most sacred spot in the world and to despise Jerusalem. What

was in her mind was this. She was saying to herself: 'I am a sinner before God; I must offer to God an offering for my sin; I must take that offering to the house of God to put myself right with him; where am I going to take it?' To her, as to all her contemporaries, the only cure for sin was sacrifice. Her great problem was: where was that sacrifice to be made? By this time, she is not arguing about the respective merits of the Temple on Mount Gerizim and the Temple on Mount Zion. All she wants to know is: where can I find God?

Jesus' answer was that the day of the old rivalries between peoples was coming to an end; and the time was on the way when God would be found everywhere. It had been Zephaniah's vision that every nation shall worship God 'each in its place' (Zephaniah 2:11). It was Malachi's dream that in every place incense would be offered as a pure offering to the name of God (Malachi 1:11). Jesus' answer to the woman was that she did not need to go anywhere special to find God, neither to Mount Gerizim nor to Mount Zion. She did not need to offer sacrifice in some special place; true worship finds God in every place.

THE TRUE WORSHIP

John 4:22–6

'You do not know what you are worshipping. We do know what we worship, because the world's salvation has its origin among the Jews. But the hour is coming – the hour is now here – when the real worshippers will worship the Father in spirit and in truth; for it is worshippers like that that the Father is looking for. God is Spirit; and those who worship him must worship him in spirit and in truth.' The woman said to him: 'I know

that the Messiah, he who is called Christ, is coming.
When he has come he will announce all things to us.'
Jesus said to her: 'I who am speaking to you am he.'

JESUS had told the Samaritan woman that the old rivalries
were on the way out, that the day was coming when controversy about the respective merits of Mount Gerizim and
Mount Zion would be an irrelevance, that those who truly
sought God would find him anywhere. For all that, Jesus still
stressed the fact that the Jewish nation had a unique place in
God's plan and revelation.

The Samaritans worshipped in ignorance, he said.
There was one sense in which that was factually true. The
Samaritans accepted only the Pentateuch, the first five books
of the Old Testament. They rejected all the rest of the Old
Testament. They had therefore rejected all the great messages
of the prophets and all the supreme devotion of the Psalms.
They had in fact a truncated religion because they had a
truncated Bible; they had rejected the knowledge that was
open to them and that they might have had. Further, the Jewish
Rabbis had always charged the Samaritans with a merely
superstitious worship of the true God. They always said
that the Samaritan worship was founded not on love and
knowledge, but on ignorance and fear. As we have seen, when
the foreign peoples were brought in to dwell in Samaria, they
brought their own gods with them (2 Kings 17:29). We are
told that a priest from Bethel came and told them how they
should fear the Lord (2 Kings 17:28). But all the probability
is that they merely added Yahweh to their list of gods because
they were superstitiously afraid to leave him out. After all,
he was the God of the land in which they were living, and it
might be dangerous not to include him in their worship.

In a false worship we may detect three faults.

(1) A false worship is a selective worship. It chooses what it wishes to know about God and omits the rest. The Samaritans took as much of Scripture as they wished and paid no attention to the rest. One of the most dangerous things in the world is a one-sided religion. It is very easy to accept and hold such parts of God's truth that suit us and to disregard the remainder. We have seen, for instance, how certain thinkers and church leaders and politicians justified *apartheid* and racial segregation by appeal to certain parts of Scripture, while they conveniently forgot the far greater parts which forbid it.

A minister in a great city organized a petition to help a man who had been condemned for a certain crime. It seemed to him that this was a case where Christian mercy ought to operate. His telephone rang, and a woman's voice said to him: 'I am astonished that you, a minister, should be lending your weight to this petition for mercy.' 'Why should you be surprised?' he asked. The voice said: 'I suppose you know your Bible.' 'I hope so,' he said. 'Then,' said the voice, 'are you not aware that the Bible says, "An eye for an eye and a tooth for a tooth"?' Here was a woman who took the part of the Bible which suited her argument and forgot the great merciful teaching of Jesus in the Sermon on the Mount.

We would do well to remember that, although no one will ever grasp truth in its entirety, it is total truth that we should aim at, not the snatching at fragments which happen to suit ourselves and our own position.

(2) A false worship is an ignorant worship. Worship ought to be the approach to God of the whole person. Each of us has a mind and we have a duty to exercise it. Religion may begin with an emotional response; but the time comes when that emotional response has to be thought out. The New Testament scholar E. F. Scott said that religion is far more than merely the strenuous exercise of the intellect, but that

nonetheless a very great part of religious failure is due to nothing other than intellectual sloth. To fail to think things out is in itself a sin. In the last analysis, religion is never safe until we can tell, not only what we believe, but why we believe it. Religion is hope, but it is hope with reason behind it (1 Peter 3:15).

(3) A false worship is a superstitious worship. It is a worship given, not out of a sense of need nor out of any real desire, but basically out of a feeling that it might be dangerous not to give it. Many people will refuse to walk beneath a ladder; many people will have a pleased feeling when a black cat crosses their path; many people will pick up a pin with the idea that good luck will follow; many people will have an uncomfortable feeling when they discover that there are thirteen sitting at a table. They do not believe in these superstitions, but they have the feeling that there might be something in them and they had better play safe. There are many people whose religion is founded on a kind of vague fear of what might happen if they leave God out of the reckoning. But real religion is founded not on fear but on the love of God and gratitude for what God has done. Too much religion is a kind of superstitious ritual to avert the possible wrath of the unpredictable gods.

Jesus pointed to the true worship. God, he said, is spirit. Immediately we grasp that, a new floodlight breaks over us. If God is spirit, God is not confined to *things*; and therefore idol-worship is not only an irrelevance, it is an insult to the very nature of God. If God is spirit, God is not confined to *places*; and therefore to limit the worship of God to Jerusalem or to any other spot is to set a limit to that which by its nature exceeds all limits. If God is spirit, our gifts to God must be gifts of the spirit. Animal sacrifices and all things of our own creating become inadequate. The only gifts that befit the nature of God are the gifts of the spirit – love, loyalty, obedience and devotion.

The spirit is the highest part of a human being. That is the part which lasts when the physical part has vanished. That is the part which dreams the dreams and sees the visions which, because of the weakness and faultiness of the body, may never be carried out. It is this spirit which is the source of our highest dreams and thoughts and ideals and desires. The true worship is when each of us, through that spirit, attains to friendship and intimacy with God. Genuine worship does not consist in coming to a certain place, nor in going through a certain ritual or liturgy, nor even in bringing certain gifts. True worship is when the spirit, the immortal and invisible part within us, speaks to and meets with God, himself immortal and invisible.

This passage closes with a great declaration. There had opened before this Samaritan woman a vista which bewildered and staggered her. Here were things beyond her understanding, things full of wonder. All that she could say was: 'When the Messiah, the Christ, the Anointed One of God comes, then we will know all about it.' Jesus said to her: 'I who am speaking to you am he.' It is as if Jesus said that this is not a dream of the truth; this *is* the truth itself.

SHARING THE WONDER

John 4:27–30

> Upon this his disciples came up; and they were in a state of amazement that he was talking to a woman; but no one said: 'What are you looking for?' or, 'Why are you talking to her?' So the woman left her water pot, and went away to the town and said to the people:

'Come and see a man who told me all things that I have
done! Can this be the Anointed One of God?' They came
out of the town and were coming to him.

THERE is little wonder that the disciples were in a state of
bewildered amazement when they returned from their errand
to the town of Sychar and found Jesus talking to the Samaritan
woman. We have already seen the Jewish idea of women.
The Rabbinic precept ran: 'Let no one talk with a woman in
the street, no, not with his own wife.' The Rabbis so despised
women and so thought them incapable of receiving any real
teaching that they said: 'Better that the words of the law
should be burned than delivered to women.' They had a
saying: 'Each time that a man prolongs converse with a
woman he causes evil to himself, and desists from the law,
and in the end inherits Gehinnom.' By Rabbinic standards,
Jesus could hardly have done a more shatteringly unconven-
tional thing than to talk to this woman. Here is Jesus taking
the barriers down.

There follows a curiously revealing touch. It is the kind
which could hardly have come from anyone except from one
who had actually shared in this scene. However staggered
the disciples might be, it did not occur to them to ask the
woman what she was looking for or to ask Jesus why he was
talking to her. They were beginning to know him; and they
had already arrived at the conclusion that however surprising
his actions were, they were not to be questioned. It is a great
step towards real discipleship to learn to say: 'It is not for me
to question the actions and the demands of Jesus. My
prejudices and my conventions must go down before them.'

By this time, the woman was on her way back to the village
without her water pot. The fact that she left her water pot
showed two things. It showed that she was in a hurry to share

this extraordinary experience, and it showed that she never dreamed of doing anything else but come back. Her whole action has much to tell us of real Christian experience.

(1) Her experience began with being compelled to face herself and to see herself as she was. The same thing happened to Peter. After the haul of fishes, when Peter suddenly discovered something of the majesty of Jesus, all he could say was: 'Go away from me, Lord, for I am a sinful man!' (Luke 5:8). Our Christian experience will often begin with a humiliating wave of self-disgust. It usually happens that the last thing people see is themselves. And it often happens that the first thing Christ does for people is to compel them to do what they have spent their lives refusing to do – look at themselves.

(2) The Samaritan woman was staggered by Christ's ability to see into her inmost being. She was amazed at his intimate knowledge of the human heart, and of her heart in particular. The psalmist was awed by that same thought. 'You discern my thoughts from far away . . . Even before a word is on my tongue, O Lord, you know it completely' (Psalm 139:1–4). It is told that once a small girl heard a sermon by C. H. Spurgeon, and whispered to her mother at the end of it: 'Mother, how does he know what goes on in our house?' There are no wrappings and disguises which are protection against the gaze of Christ. It is his power to see into the depths of the human heart. It is not that he sees only the evil there; he sees also the potential for great things in the soul of every one of us. He is like the surgeon who sees the diseased part, but who also sees the health which will follow when that part is taken away.

(3) The first instinct of the Samaritan woman was to share her discovery. Having found this amazing person, she was compelled to share her find with others. The Christian life is

based on the twin pillars of discovery and communication. No discovery is complete until the desire to share it fills our hearts; and we cannot communicate Christ to others until we have discovered him for ourselves. First to find, then to tell, are the two great steps of the Christian life.

(4) This very desire to tell others of her discovery killed in this woman the feeling of shame. She was no doubt an outcast; she was no doubt a byword; the very fact that she was drawing water from this distant well shows how she avoided her neighbours and how they avoided her. But now she ran to tell them of her discovery. Some people may have problems which they are embarrassed to mention and which they try to keep secret, but once they are behind them they are often so filled with wonder and gratitude that they tell everyone about it all. People may hide their sin; but once they discover Jesus Christ as Saviour, their first instinct is to say to others: 'Look at what I was and look at what I am; this is what Christ has done for me.'

THE MOST SATISFYING FOOD

John 4:31–4

> Meanwhile his disciples asked him: 'Rabbi! Eat something!' 'I have food,' he said to them, 'of which you do not know.' 'Surely', his disciples kept saying to each other, 'someone can't have given him something to eat?' 'My food', said Jesus to them, 'is to do the will of him who sent me and to complete his work.'

THIS passage follows the normal pattern of the conversations of the Fourth Gospel. Jesus says something which is mis-understood. He says something which has a spiritual meaning. It is at first taken with an uncomprehending literalism and then slowly he unfolds the meaning until it is grasped and realized. It is exactly the same as Jesus did when he talked to Nicodemus about being born again, and when he talked to the woman about the water which quenched the thirst of the heart forever.

By this time the disciples had come back with food, and they asked Jesus to eat. They had left him so tired and exhausted that they were worried that he did not seem to want to eat any of the provisions which they had brought back. It is strange how a great task can lift us above and beyond bodily needs. All his life William Wilberforce, who freed the slaves in the British Empire, was a little, insignificant, ailing creature. When he rose to address the House of Commons, the members at first used to smile at this strange little figure; but as the fire and the power came from the man, they used to crowd the benches whenever he rose to speak. As it was put: 'The little minnow became a whale.' His message, his task, the flame of truth and the dynamic of power conquered his physical weakness. There is a picture of John Knox preaching in his old age. He was a spent old man; he was so weak that he had to be half-lifted up the pulpit steps and left supporting himself on the bookboard; but before he had long begun his sermon the voice had regained its old trumpet-call and he was like 'to ding the pulpit into blads [to knock the pulpit into splinters] and leap out of it'. The message filled the man with a kind of supernatural strength.

Jesus' answer to his disciples was that he had food of which they knew nothing. In their simplicity, they wondered if someone had brought him food to eat. Then he told them: 'My food is to do the will of him who sent me.'

The great keynote of Jesus' life is submission to the will of God. His uniqueness lies in the very fact that he was the only person who ever was or who ever will be perfectly obedient to God's will. It can be truly said that Jesus is the only person in all the world who never did what he liked but always what God liked.

He was God-sent. Again and again, the Fourth Gospel speaks of Jesus being *sent* by God. There are two Greek words used in the Fourth Gospel for this sending. There is *apostellein* which is used seventeen times and *pempein* which is used twenty-seven times. That is to say, no fewer than forty-four times the Fourth Gospel speaks, or shows us Jesus speaking, about his being sent by God. Jesus was one who was under orders. He was God's man.

Then once Jesus had come, again and again he spoke of the work that was given him to do. In John 5:36 he speaks of the works which his Father has given him to do. In 17:4 his only claim is that he has finished the work his Father gave him to do. When he speaks of taking up and laying down his life, of living and of dying, he says: 'I have received this command from my Father' (10:18). He speaks continually, as he speaks here, of *the will of God*. 'I have come down from heaven,' he says, 'not to do my own will, but the will of him who sent me' (6:38). 'I always do', he says, 'what is pleasing to him' (8:29). In 14:23 he lays it down, out of his personal experience and on his personal example, that the only proof of love lies in the keeping of the commandments of the one a person claims to love. This obedience of Jesus was not, as it is with us, a spasmodic thing. It was the very essence and being, the mainspring and the core, the dynamic and the moving power of his life.

It is his great desire that we should be as he was.

(1) To do the will of God is the only way to peace. There can be no peace when we are at variance with the King of the universe.

(2) To do the will of God is the only way to happiness. There can be no happiness when we set our human ignorance against the divine wisdom of God.

(3) To do the will of God is the only way to power. When we go our own way, we have nothing to call on but our own power, and therefore collapse is inevitable. When we go God's way, we go in his power, and therefore victory is secure.

THE SOWER, THE HARVEST AND THE REAPERS

John 4:35–8

> 'Are you not in the habit of saying: "Four months, and the harvest will come"? Look you! I say to you, lift up your eyes and look at the fields, because they are already white for the harvesting. The harvester receives his reward and stores up fruit which makes for eternal life, so that he who sows and he who harvests may rejoice together. In this the saying is true – one sows and another harvests. I have sent you to harvest a crop which your labour did not produce. Others have laboured, and you have entered into their labours.'

ALL this that was happening in Samaria had given Jesus a vision of a world to be harvested for God. When he said: 'Four months, and the harvest will come,' we are not to think that he was speaking of the actual time of year that it was in Samaria at that time. If that were so, it would have been somewhere round about January. There would have been no exhausting heat; and there would have been no scarcity of water. One would not have needed a well to find water; it would have been the rainy season, and there would have been plenty of water.

What Jesus is doing is quoting a proverb. The Jews had a sixfold division of the agricultural year. Each division was held to last two months – seedtime, winter, spring, harvest, summer and the season of extreme heat. Jesus is saying: 'You have got a proverb; if you sow the seed, you must wait for at least four months before you can hope to begin to reap the harvest.' Then Jesus looked up. Sychar is in the midst of a region that is still famous for its corn. Agricultural land was very limited in stony, rocky Palestine; practically nowhere else in the country was it possible to look up and see the waving fields of golden corn. Jesus swept his gaze and his hand round. 'Look,' he said, 'the fields are white and ready for the harvest. They took four months to grow; but in Samaria there is a harvest for the reaping *now*.'

For once, it is the *contrast* between nature and grace of which Jesus is thinking. In the ordinary harvest, people sowed and waited; in Samaria, things had happened with such divine suddenness that the word was sown and on the spot the harvest waited. The writer and journalist H. V. Morton has a specially interesting suggestion about the fields white for the harvest. He himself was sitting at this very spot where Jacob's well is. As he sat, he saw the people come out from the village and start to climb the hill. They came in little batches; and they were all wearing white robes, and the white robes stood out against the ground and the sky. It may well be that just at this moment the people started to flock out to Jesus in response to the woman's story. As they streamed out in their white robes across the fields, perhaps Jesus said: 'Look at the fields! See them now! They are white to the harvest!' The white-robed crowd was the harvest which he was eager to reap for God.

Jesus went on to show that the incredible had happened. The sower and the harvester could rejoice at the same time. Here was something no one might expect. To the Jews, sowing

was a sad and laborious time; it was harvest which was the
time of joy. 'May those who sow in tears reap with shouts of
joy! Those who go out weeping, bearing the seed for sowing,
shall come home with shouts of joy, carrying their sheaves'
(Psalm 126:5–6).

There is something else hidden below the surface here.
The Jews had their dreams of the golden age, the age to come,
the age of God, when the world would be God's world, when
sin and sorrow would be done away with and God would
reign supreme. Amos paints his picture of it: 'The time is
surely coming, says the Lord, when the one who ploughs
shall overtake the one who reaps, and the treader of grapes
the one who sows the seed' (Amos 9:13). 'Your threshing
shall overtake the vintage, and the vintage shall overtake the
sowing' (Leviticus 26:5). It was the dream of that golden age
that sowing and reaping, planting and harvesting, would
follow hard upon the heels of each other. There would be
such fertility that the old days of waiting would be at an
end. We can see what Jesus is gently doing here. His words
are nothing less than a claim that with him the golden age
has dawned; God's time is here – the time when the word is
spoken and the seed is sown and the harvest waits.

There was another side to that – and Jesus knew it. 'There
is another proverb,' he said, 'and it too is true – one sows and
another harvests.' Then he went on to make two applications
of that.

(a) He told his disciples that they would reap a crop which
had been produced not by their labour. He meant that *he*
was sowing the seed, that in his cross, above all, the seed
of the love and the power of God would be sown, and that
the day would come when the disciples would go out into
the world and reap the harvest that his life and death had
sown.

(b) He told his disciples that the day would come when *they* would sow and others would reap. There would be a time when the Christian Church sent out its evangelists; they would never see the harvest; some of them would die as martyrs, but the blood of the martyrs would be the seed of the Church. It is as if he said: 'Some day you will labour and you will see nothing for it. Some day you will sow and you will pass from the scene before the harvest is reaped. Never fear! Never be discouraged! The sowing is not in vain; the seed is not wasted! Others will see the harvest which it was not given to you to see.'

So in this passage there are two things.

(1) There is *the reminder of an opportunity*. The harvest waits to be reaped for God. There come times in history when people are curiously and strangely sensitive to God. What a tragedy it is if Christ's Church at such a time fails to reap Christ's harvest!

(2) There is *the reminder of a challenge*. It is given to many to sow but not to reap. Many ministries succeed, not by their own force and merits, but because of some saintly men and women who lived and preached and died and left an influence which was greater in their absence than in their presence. Many have to work and never see the results of their labours. I was once taken round an estate which was famous for its rhododendrons. Its owner loved their acres and knew them all by name. He showed me certain seedlings which would take twenty-five years to flower. He was nearly seventy-five and would never see their beauty – *but someone would*. No work for Christ and no great undertaking ever fail. If we do not see the result of our labours, others will. There is no room for despair in the Christian life.

THE SAVIOUR OF THE WORLD

John 4:39–42

> Many of the Samaritans from that city believed on him,
> because of the woman's story, for she testified: 'He told
> me all things that I have done.' So when the Samaritans
> came to him, they asked him to stay among them, and
> he stayed there two days. And many more believed
> when they heard his word, and they said to the woman:
> 'No longer do we believe because of your talk. We
> ourselves have listened to him, and we know that this is
> really the Saviour of the world.'

In the events which happened at Samaria, we have the pattern
by which the gospel so often spreads. In the rise of belief
among the Samaritans, there were three stages.

(1) There was introduction. The Samaritans were introduced to Christ by the woman. Here we see full-displayed
God's need of us. Paul said: 'How are they to hear without
someone to proclaim him?' (Romans 10:14). The word of
God must be transmitted from one person to another. God
cannot deliver his message to those who have never heard it
unless there is someone to deliver it.

> He has no hands but our hands
>   To do his work today:
> He has no feet but our feet
>   To lead men in his way:
> He has no voice but our voice
>   To tell men how he died:
> He has no help but our help
>   To lead them to his side.

It is at once our precious privilege and our terrible responsibility to bring others to Christ. The introduction cannot be
made unless someone is there to make it.

Further, that introduction is made on the strength of personal witness. The cry of the Samaritan woman was: 'Look what he has done for me and to me.' It was not to a theory that she called her neighbours; it was to a dynamic and changing power. The Church can expand until the kingdoms of the world become the kingdoms of the Lord only when men and women themselves experience the power of Christ, and then transmit that experience to others.

(2) There was nearer intimacy and growing knowledge. Once the Samaritans had been introduced to Christ, they sought his company. They asked him to stay with them that they might learn of him and come to know him better. It is true that people must be introduced to Christ, but it is equally true that once they have been introduced they must themselves go on to live in the presence of Christ. No one can go through an experience for someone else. Others may lead us to the friendship of Christ, but we must claim and enjoy that friendship ourselves.

(3) There came discovery and surrender. The Samaritans discovered in Christ the Saviour of the world. It is not likely that they themselves put it exactly that way. John was writing years afterwards, and was putting the discovery of the Samaritans into his own words, words which enshrine a lifetime's living with and thinking about Jesus Christ. It is only in John that we find this tremendous title. We find it here and in 1 John 4:14. To him it was the title *par excellence* for Christ.

John did not invent the title. In the Old Testament, God had often been called the God of Salvation, the Saviour, the Saving God. Many of the Greek gods had acquired this title. At the time John was writing, the Roman emperor was invested with the title 'Saviour of the world'. It is as if John said: 'All that you have dreamed of has at last in Jesus come true.'

We do well to remember this title. Jesus was not simply a *prophet* who came with a message in words from God. He was not simply an *expert psychologist* with an uncanny faculty for seeing into the human mind. True, he showed that very skill in the case of the Samaritan woman, but he showed more than that. He was not simply *an example*. He did not come simply to show men and women the way in which life ought to be lived. A great example can be merely heart-breaking and frustrating when we find ourselves powerless to follow it.

Jesus was *Saviour*. He rescued people from the evil and hopeless situations in which they found themselves; he broke the chains that bound them to the past and gave them a power which enabled them to meet the future. The Samaritan woman is in fact the great example of his saving power. The town where she stayed would no doubt have labelled her a character beyond reformation; and she herself would no doubt have agreed that a respectable life was beyond her. But Jesus came and doubly rescued her; he enabled her to break away from the past and he opened a new future to her. There is no title adequate to describe Jesus except Saviour of the world.

THE UNANSWERABLE ARGUMENT

John 4:43–5

> Two days after, Jesus left there and went to Galilee. Jesus himself declared that a prophet has no honour in his own country. But when he came into Galilee, the Galilaeans welcomed him, because they had seen all that he had done at Jerusalem at the Feast, for they too had gone to the Feast.

ALL three synoptic gospels tell of the saying of Jesus that prophets have no honour in their own country (Mark 6:4; Matthew 13:57; Luke 4:24). It was an ancient proverb with much the same meaning as our own 'familiarity breeds contempt'. But John introduces it in a very strange place. The other gospels introduce it on occasions when Jesus was rejected by the people of his own country; John introduces it on an occasion when he was accepted.

It may be that John is reading the mind of Jesus. We have already seen that Jesus had left Judaea and set out for Galilee to avoid the controversy that an increasing publicity was bringing to him. The hour of conflict had not yet come (John 4:1-4). It may be that his astonishing success in Samaria had actually surprised him; his words about the astonishing harvest have the ring of glad surprise about them. It may well be that Jesus set out for Galilee hoping to find rest and retirement there, because he did not expect those of his native country to respond to him. And it may be that exactly the same happened in Galilee as happened in Samaria, that against all expectations there was a surge of response to his teaching. We must either explain the saying in this way or assume that somehow it has crept into the wrong place.

However that may be, this passage and the one before give us the unanswerable argument for Christ. The Samaritans believed in Jesus, not because of someone else's story but because they themselves had heard him speak things the like of which they had never heard. The Galilaeans believed in him, not because someone had told them about him but because they had seen him do in Jerusalem things the like of which they had never seen. The words he spoke and the deeds he did were arguments to which there was no answer.

Here we have one of the great truths of the Christian life. *The only real argument for Christianity is a Christian experience*. It may be that sometimes we have to argue with people until the intellectual barriers which they have erected are battered down and the citadel of their mind capitulates. But in the great majority of cases the only persuasion we can use is to say: 'I know what Jesus is like and I know what Jesus can do. All that I can ask you to do is to try him yourself and to see what happens.' Effective Christian evangelism really begins when we can say: 'I know what Christ has done for me,' and go on to say: 'Try him, and see what he can do for you.'

Here again tremendous personal responsibility is laid upon us. No one is likely to attempt the experience unless our own lives show its value. There is little use in telling people that Christ will bring them joy and peace and power, if our own lives are gloomy, worried and defeated. Other people will be persuaded to try the experiment only when they see that for us it has ended in an experience which is much to be desired.

A COURTIER'S FAITH

John 4:46–54

> So again he came to Cana in Galilee, where he had made the water into wine. Now there was a certain courtier whose son was ill in Capernaum. When this man heard that Jesus had come from Judaea into Galilee, he went to him and asked him to come down and heal his son, for he was going to die. Jesus said to him: 'Unless you see signs and wonders you will never believe.' The courtier said to him: 'Sir, come down before my little boy dies.' Jesus said to him: 'Go your way! Your son lives!' The man believed the word which Jesus spoke to him, and started on his way home. While he was still on the way down, his slaves met him and said: 'Your

son lives!' So he asked them at what hour his condition had improved. They told him: 'Yesterday, at 1 pm, the fever left him.' The father knew that that was the hour at which Jesus said to him: 'Your son lives!' And he and his whole household believed.

This is the second sign which Jesus did after he had come from Judaea into Galilee.

MOST of the commentators think this is another version of the story of the healing of the centurion's servant told in Matthew 8:5–13 and Luke 7:1–10; but there are differences which justify us in treating it as quite independent. Certain things about the conduct of this courtier are an example to us all.

(1) *Here is a courtier who came to a carpenter.* The Greek is *basilikos* which could even mean that he was a king; but it is used for a royal official, and he was a man of high standing at the court of Herod. Jesus on the other hand had no greater status than that of the village carpenter of Nazareth. Further, Jesus was in Cana and this man lived in Capernaum, almost twenty miles away. That is why he took so long to get back home.

There could be no more improbable scene in the world than an important court official hastening twenty miles to beg a favour from a village carpenter. First and foremost, this courtier swallowed his pride. He was in need, and neither convention nor custom stopped him from bringing his need to Christ. His action would cause a sensation, but he did not care what people said so long as he obtained the help he so much wanted. If we want the help which Christ can give, we must be humble enough to swallow our pride and not care what anyone else may say.

(2) *Here is a courtier who refused to be discouraged.* Jesus met him with the, at first sight, bleak statement that people

would not believe unless they were supplied with signs and wonders. It may well be that Jesus aimed that saying not so much at the courtier himself as at the crowd that must have gathered to see the outcome of this sensational happening. They would be there all agog to see what would happen.

But Jesus had a way of making sure that a person was in earnest. He did that to the Syro-Phoenician woman (Matthew 15:21–8). If the man had turned irritably and petulantly away; if he had been too proud to accept a rebuke; if he had given up despairingly on the spot – Jesus would have known that his faith was not real. People must be in earnest before the help of Christ can come to them.

(3) *Here was a courtier who had faith*. It must have been hard for him to turn away and go home with Jesus' assurance that his child would live. In recent years, people have begun to realize the power of thought and of telepathy in such a way that no one would reject this miracle simply because it was achieved at a distance; but it must have been difficult for the courtier. Yet he had faith enough to turn and walk back that twenty-mile road with nothing but Jesus' assurance to comfort his heart.

It is of the very essence of faith that we should believe that what Jesus says is true. So often we have a kind of vague, wistful longing that the promises of Jesus should be true. The only way really to enter into them is to believe in them with the clutching intensity of someone who is drowning. If Jesus says a thing, it is not a case of 'It *may* be true'; it is a case of 'It *must* be true.'

(4) *Here was a courtier who surrendered*. He was not a man who got out of Christ what he wanted and then went away to forget. He and all his household believed. That would not be easy for him, for the idea of Jesus as the Anointed One of God must have cut across all his preconceived notions.

Nor would it be easy at the court of Herod to profess faith in Jesus. He would have mockery and laughter to endure; and no doubt there would be those who thought that he had gone slightly mad.

But this courtier was a man who faced and accepted the facts. He had seen what Jesus could do; he had experienced it; and there was nothing left for it but surrender. He had begun with a sense of desperate need; that need had been supplied; and his sense of need had turned into an overwhelming love. That must always be the story of the Christian life.

Most New Testament scholars think that at this point in the Fourth Gospel the chapters have somehow become misplaced. They hold that chapter 6 should come *before* chapter 5. The reason is this. Chapter 4 finishes with Jesus in Galilee (John 4:54). Chapter 5 begins with Jesus in Jerusalem. Chapter 6 again shows us Jesus in Galilee. Chapter 7 begins with the implication that Jesus had just come into Galilee because of the opposition which he met in Jerusalem. The changes between Jerusalem and Galilee become very difficult to follow. On the other hand, chapter 4 (4:54) ends: 'Now this was the second sign that Jesus did, after coming from Judea to Galilee.' Chapter 6 begins (6:1): 'After this Jesus went to the other side of the Sea of Galilee,' which would be a natural sequence. Chapter 5 then shows us Jesus going to Jerusalem for a Feast and meeting with very serious trouble with the Jewish authorities. We are in fact told that from that time they began to persecute him (5:10). Then chapter 7 begins by saying that Jesus went about in Galilee and 'did not wish to go about in Judea because the Jews were looking for an opportunity to kill him' (7:1).

Here we have not altered the order; but we must note that to take chapter 6 before chapter 5 does give an easier and more natural order of events.

HUMAN HELPLESSNESS
AND CHRIST'S POWER

John 5:1–9

After this there was a Feast of the Jews, and Jesus went
up to Jerusalem. In Jerusalem, near the sheepgate,
there is a bathing-pool with five porches, which is
called in Hebrew Bethzatha. In these porches there lay
a crowd of people who were ill and blind and lame and
whose limbs were withered (waiting expectantly for the
moving of the water. For an angel of the Lord came
down into the pool every now and then and disturbed
the water; so the first person to go in after the disturbing
of the water regained his health from any illness which
had him in its grip.) There was a man there who had
been ill for thirty-eight years. When Jesus saw him
lying there, and since he knew that he had already
been there for a long time, he said to him: 'Do you
want to be made well?' The sick man answered: 'Sir,
I have no one to hurry me into the pool when the water
is disturbed; so, while I am on the way, someone gets
down before me.' Jesus said to him: 'Get up! Lift your
bed! and walk!' And the man was made well, and he
lifted up his bed and walked.

THERE were three Jewish feasts which were feasts of obliga-
tion – Passover, Pentecost and Tabernacles. Every adult male
Jew who lived within fifteen miles of Jerusalem was legally
bound to attend them. If we take chapter 6 before chapter 5,
we may think of this feast as Pentecost, because the events of
chapter 6 happened when the Passover was near (John 6:4).
The Passover was in mid-April, and Pentecost was seven
weeks later. John always shows us Jesus attending the great
feasts, for Jesus did not disregard the obligations of Jewish

worship. To him, it was not a duty but a delight to worship with his own people.

When Jesus arrived in Jerusalem, he was apparently alone; there is no mention of his disciples. He found his way to a famous pool. Its name was either *Bethesda*, which means House of Mercy, or more likely, *Bethzatha*, which means House of the Olive. The better manuscripts all have the second name, and we know from Josephus that there was a quarter of Jerusalem actually known as Bethzatha. The word for *pool* is *kolumbēthron*, which comes from the verb *kolumban*, *to dive*. The pool was deep enough to swim in. The passage we have put in parentheses is not in any of the greatest and best manuscripts and was probably added later as an explanation of what people were doing at the pool. Beneath the pool was a subterranean stream which every now and again bubbled up and disturbed the waters. The belief was that the disturbance was caused by an angel, and that the first person to get into the pool after the troubling of the water would be healed from any illness from which he or she was suffering.

To us, this is mere superstition. But it was the kind of belief which was spread all over the world in the past and which still exists in certain places. People believed in all kinds of spirits and demons. The air was thick with them; they had their dwellings in certain places; every tree, every river, every stream, every hill, every pool had its resident spirit.

Further, ancient peoples were specially impressed with the holiness of water and especially of rivers and springs. Water was so precious and swollen and fast-flowing rivers could be so powerful that it is not surprising that they were so impressed. In the west, we may know water only as something which comes out of a tap; but in the ancient world, as in many places still today, water was the most valuable and potentially the most dangerous of all things.

Sir J. G. Frazer in *Folk-lore in the Old Testament* (ii, 412–23) quotes many instances of this reverence for water. Hesiod, the Greek poet, said that when a man was about to ford a river, he should pray and wash his hands, for he who wades through a stream with unwashed hands incurs the wrath of the gods. When the Persian king Xerxes came to the Strymon in Thrace, his magicians offered white horses and went through other ceremonies before the army ventured to cross. Lucullus, the Roman general, offered a bull to the River Euphrates before he crossed it. Some of the Bantu tribes of south-east Africa held the belief that rivers are inhabited by malignant spirits which must be placated by flinging a handful of corn or some other offering into the river before it is crossed. Anyone who drowned in a river was said to be 'called by the spirits'. The Baganda in central Africa would not try to rescue anyone carried away by a river because they thought that the spirits had taken that person. The people who waited for the pool in Jerusalem to be disturbed were children of their time believing the things of their time.

It may be that as Jesus walked around, the man of this story was pointed out to him as a most pitiable case, because his disability made it very unlikely, even impossible, that he would ever be the first to get into the pool after it had been troubled. He had no one to help him in, and Jesus was always the friend of the friendless, and the helper of the person who has no earthly help. He did not trouble to read the man a lecture on the useless superstition of waiting for the water to be moved. His one desire was to help, and so he healed the man who had waited so long.

In this story, we see very clearly the conditions under which the power of Jesus operated. He gave his orders to people, and, in proportion as they tried to obey, power came to them.

(1) Jesus began by asking the man if he wanted to be cured. It was not so foolish a question as it may sound. The man had waited for thirty-eight years, and it might well have been that hope had died and left behind a passive and dull despair. In his heart of hearts, the man might be well content to remain an invalid for, if he was cured, he would have all the burden of making a living. He might have grown accustomed to his disability, being able to leave the working and the worrying to someone else. But his response was immediate. He wanted to be healed, though he did not see how he ever could be since he had no one to help him.

The first essential towards receiving the power of Jesus is to have intense desire for it. Jesus says: 'Do you really want to be changed?' If in our inmost hearts we are well content to stay as we are, there can be no change for us.

(2) Jesus went on to tell the man to get up. It is as if he said to him: 'Man, bend your will to it and you and I will do this thing together!' The power of God never dispenses with human effort. Nothing is truer than that we must realize our own helplessness; but in a very real sense it is true that miracles happen when our will and God's power co-operate to make them possible.

(3) In effect, Jesus was commanding the man to attempt the impossible. 'Get up!' he said. His bed would simply be a light stretcher-like frame – the Greek is *krabbatos*, a colloquial word which really means a pallet – and Jesus told him to pick it up and carry it away. The man might well have said with a kind of injured resentment that for thirty-eight years his bed had been carrying him and there was not much sense in telling him to carry it. But he made the effort along with Christ – and the thing was done.

(4) Here is the road to achievement. There are so many things in this world which defeat us. When we have intensity of desire and determination to make the effort, hopeless though it may seem, the power of Christ gets its opportunity, and with him we can conquer the things that for a long time have conquered us.

THE INNER MEANING

John 5:1–9 (*contd*)

CERTAIN scholars think this passage is an allegory.

The *man* stands for the people of Israel. The *five porches* stand for the five books of the law. In the porches, the people lay ill. The law could show people their sin, but could never mend it; the law could uncover people's weaknesses, but could never cure them. The law, like the porches, sheltered sick souls but could never heal them. The *thirty-eight years* stand for the thirty-eight years in which the Jews wandered in the desert before they entered the promised land; or for the number of the centuries they had been waiting for the Messiah. The *stirring of the waters* stands for baptism. In point of fact, in early Christian art a man is often depicted as rising from the baptismal waters carrying a bed upon his back.

It may well be that it is now possible to read all these meanings into this story; but it is highly unlikely that John wrote it as an allegory. It has the vivid stamp of factual truth. But we do well to remember that any Bible story has in it far more than fact. There are always deeper truths below the surface, and even the simple stories are meant to leave us face to face with eternal things.

HEALING AND HATRED

John 5:10–18

> It was Sabbath on that day. So the Jews said to the man
> who had been cured: 'It is Sabbath and you have no
> right to lift your bed.' He answered them: 'He who made
> me well, it was he who said to me: "Lift your bed and
> walk!"' They asked him: 'Who is the fellow who said
> to you: "Lift your bed and walk"?' The man who had
> been cured did not know who he was, for Jesus had
> slipped away, for there was a crowd in the place.
> Afterwards Jesus found him in the Temple and said to
> him: 'Look now! You have been made well. Sin no
> more in case something worse happens to you!' The
> man went away and told the Jews that it was Jesus who
> had made him well. Because of this the Jews were
> out to persecute Jesus, because he had done these
> things on the Sabbath. But Jesus answered them: 'My
> Father continues his work until now, and so do I
> continue mine.' Because of this the Jews tried all the
> harder to find a way to kill him, because not only was
> he habitually breaking the Sabbath, but he also kept on
> saying that God was his own Father, thereby making
> himself equal with God.

A MAN had been healed from a disease which, humanly speaking, was incurable. We might expect this to be an occasion of
universal joy and thanksgiving; but some met the whole
business with bleak and black looks. The man who had been
healed was walking through the streets carrying his bed; the
orthodox Jews stopped him and reminded him that he was
breaking the law by carrying a burden on the Sabbath day.

We have already seen what the Jews did with the law of
God. It was a series of great wide principles which men and

women were left to apply and carry out, but throughout the years the Jews had made it into thousands of little rules and regulations. The law simply said that the Sabbath day must be different from other days and that on it neither a man nor his servants nor his animals must work; the Jews set out thirty-nine different classifications of work, one of which was that it consisted in carrying a burden.

They were founded particularly on two passages. Jeremiah had said: 'Thus says the Lord: For the sake of your lives, take care that you do not bear a burden on the sabbath day or bring it in by the gates of Jerusalem. And do not carry a burden out of your houses on the sabbath or do any work, but keep the sabbath day holy, as I commanded your ancestors' (Jeremiah 17:21–2). Nehemiah had been worried at the work and the trading that took place on the Sabbath day and had stationed servants at the gates of Jerusalem to see that no burdens were carried in or out on the Sabbath (Nehemiah 13:15–19).

Nehemiah 13:15 makes it perfectly clear that what was in question was trading on the Sabbath as if it had been an ordinary day. But the Rabbis of Jesus' day solemnly argued that a man was sinning if he carried a needle in his robe on the Sabbath. They even argued as to whether he could wear his false teeth or his artificial leg. They were quite clear that any kind of brooch could not be worn on the Sabbath. To them, all this petty detail was a matter of life and death – and certainly this man was breaking the Rabbinic law by carrying his bed on the Sabbath day.

His defence was that the man who had healed him had told him to do it, but he did not know his identity. Later Jesus met him in the Temple; at once the man hastened to tell the authorities that Jesus was the one in question. He was not seeking to get Jesus into trouble, but the actual words of the law were: 'If anyone carries anything from a public place to a private house on the Sabbath intentionally he is punishable by death by stoning.' He was simply trying to explain that it was not his fault that he had broken the law.

So the authorities levelled their accusations against Jesus. The verbs in verse 18 are *imperfect tense*, which describes repeated action in past time. Clearly this story is only a sample of what Jesus habitually did.

His defence was shattering. God did not stop working on the Sabbath day and neither did he. Any scholarly Jew would grasp its full force. Philo had said: 'God never ceases doing, but as it is the property of fire to burn and snow to chill, so it is the property of God to do.' Another writer said: 'The sun shines; the rivers flow; the processes of birth and death go on on the Sabbath as on any other day; and that is the work of God.' True, according to the creation story, God rested on the seventh day; but he rested from *creation*; his higher works of judgment and mercy and compassion and love still went on.

Jesus said: 'Even on the Sabbath God's love and mercy and compassion act; *and so do mine.*' It was this last passage which shattered the Jews, for it meant nothing less than that the work of Jesus and the work of God were the same. It seemed that Jesus was putting himself on an equality with God. What Jesus was really saying, we shall see in our next section; but at the moment we must note this – Jesus teaches that human need must always be helped; that there is no greater task than to relieve someone's pain and distress, and that the Christian's compassion must be like God's – unceasing. Other work may be laid aside, but the work of compassion never.

Another Jewish belief enters into this passage. When Jesus met the man in the Temple, he told him to sin no more in case something worse might happen to him. To the Jews, sin and suffering were inextricably connected. If people suffered, necessarily they had sinned; nor could they ever be cured until their sins were forgiven. The Rabbis said: 'The sick arises not from sickness, until his sins be forgiven.' The man might argue that he had sinned and been forgiven and had, so to speak, got away with it; and he might go on to argue that, since he had found someone who could release him from the consequences of sin, he could very well go on sinning and escaping. There were those in the Church who used their liberty as an excuse for self-indulgence (Galatians 5:13). There were those who sinned in the confidence that grace would abound (Romans 6:1–18). There have always been those who have used the love and the forgiveness and the grace of God as an excuse to sin. But we have only to think what God's forgiveness cost, we have only to look at the cross of Calvary, to know that we must always hate sin because every sin breaks again the heart of God.

THE TREMENDOUS CLAIMS

John 5:19–29

'This is the truth I tell you – the Son cannot do anything which proceeds from himself. He can only do what he sees the Father doing. In whatever way the Father acts, the Son likewise acts in the same way; for the Father loves the Son and has shown him everything that he does. And he will show him greater works than these, so that you will be moved to wondering amazement. For, as the Father raises the dead and makes them alive, so also the Son makes alive those whom he wishes. Neither does the Father judge anyone, but he has given the whole process of judging to the Son, that all may honour the Son, as they honour the Father. He who does not honour the Son does not honour the Father who sent him.

This is the truth I tell you – he who listens to my word and believes on him who sent me has eternal life, and is not on the way to judgment, but he has crossed from death to life.

This is the truth I tell you – the hour is coming and now is when the dead will hear the voice of the Son of God, and, when they have heard, they will live. For, as the Father has life in himself, so he has given to the Son to have life in himself. And he has given him authority to exercise the process of judgment, because he is the Son of Man. Do not be astonished at this, for the hour is coming when everyone in the tombs will hear his voice and will come forth; those who have done good will come out to a resurrection which will give them life, but those whose actions were base will come out to a resurrection which will issue in judgment.'

HERE we come to the first of the long discourses of the Fourth Gospel. When we read passages like this, we must remember that John is not seeking so much to give us the words that Jesus spoke as the things which Jesus meant. He was writing somewhere round about AD 100. For seventy years, he had thought about Jesus and the wonderful things which Jesus had said. Many of these things he had not fully understood when he had heard them. But more than half a century of thinking under the guidance of the Holy Spirit had shown him deeper and deeper meaning in the words of Jesus. And so he sets down for us not only what Jesus said, but also what Jesus meant.

This passage is so important that we must first study it as a whole and then take it in shorter sections.

First, then, let us look at it as a whole. We must try to think not only how it sounds to us, but also how it sounded to the Jews who heard it for the first time. They had a background of thoughts and ideas, of theology and belief, of literature and religion which is very far from our background; and, to understand a passage like this, we must try to think ourselves into the mind of a Jew who listened to it for the first time.

This is an amazing passage, because it is woven together of thoughts and expressions which are all claims by Jesus to be the promised Messiah. Many of these claims we do not now readily see, but they would be crystal clear to the Jews and would leave them aghast.

(1) The clearest claim is the statement that Jesus is the Son of Man. We know how common that strange title is in the gospels. It has a long history. It was born in Daniel 7:1–14. The Authorized Version mistranslates *the Son of Man* for *a* son of man (Daniel 7:13).

The point of the passage is this. Daniel was written in days of terror and of persecution, and it is a vision of the glory which will some day replace the suffering which the people are undergoing. In Daniel 7:1–7, the seer describes the great pagan empires which have held sway under the symbolism of animals. There is the lion with eagle's wings (7:4), which stands for the Babylonian Empire; the bear with the three ribs in his mouth, as one devouring the carcass (7:5), which stands for the Median Empire; the leopard with four wings and four heads (7:6), which stands for the Persian Empire; and the beast, great and terrible, with iron teeth and with ten horns (7:7), which stands for the Macedonian Empire. All these terrible powers will pass away, and the power and the dominion will be given to one *like a son of man*. The meaning is that the Empires which have held sway have been so savage that they could be described only in terms of wild animals; but into the world there is going to come a power so gentle and kind that it will be human and not bestial. In Daniel, the phrase describes the kind of power which is going to rule the world.

Someone has to introduce and exercise that power; and the Jews took this title and gave it to the chosen one of God who some day would bring in the new age of gentleness and love and peace; and so they came to call the Messiah *Son of Man*. Between the Old and the New Testaments, there arose a whole literature which dealt with the golden age which was to come.

One book which was specially influential was the *Book of Enoch*, and in it there appears again and again a great figure called *That Son of Man*, who is waiting in heaven until God sends him to earth to bring in his kingdom and rule over it. So when Jesus called himself the Son of Man, he was doing nothing less than call himself the Messiah. Here was a claim so clear that it could not be misunderstood.

(2) But not only is this claim to be God's Messiah made in so many words; in phrase after phrase it is implicit. The very miracle which had happened to the paralysed man was a sign that Jesus was the Messiah. It was Isaiah's picture of the new age of God that 'then the lame shall leap like a deer' (Isaiah 35:6). It was Jeremiah's vision that the blind and the lame would be gathered in (Jeremiah 31:8–9).

(3) There is Jesus' repeated claim to raise the dead and to be their judge when they are raised. In the Old Testament, God alone can raise the dead and alone has the right to judge. 'I, even I, am he; there is no god besides me. I kill and I make alive' (Deuteronomy 32:39). 'The Lord kills and brings to life' (1 Samuel 2:6). When Naaman, the Syrian, came seeking to be cured from leprosy, the king of Israel said in bewildered despair: 'Am I God, to give death or life?' (2 Kings 5:7). The function of killing and making alive belonged inalienably to God. It is the same with judgment. 'The judgement is God's' (Deuteronomy 1:17).

In later thought, this function of resurrecting the dead and then acting as judge became part of the duty of God's chosen one when he brought in the new age of God. First Enoch says of the Son of Man: 'The sum of judgment was committed to him' (1 Enoch 69:27). Jesus in our passage speaks of those who have done good being resurrected to life and of those who have done evil being resurrected to death. The Apocalypse of Baruch lays it down that when God's age comes, 'The aspect of those who now act wickedly shall become worse than it is, as they shall suffer torment,' whereas those who have trusted in the law and acted upon it shall be clothed in beauty and in splendour (2 Baruch 51:1–4). First Enoch has it that in that day: 'The earth shall be wholly rent asunder, and all that is on earth shall perish, and there shall be judgment on all men' (1 Enoch 1:7–8). The Testament of Benjamin has it: 'All men shall rise, some to be exalted, and some to be humbled and put to shame' (10:7–8).

For Jesus to speak like this was an act of the most extraordinary and unique courage. He must have known well that to make claims like this would sound the sheerest blasphemy to the orthodox Jewish leaders and was to court death. Those who listened to words like this had only two alternatives – they must either accept Jesus as the Son of God or hate him as a blasphemer.

We now go on to take this passage section by section.

THE FATHER AND THE SON

John 5:19–20

'This is the truth I tell you – the Son cannot do anything which proceeds from himself. He can only do what he

sees the Father doing. In whatever way the Father
acts, the Son likewise acts in the same way; for the
Father loves the Son and has shown him everything
that he does. And he will show him greater works
than these, so that you will be moved to wondering
amazement.'

THIS is the beginning of Jesus' answer to the Jews' charge
that he was making himself equal to God. He lays down three
things about his relationship with God.

(1) He lays down his *identity* with God. The salient truth
about Jesus is that in him we see God. If we wish to see how
God feels to human beings, if we wish to see how God reacts
to sin, if we wish to see how God regards the human situation,
we must look at Jesus. The mind of Jesus is the mind of God;
the words of Jesus are the words of God; the actions of Jesus
are the actions of God.

(2) This identity is based not so much on equality as on
complete *obedience*. Jesus never did what he wanted to do
but always what God wanted him to do. It is because his will
was completely submitted to God's will that we see God in
him. Jesus is to God as we must be to Jesus.

(3) This obedience is not based on submission to power;
it is based on *love*. The unity between Jesus and God is a
unity of love. We speak of two minds having only a single
thought and two hearts beating as one. In human terms, that
is a perfect description of the relationship between Jesus and
God. There is such complete identity of mind and will and
heart that Father and Son are one.

But this passage has something still more to tell us about
Jesus.

(1) It tells us of his complete *confidence*. He is quite sure
that what people were seeing then was only a beginning. On

purely human grounds, the one thing Jesus might reasonably expect was death. The forces of Jewish orthodoxy were gathering against him and the end was already sure. But Jesus was quite certain that the future was in the hands of God and that what God had sent him to do could not be stopped by any human means.

(2) It tells of his complete *fearlessness*. That he would be misunderstood was certain. That his words would inflame the minds of his hearers and endanger his own life was beyond argument. There was no human situation in which Jesus would lower his claims or adulterate the truth. He would make his claim and speak his truth no matter what people might threaten to do. To him, it was much more important to be true to God than to fear human actions.

LIFE, JUDGMENT AND HONOUR

John 5:21–3

> 'For, as the Father raises the dead and makes them alive, so also the Son makes alive those whom he wishes. Neither does the Father judge anyone, but he has given the whole process of judging to the Son, that all may honour the Son, as they honour the Father. He who does not honour the Son does not honour the Father who sent him.'

HERE we see three great functions which belong to Jesus Christ as the Son of God.

(1) He is *the giver of life*. John meant this in a double sense. He meant it *in time*. We are not fully alive until Jesus Christ enters into us and we enter into Jesus Christ. When we make the discovery of the realm of music or of literature or

of art or of travel, we sometimes speak of a new world opening out to us. People into whose lives Jesus Christ has entered find life made new. They are changed people; their personal relationships are changed; their conception of work and duty and pleasure is changed; their relationship to God is changed. He meant it in *eternity*. After this life is ended, for those who have accepted Jesus Christ there opens life still more full and still more wonderful; while for those who have refused Jesus Christ, there comes that death which is separation from God. Jesus Christ gives life both in this world and in the world to come.

(2) He is *the bringer of judgment*. John says that God committed the whole process of judgment to Jesus Christ. What he means is this – our judgment depends on our reaction to Jesus. If we find in Jesus the one person to be loved and followed, we are on the way to life. If we see in Jesus an enemy, we have condemned ourselves. Jesus is the touchstone by which all are tested; reaction to him is the test by which all are divided.

(3) He is *the receiver of honour*. The most uplifting thing about the New Testament is its unquenchable hope and its unconquerable certainty. It tells the story of a crucified Christ and yet never has any doubt that at the end all people will be drawn to that crucified figure and that all people will know him and acknowledge him and love him. Amid persecution and disregard, in spite of smallness of numbers and poverty of influence, in the face of failure and disloyalty, the New Testament and the early Church never doubted the ultimate triumph of Christ. When we are tempted to despair, we would do well to remember that human salvation is the purpose of God and that nothing, in the end, can frustrate his will. The evil will of men and women may delay God's purpose; it cannot defeat it.

ACCEPTANCE MEANS LIFE

John 5:24

> 'This is the truth I tell you – he who listens to my word
> and believes on him who sent me has eternal life, and is
> not on the way to judgment, but he has crossed from
> death to life.'

JESUS says quite simply that to accept him is life; and to reject
him is death. What does it mean to listen to Jesus' word and
to believe in the Father who sent him? To put it at its briefest,
it means three things. (1) It means to believe that God is as
Jesus says he is; that he is love; and so to enter into a new
relationship with him in which fear is banished. (2) It means
to accept the way of life that Jesus offers us, however difficult
it may be and whatever sacrifices it may involve, certain that
to accept it is the ultimate way to peace and to happiness, and
to refuse it the ultimate way to death and judgment. (3) It
means to accept the help that the risen Christ gives and the
guidance that the Holy Spirit offers, and so to find strength
for all that the way of Christ involves.

When we do that, we enter into three new relationships.
(1) We enter into a new relationship with God. The judge
becomes the father, the distant becomes the near, strangeness
becomes intimacy and fear becomes love. (2) We enter into a
new relationship with our neighbours. Hatred becomes love,
selfishness becomes service and bitterness becomes forgiveness. (3) We enter into a new relationship with ourselves.
Weakness becomes strength, frustration becomes achievement and tension becomes peace.

To accept the offer of Jesus Christ is to find life. Everyone
in one sense may be said to be alive; but there are few who
can be said to know life in the real sense of the term. When

Sir Wilfred Grenfell was writing to a nursing sister about her decision to come out to Labrador to help in his work there, he told her that he could not offer her much money, but that if she came she would discover that in serving Christ and the people of the country she would have the time of her life. Robert Browning describes the meeting of two people into whose hearts love had entered. She looked at him, he looked at her, and 'suddenly life awoke'. A novelist makes one character say to another: 'I never knew what life was till I saw it in your eyes.'

The person who accepts the way of Christ has passed from death to life. In this world, life becomes new and thrilling; in the world to come, eternal life with God becomes a certainty.

DEATH AND LIFE

John 5:25-9

> 'This is the truth I tell you – the hour is coming and now is when the dead will hear the voice of the Son of God, and, when they have heard, they will live. For, as the Father has life in himself, so he has given to the Son to have life in himself. And he has given him authority to exercise the process of judgment, because he is the Son of Man. Do not be astonished at this, for the hour is coming when everyone in the tombs will hear his voice and will come forth; those who have done good will come out to a resurrection which will give them life, but those whose actions were base will come out to a resurrection which will issue in judgment.'

HERE, the messianic claims of Jesus stand out most clearly. He is the Son of Man; he is the life-giver and the life-bringer;

he will raise the dead to life and, when they are raised, he will be their judge.

In this passage, John seems to use the word *dead* in two senses.

(1) He uses it of those who are spiritually dead; to them, Jesus will bring new life. What does it mean?

(a) To be spiritually dead is *to have stopped trying.* It is to have come to look on all faults as ineradicable and all virtues as unattainable. But the Christian life cannot stand still; it must either go on or slip back; and to stop trying is therefore to slip back to death.

(b) To be spiritually dead is *to have stopped feeling.* There are many people who at one time felt intensely in face of the sin and the sorrow and the suffering of the world; but slowly they have become insensitive. They can look at evil and feel no indignation; they can look at sorrow and suffering and feel no answering sword of grief and pity pierce their heart. When compassion goes, the heart is dead.

(c) To be spiritually dead is *to have stopped thinking.* J. Alexander Findlay, Principal of Didsbury Methodist College, Manchester, told of a saying of a friend of his – 'When you reach a conclusion you're dead.' He meant that when someone's mind becomes so shut that it can accept no new truth, that person is mentally and spiritually dead. The day when the desire to learn leaves us, the day when new truth, new methods, new thought become simply a disturbance with which we cannot be bothered, is the day of our spiritual death.

(d) To be spiritually dead is *to have stopped repenting.* The day when someone is able to sin in peace is the day of that person's spiritual death; and it is easy to slip into that frame of mind. The first time we do a wrong thing, we do it with fear and regret. If we do it a second time, it is easier to do it. If we do it a third time, it is easier still. If we go on doing it, the time comes when we scarcely give it a thought. To avoid spiritual death, we must keep ourselves sensitive to sin by keeping ourselves sensitive to the presence of Jesus Christ.

(2) John also uses the word *dead* literally. Jesus teaches that the resurrection will come and that what happens to someone in the afterlife is inextricably bound up with what that person has done in this life. The awful importance of this life is that it determines eternity. All through it, we are fitting or unfitting ourselves for the life to come, making ourselves fit or unfit for the presence of God. We choose either the way which leads to life or the way which leads to death.

THE ONLY TRUE JUDGMENT

John 5:30

> 'I cannot do anything which originates in myself. As I hear, so I judge. But the judgment which I exercise is just, because I do not seek to do what I wish to do, but I seek to do what he who sent me wishes to do.'

In the preceding passage, Jesus has claimed the right of judgment. It was not unnatural that people should ask by what right he proposed to judge others. His answer was that his judgment was true and final because he had no desire to do anything other than the will of God. His claim was that his judgment was the judgment of God.

It is very difficult for anyone to judge another person fairly. If we examine ourselves honestly, we will see that many motives may affect our judgment. It may be rendered unfair by *injured pride*. It may be rendered blind by our *prejudices*. It may be made bitter by *jealousy*. It may be made arrogant by *contempt*. It may be made harsh by *intolerance*. It may be made condemnatory by *self-righteousness*. It may be affected by our own *self-conceit*. It may be based on *envy*. It may be impaired by an insensitive or deliberate *ignorance*. Only someone whose heart is pure and whose motives are completely unmixed can rightly judge another person – which means to say that no one can.

On the other hand, the judgment of God is perfect.

God alone is *holy*, and therefore he alone knows the standards by which everyone must be judged. God alone is perfectly *loving*, and his judgment alone is delivered in the charity in which all true judgment must be given. God alone has full *knowledge*, and judgment can be perfect only when it takes into account *all* the circumstances. The claim of Jesus to judge is based on the claim that in him is the perfect mind of God. He does not judge with the inevitable mixture of human motives; he judges with the perfect holiness, the perfect love and the perfect sympathy of God.

WITNESS TO CHRIST

John 5:31–6

'If I bear witness about myself, my witness need not be accepted as true; but it is Another who is bearing witness about me, and I know that the witness which he bears about me is true. You sent your envoys to John, and he bore witness to the truth; but the testimony which I receive is not from any man, but I say these things that you may be saved. He was the lamp which burns and shines. For a time you were pleased to take pleasure in his light. But I have a greater testimony than John's. The works which the Father granted to me to

accomplish, the very works which I do, are evidence
about me to prove that my Father has sent me.'

ONCE again, Jesus is answering the charges of his opponents.
His opponents are demanding: 'What evidence can you
produce that your claims are true?' Jesus argues in a way that
the Rabbis would understand, for he uses their own methods.

(1) He begins by admitting the universal principle that
the unsupported evidence of one person cannot be taken as
proof. There must be at least two witnesses. 'On the evidence
of two or three witnesses the death sentence shall be executed;
a person must not be put to death on the evidence of only one
witness' (Deuteronomy 17:6). 'A single witness shall not
suffice to convict a person of any crime or wrongdoing in
connection with any offence that may be committed. Only
on the evidence of two or three witnesses shall a charge be
sustained' (Deuteronomy 19:15). When Paul threatens to
come to the Corinthians with rebuke and discipline, he says
that all his charges will be confirmed by two or three witnesses
(2 Corinthians 13:1). Jesus says that when a Christian has a
legitimate complaint against a member of the church, that
person must take along some others to confirm the charge
(Matthew 18:16). In the early Church, it was the rule that
no charge against an elder was entertained unless it was
supported by two or three witnesses (1 Timothy 5:19). Jesus
began by fully admitting the normal Jewish law of evidence.

Further, it was universally held that a man's evidence about
himself could not be accepted. The Mishnah said: 'A man is
not worthy of belief when he is speaking about himself.'
Demosthenes, the great Greek orator, laid it down as a
principle of justice: 'The laws do not allow a man to give
evidence on his own behalf.' Ancient law knew well that
self-interest had an effect on people's statements about

themselves. So Jesus agrees that his own unsupported testimony to himself need not be true.

(2) But there are other witnesses to him. He says that 'Another' is his witness, meaning God. He will return to that, but for the moment he cites John the Baptist who had repeatedly borne witness to him (John 1:19–20, 26, 29, 35–6). Then Jesus pays a tribute to John and issues a rebuke to the Jewish authorities.

He says that John was the lamp which burns and shines. That was the perfect tribute to him. (a) A lamp bears a borrowed light. It does not light itself; it is lit. (b) John had warmth, for his was not the cold message of the intellect but the burning message of the heart set on fire. (c) John had light. The function of light is to guide, and John pointed men and women on the way to repentance and to God. (d) In the nature of things a lamp burns itself out; in giving light it consumes itself. John was to decrease while Jesus increased. True witnesses burn themselves out for God.

In paying tribute to John, Jesus rebukes the Jews. They were pleased to take pleasure in John for a time, but they never really took him seriously. They were, as one has put it, like 'gnats dancing in the sunlight', or like children playing while the sun shone. John was a pleasant diversion, to be listened to as long as he said the things they liked, and to be abandoned whenever he became awkward. Many people listen to God's truth like that; they enjoy a sermon as a performance. A famous preacher tells how, after he had preached a sombre sermon on judgment, he was greeted with the comment: 'That sermon was sure cute!' God's truth is not a thing by which to be pleasantly titillated; it is often something to be received in the dust and ashes of humiliation and repentance.

But Jesus does not even plead John's evidence. He says it is not the human evidence of any fallible person he is going to produce to support his claims.

(3) So he produces the witness of his works. He had done that when John sent from prison to ask if he was the Messiah. He had told John's inquiring envoys to go back and tell him what they saw happening (Matthew 11:4; Luke 7:22). But Jesus cites his works, not to point to himself but to point to the power of God working in him and through him. His supreme witness is God.

THE WITNESS OF GOD

John 5:37–43

'And the Father who sent me has borne witness about me. You have never heard his voice, nor have you ever seen his form. You do not have his word dwelling in you, because you do not believe in the One whom he sent. You search the Scriptures, because you think that in them you have eternal life. It is they which bear witness about me, yet you refuse to come to me that you may have life. I receive no glory from men; but I know you and I know that you do not have the love of God in you. I came in the name of my Father and yet you do not receive me. If another comes in his own name, you will receive him.'

THE early part of this section may be taken in two ways.

(1) It may be that it refers to the unseen witness of God in the heart of every individual. In his First Letter, John writes: 'Those who believe in the Son of God have the testimony [of God] in their hearts' (1 John 5:10). A Jew would have insisted that no one can ever see God. Even in the giving of the Ten

Commandments, 'You heard the sound of words but saw no form; there was only a voice' (Deuteronomy 4:12). So this may mean: 'It is true that God is invisible; and so is his witness, for it is the response which rises in the human heart when anyone is confronted with me.' When we are confronted with Christ, we see in him the altogether lovely and the altogether wise; that conviction is the witness of God in our hearts. The Stoics held that the highest kind of knowledge comes not by thought but by what they called 'arresting impressions' – being seized by a conviction like someone laying an arresting hand on the shoulder. It may be that Jesus here means that the conviction in our hearts of his supremacy is the witness of God within.

(2) It may be that John is really meaning that God's witness to Christ is to be found in the Scriptures. To Jews, the Scriptures were all in all. 'He who has acquired the words of the law has acquired eternal life.' 'He who has the law has a cord of grace drawn around him in this world and in the world to come.' 'He who says that Moses wrote even one verse of the law in his own knowledge is a despiser of God.' 'She is the book of the commandments of God, the law that endures forever. All who hold her fast will live and those who forsake her shall die' (Baruch 4:1–2). 'If food, which is your life but for an hour, requires a blessing before and after it be eaten, how much more does the law, in which lies the world that is to be, require a blessing?' The Jews searched the law and yet failed to recognize Christ when he came. What was wrong? The best Bible students in the world, people who meticulously and continuously read Scripture, rejected Jesus. How could that happen?

One thing is clear – they read Scripture in the wrong way.

(1) They read it with a shut mind. They read it not to search for God but to find arguments to support their own positions.

They did not really love God; they loved their own ideas about him. Water has as much chance of getting into concrete as the word of God had of getting into their minds. They did not humbly learn a theology from Scripture; they used Scripture to defend a theology which they themselves had produced. There is still danger that we should use the Bible to prove our beliefs and not to test them.

(2) They made a still bigger mistake – they regarded God as having given a written revelation. The revelation of God is a revelation in history. It is not God speaking, but God acting. The Bible itself is not his revelation; it is *the record of* his revelation. But they worshipped the Bible's words.

There is only one proper way to read the Bible – to read it as all pointing to Jesus Christ. Then many of the things which puzzle us, and sometimes distress us, are clearly seen as stages on the way, a pointing forward to Jesus Christ, who *is* the supreme revelation and by whose light all other revelation is to be tested. The Jews worshipped a God who wrote rather than a God who acted, and therefore when Christ came they did not recognize him. The function of the Scriptures is not to give life but to point to him who can.

There are two most revealing things here.

(1) In verse 34, Jesus had said the purpose of his words was 'that you may be saved'. Here he says: 'I am not looking for any glory from human beings.' That is to say: 'I am not arguing like this because I want to win an argument. I am not talking like this because I want to score off you and win the applause of others. It is because I love you and want to save you.'

There is something tremendous here. When people oppose us and we argue back, what is our main feeling? Wounded pride? The conceit that hates any kind of failure? Annoyance? A desire to cram our opinions down other people's throats because we think them fools? Jesus talked as he did only because he loved men and women. His voice might be stern, but in the sternness there was still the accent of yearning love; his eyes might flash fire, but the flame was the flame of love.

(2) Jesus says: 'If another comes in his own name, him you will receive.' The Jews had their succession of impostors claiming to be the Messiah, and every one had his following (cf. Mark 13:6, 22; Matthew 24:5, 24). Why do people follow impostors? Because they make claims that correspond with people's own desires. The impostors came promising empires and victory and material prosperity; Jesus came offering a cross. The characteristic of the impostor is the offer of the easy way; Jesus offered men and women the hard way of God. The impostors perished and Christ lives on.

THE ULTIMATE CONDEMNATION

John 5:44–7

> 'How can you believe when you are out for the glory that you get from each other, and when you do not search for the glory which comes from the only God? Do not think that it is I who will accuse you to the Father. You have an accuser – it is Moses I mean – on whom you set your hopes. If you had believed in Moses, you would have believed in me, for he wrote about me. If you do not believe in his writings, how will you believe in my words?'

THE scribes and Pharisees desired the praise of the people. They dressed in such a way that everyone would recognize them. They prayed in such a way that everyone would see. They loved the front seats in the synagogue. They loved the deferential greetings of men on the street. And just because of that, they could not hear the voice of God. Why? As long as people measure themselves against one another, they will be well content. But the point is not: 'Am I as good as my neighbour?' The point is: 'Am I as good as God?' 'What do I look like to him?' As long as we judge ourselves by human comparisons, there is plenty of room for self-satisfaction; and that kills faith, for faith is born of the sense of need. But when we compare ourselves with Jesus Christ, we are humbled to the dust, and then faith is born, for there is nothing left to do but trust to the mercy of God.

Jesus finishes with a charge that would strike home. The Jews believed the books which they believed Moses had given them to be the very word of God. Jesus said: 'If you had read these books aright, you would have seen that they all pointed to me.' He went on: 'You think that because you have Moses to be your mediator you are safe; but Moses is the very one who will condemn you. Maybe you could not be expected to listen to me, but you are bound to listen to the words of Moses to which you attach such value – and they all spoke of me.'

Here is the great and threatening truth. What had been the greatest privilege of the Jews had become their greatest condemnation. No one could condemn anyone who had never had a chance. But knowledge had been given to the Jews; and the knowledge they had failed to use had become their condemnation. Responsibility is always the other side of privilege.

THE LOAVES AND FISHES

John 6:1–13

After these things Jesus went away across the Sea of Galilee, that is, the Sea of Tiberias. A great crowd was

following him, because they were watching the signs
which he did on those who were ill. Jesus went up into
the hill and he was sitting there with his disciples. The
Passover, the Feast of the Jews, was near. When Jesus
lifted up his eyes and saw that a great crowd was coming
to him, he said to Philip: 'Where are we to buy bread
for these to eat?' He was testing Philip when he said
this, for he himself knew what he was going to do. Philip
answered him: 'Even 200 denarii worth of bread is not
enough to give each of them a little to eat.' One of the
disciples said to him – it was Andrew, Simon Peter's
brother – 'There is a lad here who has five barley loaves
and two little fishes. But what use are they among so
many?' Jesus said: 'Make the men sit down.' There was
much grass in the place. So the men sat down to the
number of about 5,000. So Jesus took the loaves and
gave thanks for them, and divided them up among
those who were reclining there. So too he gave them
of the fishes, as much as they wished. When they were
satisfied, he said to the disciples: 'Collect the broken
pieces that are left over, so that nothing may be wasted.'
So they collected them, and they filled twelve baskets
with the broken pieces of the loaves which remained
over after the people had eaten.

THERE were times when Jesus desired to withdraw from the
crowds. He was under continuous strain and needed rest.
Moreover, it was necessary that sometimes he should get his
disciples alone to lead them into a deeper understanding of
himself. In addition, he needed time for prayer. On this
particular occasion, it was wise to go away before a head-on
collision with the authorities took place, for the time of the
final conflict had not yet come.

From Capernaum to the other side of the Sea of Galilee
was a distance of about four miles, and Jesus set sail. The

people had been watching with astonishment the things he did; it was easy to see the direction the boat was taking; and they hastened round the top of the lake by land. The River Jordan flows into the north end of the Sea of Galilee. Two miles up the river were the fords of Jordan. Near the fords was a village called Bethsaida Julias, to distinguish it from the other Bethsaida in Galilee, and it was for that place that Jesus was making (Luke 9:10). Near Bethsaida Julias, almost on the lakeside, was a little plain where the grass always grew. It was to be the scene of a wondrous happening.

At first, Jesus went up into the hill behind the plain and he was sitting there with his disciples. Then the crowd began to appear in droves. It was nine miles round the top of the lake and across the ford, and they had made the journey with all speed. We are told that the Feast of the Passover was near and there would be even bigger crowds on the roads at that time. Possibly many were on the way to Jerusalem by that route. Many Galilaean pilgrims travelled north and crossed the ford and went through Peraea, and then recrossed the Jordan near Jericho. The way was longer, but it avoided the territory of the hated and dangerous Samaritans. It is likely that the great crowd was swelled by detachments of pilgrims on their way to the Passover Feast.

At the sight of the crowd, Jesus' sympathy was kindled. They were hungry and tired, and they must be fed. Philip was the natural man to whom to turn, for he came from Bethsaida (John 1:44) and would have local knowledge. Jesus asked him where food could be got. Philip's answer was despairing. He said that even if food could be got it would cost more than 200 denarii to give this vast crowd even a little each. A denarius was the standard day's wage for a working man. Philip calculated that it would take more than six months' wages to begin to feed a crowd like this.

Then Andrew appeared on the scene. He had discovered a young boy with five barley loaves and two little fishes. Quite likely the boy had brought them as a picnic lunch. Maybe he was out for the day, and as a boy might, had attached himself to the crowd. Andrew, as usual, was bringing people to Jesus.

The boy had not much to bring. Barley bread was the cheapest of all bread and was held in contempt. There is a regulation in the Mishnah about the offering that a woman who has committed adultery must bring. She must, of course, bring a trespass offering. With all offerings a food offering was made, and the food offering consisted of flour and wine and oil intermixed. Ordinarily the flour used was made of wheat; but it was laid down that, in the case of an offering for adultery, the flour could be barley flour, for barley is the food of animals, and the woman's sin was the sin of an animal. Barley bread was the bread of the very poor.

The fishes would be no bigger than sardines. Pickled fish from Galilee were known all over the Roman Empire. In those days, fresh fish was an unheard-of luxury, for there was no means of transporting it any distance and keeping it in an eatable condition. Small sardine-like fish swarmed in the Sea of Galilee. They were caught and pickled and made into a kind of savoury. The boy had his little pickled fish to help the dry barley bread down.

Jesus told the disciples to make the people sit down. He took the loaves and the fishes and he blessed them. When he did that, he was acting as father of the family. The grace he used would be the one that was used in every home: 'Blessed art Thou, O Lord, our God, who causest to come forth bread from the earth.' The people ate and were filled. Even the word that is used for *filled* (*chortazesthai*) is suggestive. Originally, in classical Greek, it was a word used for feeding animals

with fodder. When used of people, it meant that they were
fed to repletion.

When the people had eaten their fill, Jesus bade his
disciples gather up the fragments left. Why the fragments?
At Jewish feasts, the regular practice was to leave something
for the servants. That which was left was called the *Peah*;
and no doubt the people left their usual part for those who
had served them with the meal.

Of the fragments, twelve baskets were taken up. No doubt
each of the disciples had his basket (*kophinos*). It was bottle-
shaped, and no Jew ever travelled without one. Twice the
Roman satirist Juvenal (3:14, 6:542) talks of 'the Jew with
his basket and his truss of hay'. (The truss of hay was to use
as a bed, for many of the Jews lived a nomadic life.) The Jew
with his basket was a well-recognized figure. He carried it
because he needed to carry his own food if he was going to
observe the Jewish rules of cleanness and uncleanness. From
the fragments, each of the disciples filled his basket. And so
the hungry crowd were fed and more than fed.

THE MEANING OF A MIRACLE

John 6:1–13 (*contd*)

WE will never know exactly what happened on that grassy
plain near Bethsaida Julias. We may look at it in three ways.

(a) We may regard it simply as a miracle in which Jesus
multiplied loaves and fishes. Some may find that hard to
conceive of; and some may find it hard to reconcile with the
fact that that is just what Jesus refused to do at his temptations
(Matthew 4:3–4). If we can believe in the sheer miraculous
character of this miracle, then let us continue to do so. But if
we are puzzled, there are two other explanations.

(b) It may be that this was really a sacramental meal. In the rest of the chapter, the language of Jesus is exactly that of the Last Supper, when he speaks about eating his flesh and drinking his blood. It could be that at this meal it was but a morsel, like the sacrament, that each person received; and that the thrill and wonder of the presence of Jesus and the reality of God turned the sacramental crumb into something which richly nourished their hearts and souls – as happens at every communion service to this day.

(c) There may be another and very lovely explanation. It is scarcely to be thought that the crowd left on a nine-mile expedition without making any preparations at all. If there were pilgrims with them, they would certainly possess supplies for the way. But it may be that they would not produce what they had, for they selfishly – and very humanly – wished to keep it all for themselves. It may then be that Jesus, with that rare smile of his, produced the little store that he and his disciples had; with sunny faith he thanked God for it and shared it out. Moved by his example, everyone who had anything did the same; and in the end there was enough, and more than enough, for all.

It may be that this is a miracle in which the presence of Jesus turned a crowd of selfish men and women into a fellowship of sharers. It may be that this story represents the biggest miracle of all – one which changed not loaves and fishes, but men and women.

However that may be, there were certain people there without whom the miracle would not have been possible.

(1) There was Andrew. There is a contrast between Andrew and Philip. Philip was the man who said: 'The situation is hopeless; nothing can be done.' Andrew was the man who said: 'I'll see what I can do; and I'll trust Jesus to do the rest.'

It was Andrew who brought that young boy to Jesus, and by bringing him made the miracle possible. No one ever knows what will come out of it when we bring someone to Jesus. If parents train up their children in the knowledge and the love and the fear of God, no one can say what mighty things those children may some day do for God and for others. If a Sunday School teacher brings a child to Christ, no one knows what that child may some day do for Christ and his Church.

There is a tale of an old German schoolmaster who, when he entered his class of boys in the morning, used to remove his cap and bow ceremoniously to them. One asked him why he did this. His answer was: 'You never know what one of these boys may some day become.' He was right – one of them was the founder of the Reformation, Martin Luther.

Andrew did not know what he was doing when he brought that boy to Jesus that day, but he was providing material for a miracle. We never know what possibilities we are releasing when we bring someone to Jesus.

(2) There was the boy. He had not much to offer, but in what he had Jesus found the materials of a miracle. There would have been one great deed fewer in history if that boy had withheld his loaves and fishes.

Jesus needs what we can bring him. It may not be much, but he needs it. It may well be that the world is denied miracle after miracle and triumph after triumph because we will not bring to Jesus what we have and what we are. If we would lay ourselves on the altar of his service, there is no saying what he could do with us and through us. We may be sorry and embarrassed that we have not more to bring – and rightly so; but that is no reason for failing to bring what we have. Little is always much in the hands of Christ.

THE RESPONSE OF THE CROWD

John 6:14–15

> So when the men had seen the sign which he had done,
> they said: 'Truly, this is the prophet who is to come
> into the world.' So Jesus, aware that they were going to
> come and seize him to make him king, withdrew again
> to the mountain alone.

HERE we have the reaction of the crowd. The Jews were waiting for the prophet whom they believed Moses had promised to them. 'The Lord your God will raise up for you a prophet like me from among your own people; you shall heed such a prophet' (Deuteronomy 18:15). In that moment at Bethsaida Julias, they were willing to accept Jesus as that prophet and to carry him to power on a wave of popular acclaim. But it was not so very long before another crowd was clamouring: 'Crucify him! Crucify him!' Why was it at that moment that the crowd acclaimed Jesus?

For one thing, they were eager to support Jesus when he gave them what they wanted. He had healed them and fed them; and they would thereupon have made him their leader. There is such a thing as a bought loyalty. There is such a thing as cupboard love. Dr Johnson, the great eighteenth-century man of letters, in one of his more cynical moments, defined gratitude as 'a lively sense of favours still to come'.

The attitude of that crowd disgusts us. But are we so very different? When we want comfort in sorrow, when we want strength in difficulty, when we want peace in turmoil, when we want help in the face of depression, there is no one so wonderful as Jesus, and we talk to him and walk with him and open our hearts to him. But when he comes to us with some stern demand for sacrifice, with some challenge to effort, with the offer of some cross, we will have nothing to do with him. When we examine our hearts, it may be that we will find that we too love Jesus for what we can get out of him.

For another thing, they wished to use him for their own purposes and to mould him to their own dreams. They were waiting for the Messiah; but they visualized him in their own way. They looked for a Messiah who would be king and conqueror, who would set his foot upon the eagle's neck and drive the Romans from the land. They had seen what Jesus could do; and the thought in their minds was: 'This man has power, marvellous power. If we can harness him and his power to our dreams, things will begin to happen.' If they had been honest, they would have had to admit that they wished to make use of him.

Again, are we so very different? When we appeal to Christ, is it for strength to go on with our own schemes and ideas, or is it for humility and obedience to accept his plans and wishes? Is our prayer: 'Lord, give me strength to do what you want me to do,' or is it in reality: 'Lord, give me strength to do what I want to do'?

That crowd would have followed Jesus at that moment because he was giving them what they wanted and they wished to use him for their own purposes. That attitude still lingers. We would like Christ's gifts without his cross; we would like to use him instead of allowing him to use us.

A VERY PRESENT HELP IN
TIME OF TROUBLE

John 6:16–21

When evening came, his disciples went down to the sea, and, when they had embarked upon a boat, they

> started across the sea to Capernaum. By this time
> darkness had come on, and Jesus had not yet come to
> them; and the sea was roused because a great wind was
> blowing. So, when they had rowed between three and
> four miles, they saw Jesus walking on the sea, and
> coming near the boat, and they were afraid. But he said
> to them: 'It is I; don't be afraid.' So they wished to take
> him on board the boat; and immediately the boat reached
> the land for which they were making.

THIS is one of the most wonderful stories in the Fourth Gospel,
and it is all the more wonderful when we press behind the
meaning of the Greek to find that it really describes not some
extraordinary miracle, but a simple incident in which John
found, in a way he never forgot, what Jesus was like.

Let us reconstruct the story. After the feeding of the 5,000
and the attempt to make him king, Jesus slipped away to the
hills alone. The day wore on. It came to the time which the
Jews described as 'the second evening', the time between the
twilight and the dark. Jesus had still not arrived. We must not
think that the disciples were forgetful or discourteous in
leaving Jesus behind, for, as Mark tells the story, Jesus sent
them on ahead (Mark 6:45), while he persuaded the crowds
to go home. Doubtless it was his intention to walk round the
head of the lake while they rowed across and to rejoin them
in Capernaum.

The disciples set sail. The wind got up, as it can in the
narrow, land-locked lake; and the waters were whipped to
foam. It was Passover time, and that was the time of the full
moon (John 6:4). Up on the hillside, Jesus had prayed and
communed with God; as he set out, the silver moon made the
scene almost like daylight; and down on the lake below he
could see the boat and the rowers toiling at the oars, making
heavy weather of it. So he came down.

We must remember two facts. At the north end, the lake was no more than four miles across; and John tells us that the disciples had rowed between three and four miles; that is to say, they were very nearly at their journey's end. It is natural to suppose that in the wind they hugged the shore of the lake, seeking what shelter they might find. That is the first fact, and now we come to the second. They saw Jesus, as the Authorized Version and Revised Standard Version have it, walking *on the sea*. The Greek is *epi tēs thalassēs*, which is precisely the phrase used in John 21:1, where it means – it has never been questioned – that Jesus was walking on the seashore. That is what the phrase means in our passage, too.

Jesus was walking *epi tēs thalassēs*, by the seashore. The toiling disciples looked up and suddenly saw him. It was all so unexpected, they had been bent so long over their oars, that they were alarmed because they thought it was a spirit they were seeing. Then across the waters came that well-loved voice – 'It is I; don't be afraid.' They wanted him to come on board; the Greek most naturally means that their wish was not fulfilled. Why? Remember the breadth of the lake was four miles and they had rowed about that distance. The simple reason was that, before they could take Jesus on board, the boat grounded on the shingle, and they were there.

Here is just the kind of story that a fisherman like John would have loved and remembered. Every time he thought of it, he would feel that night again – the grey silver of the moonlight, the rough oar against his hand, the flapping sail, the shriek of the wind, the sound of the surging water, the astonishingly unexpected appearance of Jesus, the sound of his voice across the waves and the crunch of the boat as it reached the Galilaean side.

As he remembered, John saw wonders which are still there for us.

(1) He saw that Jesus *watches*. Up on the hill, Jesus had been watching them. He had not forgotten. He was not too busy with God to think of them. John suddenly realized that all the time they had pulled at the oars, Jesus' loving look was on them. When we are up against it, Jesus watches. He does not make things easy for us. He lets us fight our own battles. Like a parent watching a son or daughter put up a splendid effort in some athletic contest, he is proud of us; or, like a parent watching a son or daughter let the side down, he is sad. Life is lived with the loving eye of Jesus upon us.

(2) He saw that Jesus *comes*. Down from the hillside Jesus came to enable the disciples make the last pull that would reach safety. He does not watch us with serene detachment; when strength is failing, he comes with strength for the last effort which leads to victory.

(3) He saw that Jesus *helps*. He watches, he comes and he helps. It is the wonder of the Christian life that there is nothing that we are left to do alone. A teacher in a little country school told this story to her children, and she must have told it well. Some short time afterwards, there was a blizzard of wind and snow. When school finished, the teacher was helping the children home. Sometimes she had practically to drag them through the drifts. When they were all very nearly exhausted with the struggle, she overheard a little boy say, half to himself: 'We could be doing with that chap Jesus here now.' We could always be doing with Jesus, and we never need to do without him.

(4) He saw that Jesus *brings us to the haven*. It seemed to John, as he remembered it, that, as soon as Jesus arrived, the keel of the boat grated on the shingle – and they were there. As the psalmist had it: 'Then they were glad because they

had quiet, and he brought them to their desired haven' (Psalm 107:30). Somehow in the presence of Jesus the longest journey is shorter and the hardest battle easier.

One of the loveliest things in the Fourth Gospel is that John, the old fisherman turned evangelist, found all the wealth of Christ in the memory of a fisherman's story.

THE MISTAKEN SEARCH

John 6:22–7

> On the next day, the crowd, which was still standing on the far side of the sea, saw that there had been only one boat, and that Jesus had not gone into the boat with his disciples, but that the disciples had gone away alone. But some boats from Tiberias put in near the place where they had eaten the bread, after the Lord had given thanks. So when they saw that Jesus was not there, nor his disciples either, they embarked on the boats, and came to Capernaum, looking for Jesus. When they had found him on the other side of the sea, they said to him: 'Rabbi, when did you get here?' Jesus answered: 'This is the truth I tell you – you are looking for me, not because you saw signs, but because you ate of the loaves until your stomachs were filled. Do not work for the food which perishes, but work for the food which lasts, and which gives eternal life, that food which the Son of Man will give you; for the Father – God – has set his seal upon him.'

THE crowd had lingered on the far side of the lake. In the time of Jesus, people did not need to keep office hours. They had time to wait until he came back to them. They waited because, having seen that there was only one boat and that the disciples had gone off in it without Jesus, they deduced that he must still be somewhere near at hand. After they had waited for some time, they began to realize that he was not coming back. Into the bay came some little boats from Tiberias. No doubt they had taken shelter from the storm of the night. The waiting people embarked on them and made the crossing of the lake back to Capernaum.

Discovering to their surprise that Jesus was already there, they asked him when he had arrived. To that question, Jesus simply did not reply. This was no time to talk of things like that; life was too short for pleasant gossip about journeys. He went straight to the heart of the matter. 'You have seen', he said, 'wonderful things. You have seen how God's grace enabled a crowd to be fed. Your thoughts ought to have been turned to the God who did these things; but instead all that you are thinking about is bread.' It is as if Jesus said: 'You cannot think about your souls for thinking of your stomachs.'

'Men', as the fourth-century theologian John Chrysostom said, 'are nailed to the things of this life.' Here were people whose eyes never lifted beyond the ramparts of the world to the eternities beyond. Once Napoleon and an acquaintance were talking of life. It was dark; they walked to the window and looked out. There in the sky were distant stars, little more than pinpoints of light. Napoleon, who had sharp eyes while his friend was dim-sighted, pointed to the sky: 'Do you see these stars?' he asked. 'No,' his friend answered. 'I can't see them.' 'That', said Napoleon, 'is the difference between you and me.' The person who is earthbound is living half a life. It is the person with vision, who looks at the horizon and sees the stars, who is truly alive.

Jesus put his command in one sentence. 'Don't work for the food which perishes but for that which lasts forever and gives eternal life.' Long ago, a prophet called Isaiah had asked: 'Why do you spend your money for that which is not bread, and your labour for that which does not satisfy?' (Isaiah 55:2). There are two kinds of hunger. There is physical hunger which physical food can satisfy; but there is a spiritual hunger which that food can never satisfy. It is possible to have amassed great wealth and still feel that there is incompleteness in life.

In the years just after AD 60, the luxury of Roman society was unparalleled. It was at this time that they served feasts of peacocks' brains and nightingales' tongues; that they cultivated the odd habit of taking emetics between courses so that the next might taste better; that meals costing thousands of pounds were commonplace. It was at this time that Pliny tells of a Roman lady who was married in a robe so richly jewelled and gilded that it cost the equivalent of about £500,000. There was a reason for all this, and the reason was a deep dissatisfaction with life, a hunger that nothing could satisfy. They would try anything for a new thrill, because they were both appallingly rich and appallingly hungry. As Matthew Arnold wrote in his poem 'Obermann Once More':

> In his cool hall with haggard eyes,
>   The Roman noble lay;
> He drove abroad in furious guise
>   Along the Appian Way;
> He made a feast, drank fierce and fast,
>   He crowned his hair with flowers –
> *No easier nor no quicker passed*
>   The impracticable hours.

Jesus' point was that all that the crowd were interested in was physical satisfaction. They had received an unexpectedly free and lavish meal; and they wanted more. But there are other hungers which can be satisfied only by him. There is the hunger for truth – in him alone is the truth of God. There is the hunger for life – in him alone is life more abundant. There is the hunger for love – in him alone is the love that outlasts sin and death. Christ alone can satisfy the hunger of the human heart and soul.

Why is this so? There is a wealth of meaning in the phrase: 'God has set his seal upon him.' H. B. Tristram in *Eastern Customs in Bible Lands* has a most interesting section on seals in the ancient world. It was not the *signature*, but the *seal* that authenticated. In commercial and political documents it was the seal, imprinted with the signet ring, which made the document valid; it was the seal which authenticated a will; it was the seal on the mouth of a sack or a crate that guaranteed the contents. Tristram tells how on his own journeys, when he made an agreement with his mule-drivers and his porters, they set the impression of their seal upon it to show that it was binding. Seals were made of pottery or metal or jewels. In the British Museum, there are the seals of most of the Assyrian kings. The seal was fixed on clay and the clay was attached to the document.

The Rabbis had a saying: 'The seal of God is truth.' 'One day', says the Talmud, 'the great synagogue [the assembly of the Jewish experts in the law] were weeping, praying and fasting together, when a little scroll fell from the firmament among them. They opened it and on it was only one word, *Ameth*, which means *truth*. "That", said the Rabbi, "is the seal of God."' *Ameth* is spelt with three Hebrew letters – *aleph*, which is the first letter of the alphabet, *min* the middle letter, and *tau* the last. The truth of God is the beginning, the middle and the end of life.

That is why Jesus can satisfy the eternal hunger. He is sealed by God, he is God's truth incarnate and it is God alone who can truly satisfy the hunger of the soul which he created.

THE ONLY TRUE WORK

John 6:28–9

> They said to him: 'What are we to do to work the works
> of God?' Jesus answered: 'This is the work of God, to
> believe in him whom he has sent.'

WHEN Jesus spoke about the works of God, the Jews
immediately thought in terms of 'good' works. It was their
conviction that by living a good life it was possible to earn
the favour of God. They held that people could be divided
into three classes – those who were good, those who were
bad and those who were in between, who, by doing one more
good work, could be transferred to the category of the good.
So, when the Jews asked Jesus about the work of God, they
expected him to lay down lists of things to do. But that is not
what Jesus says at all.

Jesus' answer is extremely compressed, and we must
expand it and see what lies behind it. He said that God's
work was to believe in him whom he had sent. Paul would
have put it this way – the one work that God desires from us
is *faith*. Now what does faith mean? It means being in such a
relationship with God that we are his friends, not terrified of
him any more but knowing him as our Father and our friend
and giving him the trust and the obedience and the submission
which naturally arise from this new relationship. How does
believing in Jesus tie up with that? It is only because Jesus
came to tell us that God is our Father and loves us and wants
nothing more than to forgive, that the old distance and enmity
are taken away and the new relationship with him is made
possible.

But that new relationship issues in a certain kind of life.
Now we know what God is like, our lives must answer to

that knowledge. That answer will be in three directions, each
of which corresponds to what Jesus told us of God.

(1) God is love. Therefore in our lives there must be love
and service of others corresponding to the love and the service
of God, and forgiveness of others corresponding to the forgiveness of God.

(2) God is holiness. Therefore in our lives there must be
purity corresponding to the holiness of God.

(3) God is wisdom. Therefore in our lives there must be
complete submission and trust corresponding to the wisdom
of God.

The essence of the Christian life is a new relationship to
God, a relationship offered by him and made possible by the
revelation which Jesus gave us of him, a relationship which
issues in that service, purity and trust which are the reflection
of God. This is the work which God wishes us and enables us
to perform.

THE DEMAND FOR A SIGN

John 6:30–4

> They said to him: 'What sign are you going to perform
> that we may see it and believe in you? What is your
> work? Our fathers ate the manna in the wilderness. As
> it stands written: "He gave them bread from heaven to
> eat."' Jesus said to them: 'This is the truth I tell you –
> Moses did not give you bread from heaven, but my
> Father gives you the real bread from heaven. The bread
> of God is he who comes down from heaven, and gives
> life to the world.' They said to him: 'Sir, always give
> us that bread.'

HERE the argument becomes specifically Jewish in its
expression and assumptions and allusions. Jesus had just

made a great claim. The true work of God was to believe in him. 'Very well,' said the Jews, 'this is in effect a claim to be the Messiah. Prove it.'

Their minds were still on the feeding of the crowd, and inevitably that turned their thoughts to the manna in the wilderness. They could hardly help connecting the two things. The manna had always been regarded as the bread of God (Psalm 78:24; Exodus 16:15); and there was a strong Rabbinic belief that when the Messiah came he would again give the manna. The giving of the manna was held to be the supreme work in the life of Moses, and the Messiah was bound to surpass it. 'As was the first redeemer so was the final redeemer; as the first redeemer caused the manna to fall from heaven, even so shall the second redeemer cause the manna to fall.' 'Ye shall not find the manna in this age, but ye shall find it in the age that is to come.' 'For whom has the manna been prepared? For the righteous in the age that is coming. Everyone who believes is worthy and eateth of it.' It was the belief that a pot of the manna had been hidden in the ark in the first Temple, and that, when the Temple was destroyed, Jeremiah had hidden it away and would produce it again when the Messiah came. In other words, the Jews were challenging Jesus to produce bread from God in order to substantiate his claims. They did not regard the bread which had fed the 5,000 as bread from God; it had begun in earthly loaves and issued in earthly loaves. The manna, they held, was a different thing and a real test.

Jesus' answer was twofold. First, he reminded them that it was not *Moses* who had given them the manna; it was *God*. Second, he told them that the manna was not really the bread of God; it was only the symbol of the bread of God. The bread of God was he who came down from heaven and gave men and women not simply satisfaction from physical hunger,

but life. Jesus was claiming that the only real satisfaction
was in him.

THE BREAD OF LIFE

John 6:35–40

> Jesus said to them: 'I am the bread of life. He who comes
> to me will never hunger, and he who believes in me
> will never thirst any more. But I tell you, though you
> have seen me, yet you do not believe in me. All that the
> Father gives me will come to me, because I came down
> from heaven, not to do my will, but to do the will of
> him who sent me. This is the will of him who sent me –
> that I should lose none of those he gave to me, but that
> I should raise them all up on the last day. This is the
> will of my Father, that everyone who believes on the
> Son, when he sees him, should have everlasting life.
> And I will raise him up on the last day.'

THIS is one of the great passages of the Fourth Gospel, and
indeed of the New Testament. In it there are two great lines
of thought that we must try to analyse.

First, what did Jesus mean when he said: 'I am the bread
of life'? It is not enough to regard this as simply a beautiful
and poetical phrase. Let us analyse it step by step. (1) Bread
sustains life. It is that without which life cannot go on. (2)
But what is life? Clearly by life is meant something far more
than mere physical existence. What is this new spiritual
meaning of life? (3) Real life is the new relationship with
God, that relationship of trust and obedience and love of
which we have already thought. (4) That relationship is made
possible only by Jesus Christ. Apart from him, no one can
enter into it. (5) That is to say, without Jesus there may be

existence, but not life. (6) Therefore, if Jesus is the essential of life, he may be described as the bread of life. The hunger of the human situation is ended when we know Christ and through him know God. The restless soul is at rest; the hungry heart is satisfied.

Second, this passage opens out to us the stages of the Christian life. (1) We see Jesus. We see him in the pages of the New Testament, in the teaching of the Church, sometimes even face to face. (2) Having seen him, we come to him. We regard him not as some distant hero and pattern, not as a figure in a book, but as someone accessible. (3) We believe in him. That is to say, we accept him as the final authority on God, on all humanity, on life. That means that our coming is not a matter of mere interest, nor a meeting on equal terms; it is essentially a submission. (4) This process gives us life. That is to say, it puts us into a new and lovely relationship with God, wherein he becomes an intimate friend; we are now at home with the one whom we feared or never knew. (5) The possibility of this is free and universal. The invitation is to everyone. The bread of life is ours for the taking. (6) The only way to that new relationship is through Jesus. Without him, it would never have been possible; and apart from him, it is still impossible. No searching of the human mind or longing of the human heart can fully find God apart from Jesus. (7) At the back of the whole process is God. It is those whom God has given him who come to Christ. God not only provides the goal; he moves in the human heart to awaken desire for him; and he works in the human heart to take away the rebellion and the pride which would hinder the great submission. We could never even have sought him unless he had already found us. (8) There remains that stubborn something which enables us to refuse the offer of God. In the last analysis, the one thing which defeats God is the defiance of the human heart. Life is there for the taking – or the refusing.

When we take, two things happen.

First, into life enters new satisfaction. The hunger and the thirst are gone. The human heart finds what it was searching for, and life ceases to be mere existence and becomes a thing at once of thrill and of peace.

Second, even beyond life we are safe. Even on the last day when all things end, we are still secure. As one great commentator said: 'Christ brings us to the haven beyond which there is no danger.'

The offer of Christ is life in time and life in eternity. That is the greatness and glory of which we cheat ourselves when we refuse his invitation.

THE FAILURE OF THE JEWS

John 6:41–51

So the Jews kept murmuring about him, because he said: 'I am the bread which came down from heaven.' They kept saying: 'Is this not Jesus, the son of Joseph, whose father and mother we know? How can he now say: "I have come down from heaven"?' Jesus answered: 'Stop murmuring to each other. No one can come to me except the Father who sent me draws him; and I will raise him up on the last day. It stands written in the prophets: "And all will be taught by God." Everyone who has listened and learned from my Father comes to me. Not that anyone has seen the Father, except he who is from God – *he* has seen the Father. This is the truth I tell you – he who believes has eternal life. I am the bread of life. Your fathers ate the manna in the wilderness, and died. This is the bread of life which comes down from

heaven that a man may eat of him and not die. I am the
bread of life which came down from heaven. If anyone
eats of this bread he will live forever.'

THIS passage shows the reasons why the Jews rejected Jesus
and, in rejecting him, rejected eternal life.

(1) They judged things by human values and by external
standards. Their reaction in face of the claim of Jesus was to
produce the fact that he was a carpenter's son and that they
had seen him grow up in Nazareth. They were unable to
understand how one who was a tradesman and who came
from a poor home could possibly be a special messenger from
God.

T. E. Lawrence, better known as Lawrence of Arabia, was
a close personal friend of Thomas Hardy, the poet and
novelist. In the days when Lawrence was serving as an aircraftman in the Royal Air Force, he sometimes used to visit
Hardy and his wife in his aircraftman's uniform. On one
occasion, his visit coincided with a visit of the Mayoress of
Dorchester. She was bitterly affronted that she had to submit
to meeting a common aircraftman, for she had no idea who
he was. In French, she said to Mrs Hardy that never in all her
born days had she had to sit down to tea with a private soldier.
No one said anything; then Lawrence said in perfect French:
'I beg your pardon, Madame, but can I be of any use as an
interpreter? Mrs Hardy knows no French.' A snobbish and
discourteous woman had made a shattering mistake because
she judged by externals.

That is what the Jews did with Jesus. We must take
care that we never neglect a message from God because
we despise or do not care for the messenger. We would
hardly refuse a sizable cheque because it happened to be
enclosed in an envelope which did not conform to the most

aristocratic standards of notepaper. God has many messengers. His greatest message came through a Galilaean
carpenter, and for that very reason the Jews disregarded it.

(2) The Jews argued *with each other*. They were so taken
up with their private arguments that it never struck them to
refer the decision to God. They were exceedingly eager to let
everyone know what they thought about the matter; but not
in the least anxious to know what God thought. It might well
be that sometimes in a court or committee, when those present
are desirous of pushing their opinions down one another's
throats, we would be better to be quiet and ask God what he
thinks and what he wants us to do. After all, it does not matter
so very much what we think; but what God thinks matters
intensely; and we so seldom take steps to find it out.

(3) The Jews listened, *but they did not learn*. There are
different kinds of listening. There is the listening of criticism;
there is the listening of resentment; there is the listening of
superiority; there is the listening of indifference; there is the
listening of those who listen only because for the moment
they cannot get the chance to speak. The only listening that is
worth while is that which hears and learns; and that is the
only way to listen to God.

(4) The Jews resisted *being drawn to God*. Only those
accept Jesus whom God draws to him. The word which John
uses for *to draw* is *helkuein*. It is the word used in the Greek
translation of the Hebrew when Jeremiah hears God say, as
the Authorized Version has it: 'With lovingkindness have I
drawn thee' (Jeremiah 31:3). The interesting thing about the
word is that it almost always implies some kind of resistance.
It is the word for drawing a heavily laden net to the shore
(John 21:6, 11). It is used of Paul and Silas being dragged
before the magistrates in Philippi (Acts 16:19). It is the word
for drawing a sword from the belt or from its scabbard (John

18:10). Always there is this idea of resistance. God can draw men and women, but their resistance can defeat God's pull.

Jesus is the bread of life; which means that he is the essential for life; therefore to refuse the invitation and command of Jesus is to miss life and to die. The Rabbis had a saying: 'The generation in the wilderness have no part in the life to come.' In the old story in Numbers, the people who cravenly refused to brave the dangers of the promised land, after the report of the scouts, were condemned to wander in the wilderness until they died. Because they would not accept the guidance of God, they were forever shut out from the promised land. The Rabbis believed that their ancestors who died in the wilderness not only missed the promised land but also missed the life to come. To refuse the offer of Jesus is to miss life in this world and in the world to come; whereas to accept his offer is to find real life in this world and glory in the world to come.

HIS BODY AND HIS BLOOD

John 6:51–9

'The bread which I will give him is my flesh, which is given that the world may have life.' So the Jews argued with each other. 'How', they said, 'can this man give us his flesh to eat?' Jesus said to them: 'This is the truth I tell you – unless you eat the flesh of the Son of Man and drink his blood, you cannot possess eternal life within yourselves. He who eats my flesh and drinks my blood has eternal life, and I will raise him up on the last day. My flesh is the real food and my blood is the real drink. He who eats my flesh and drinks my blood remains in me and I in him. As the living Father has sent me, so I live through him; and he who eats me will

> live through me. This is the bread which came down
> from heaven. It is not a case of eating, as your fathers
> ate and died. He who eats this bread lives forever.' He
> said these things when he was teaching in the synagogue
> at Capernaum.

To most of us, this is a very difficult passage. It speaks in language and moves in a world of ideas which are quite strange to us and which may seem even fantastic and grotesque. But to those who heard it first, it was moving among familiar ideas which went back to the very childhood of the race.

These ideas would be quite normal to anyone brought up in ancient sacrifice. The animal was very seldom burned in its entirety. Usually only a token part was burned on the altar, although the whole animal was offered to the god. Part of the flesh was given to the priests as their 'perk', and part to the worshippers to make a feast for themselves and their friends within the temple precincts. At that feast, the god himself was held to be a guest. More, once the flesh had been offered to the god, it was held that he had entered into it; and therefore when the worshipper ate it he was literally eating the god. When people rose from such a feast they went out, as they believed, literally god-filled. We may think of it as idolatrous worship, we may think of it as a vast delusion; yet the fact remains that these people went out quite certain that in them there was now the dynamic vitality of their god. To people used to that kind of experience, a section like this presented no difficulties at all.

Further, in that ancient world, the one live form of religion was to be found in the mystery religions. The one thing the mystery religions offered was communion and even identity with some god. The way it was done was this. All the mystery religions were essentially passion plays. They were stories of a god who had lived and suffered terribly and who died and rose again. The story was turned into a moving play. Before the initiate could see it, he had to undergo a long course of instruction in the inner meaning of the story. He had to undergo all kinds of ceremonial purifications. He had to pass through a long period of fasting and abstention from sexual relationships.

At the actual presentation of a passion play, everything was designed to produce a highly emotional atmosphere. There was carefully calculated lighting, sensuous incense, exciting music, a wonderful liturgy; everything was designed to work up the initiate to a height of emotion and expectation that he had never experienced before. Call it hallucination if you like; call it a combination of hypnotism and self-hypnotism. But something happened; and that something was identity with the god. As the carefully prepared initiate watched, he became one with the god. He shared the sorrows and the griefs; he shared the death and the resurrection. He and the god became forever one; and he was safe in life and in death.

Some of the sayings and prayers of the mystery religions are very beautiful. In the Mysteries of Mithra, the initiate prayed: 'Abide with my soul; leave me not, that I may be initiated and that the holy spirit may dwell within me.' In the Hermetic Mysteries, the initiate said: 'I know thee Hermes, and thou knowest me; *I am thou and thou art I.*' In the same mysteries, a prayer runs: 'Come to me, Lord Hermes, as babes to mothers' wombs.' In the Mysteries of Isis, the worshipper said: 'As truly as Osiris lives, so shall his followers live. As truly as Osiris is not dead, his followers shall die no more.'

We must remember that those ancient people knew all about the striving, the longing, the dreaming for identity with their god and for the bliss of taking him into themselves. They would not read phrases like eating Christ's body and drinking his blood with crude and shocked literalism. They would know something of that ineffable experience of union, closer than any earthly union, of which these words speak. This is language that the ancient world could understand – and so can we.

It may be well that we should remember that here John is doing what he so often does. He is not giving, or trying to give, the actual words of Jesus. He has been thinking for seventy years about what Jesus said; and now, led by the Holy Spirit, he is giving the *inner significance* of his words. It is not the words that he reports; that would merely have been a feat of memory. It is the essential meaning of the words; that is the guidance of the Holy Spirit.

HIS BODY AND HIS BLOOD

John 6:51-9 (*contd*)

LET us see now if we can find out something of what Jesus meant and of what John understood from words like this. There are two ways in which we may take this passage.

(1) We may take it in a quite general sense. Jesus spoke about eating his flesh and drinking his blood.

Now the flesh of Jesus was his complete humanity. John in his First Letter lays it down almost passionately: 'Every spirit that confesses that Jesus Christ has come in the flesh is from God, and every spirit that does not confess Jesus is not from God.' In fact, the spirit which denies that Jesus has come in the flesh is of the antichrist (1 John 4:2-3). John insisted that we must grasp and never let go the full humanity of Jesus, that he was bone of our bone and flesh of our flesh. What does this mean? Jesus, as we have seen again and again, was the mind of God become a person. This means that in

Jesus we see God taking human life upon him, facing our human situation, struggling with our human problems, battling with our human temptations, working out our human relationships.

Therefore it is as if Jesus said: 'Feed your heart, feed your mind, feed your soul on the thought of my humanity. When you are discouraged and in despair, when you are beaten to your knees and disgusted with life and living – remember *I* took that life of yours and these struggles of yours on me.' Suddenly life and the flesh are clad with glory, for they are touched with God. It was and is the great belief of the Greek Orthodox christology that Jesus deified our flesh by taking it on himself. To eat Christ's body is to feed on the thought of his humanity until our own humanity is strengthened and cleansed and irradiated by his.

Jesus said we must drink his blood. In Jewish thought, *the blood stands for the life*. It is easy to understand why. As the blood flows from a wound, life ebbs away; and to the Jews, *the blood belonged to God*. That is why to this day a true Jew will never eat any meat which has not been completely drained of blood. 'Only, you shall not eat flesh with its life, that is, its blood' (Genesis 9:4). 'Its blood, however, you must not eat' (Deuteronomy 15:23). Now see what Jesus is saying – 'You must drink my blood – you must take my life into the very centre of your being – and that life of mine is the life which belongs to God.' When Jesus said we must drink his blood, he meant that we must take his life into the very core of our hearts.

What does that mean? Think of it this way. Here in a bookcase is a book which you never read. It may be the glory and the wonder of the tragedies of Shakespeare; but as long as it remains unread upon your bookshelves, it is external to you. One day, you take it down and read it. You are thrilled and fascinated and moved. The story sticks to you; the great lines remain in your memory; now when you want to, you can take that wonder out from inside yourself and remember it and think about it and feed your mind and your heart upon it. Once the book was outside you. Now it is inside you and you can feed upon it. It is that way with any great experience in life. It remains external until we take it within ourselves.

It is so with Jesus. As long as he remains a figure in a book, he is external to us; but when he enters into our hearts, we can feed upon the life and the strength and the dynamic vitality that he gives to us. Jesus said that we must drink his blood. He is saying: 'You must stop thinking of me as a subject for theological debate; you must take me into you, and you must come into me; and then you will have real life.' That is what Jesus meant when he spoke about us abiding in him and himself abiding in us.

When he told us to eat his flesh and drink his blood, he was telling us to feed our hearts and souls and minds on his humanity, and to revitalize our lives with his life until we are filled with the life of God.

(2) But John meant more than that, and was thinking also of the Lord's Supper. He was saying: 'If you want life, you must come and sit at that table where you eat that broken bread and drink that poured-out wine which somehow, in the grace of God, bring you into contact with the love and the life of Jesus Christ.' But – and here is the sheer wonder of his point of view – *John has no account of the Last Supper*. He brings in his teaching about it, not in the narrative of the upper room, but in the story of a picnic meal on a hillside near Bethsaida Julias by the blue waters of the Sea of Galilee.

There is no doubt that John is saying that for the true Christian *every meal has become a sacrament*. It may well be that there were those who – if the phrase is allowed – were making too much of the sacrament within the Church, making a magic of it, implying that it was the only place where we might enter into the nearer presence of the risen Christ. It is true that the sacrament is a special appointment with God; but John held with all his heart that every meal in the humblest home, in the richest palace, beneath the canopy of the sky with only the grass for carpet, was a sacrament. He refused to limit the presence of Christ to an ecclesiastical environment and a correctly liturgical service. He said: 'At any meal you can find again that bread which speaks of the humanity of the Master, that wine which speaks of the blood which is life.'

In John's thought, the communion table and the dinner table and the picnic on the seashore or the hillside are all alike in that at all of them we may taste and touch and handle the bread and the wine which brings us Christ. Christianity would be a poor thing if Christ were confined to churches. It is John's belief that we can find him anywhere in a Christ-filled world. It is not that he belittles the sacrament; but he expands it, so that we find Christ at his table in church, and then go out to find him everywhere where men and women meet together to enjoy the gifts of God.

THE ALL-IMPORTANT SPIRIT

John 6:59–65

> When they had heard this discourse many of his disciples said: 'This word is hard! Who is able to listen to it?' Jesus well knew within himself that his disciples were murmuring about this; so he said to them: 'Does this cause you to stumble? What then if you were to see the Son of Man ascending to where he formerly was?

The life-giving power is the Spirit; the flesh is of no
help. The words which I have spoken to you are spirit
and life. But there are some who do not believe.' For
Jesus knew from the beginning who they were who did
not believe, and who it was who was going to betray
him. So that was why he often said: 'No man can come
to me, except it has been given to him by the Father to
do so.'

It is little wonder that the disciples found the discourse of
Jesus hard. The Greek word is *sklēros*, which means not *hard
to understand* but *hard to accept*. The disciples knew quite
well that Jesus had been claiming to be the very life of God
come down from heaven, and that no one could live this life
or face eternity without submitting to him.

Here we come upon a truth that re-emerges in every age.
Time and again it is not the intellectual difficulty which keeps
men and women from becoming Christians; it is the height
of Christ's moral demand. At the heart of all religion there
must be mystery, for the simple reason that at that heart there
is God. In the nature of things, we cannot ever fully understand God. Any honest thinker will accept that there must be
mystery.

The real difficulty of Christianity is twofold. It demands
an act of surrender to Christ, an acceptance of him as the
final authority; and it demands a moral standard of the
highest level. The disciples were well aware that Jesus had
claimed to be the very life and mind of God come down
to earth; their difficulty was to accept that as true, with all
its implications. To this day many refuse Christ, not
because he puzzles intellect, but because he challenges their
lives.

Jesus goes on, not to try to prove his claim, but to state
that some day events will prove it. What he is saying is this:

'You find it difficult to believe that I am the bread, the essential of life, which *came down* from heaven. Well then, you will have no difficulty in accepting that claim when some day you see me *ascending back* to heaven.' It is a forecast of the ascension. It means that the resurrection is the guarantee of the claims of Jesus. He was not one who lived nobly and died gallantly for a lost cause; he was the one whose claims were vindicated by the fact that he rose again.

Jesus goes on to say that the all-important thing is the life-giving power of the Spirit; the flesh is of no help. We can put that very simply in a way which will give us at least something of its meaning – the most important thing is the spirit in which any action is done. It has been put this way: 'All human things are trivial if they exist for nothing beyond themselves.' The real value of anything depends on its aim. If we eat simply for the sake of eating, we become gluttons, and it is likely to do us far more harm than good; if we eat to sustain life, to do our work better, to maintain the fitness of our body at its highest peak, food has a real significance. If people spend a great deal of time on sport simply for the sake of sport, they are at least to some extent wasting their time. But if they spend that time in order to keep their bodies fit and thereby to do their work for God and for others better, sport ceases to be trivial and becomes important. The things of the flesh all gain their value from the spirit in which they are done.

Jesus goes on: 'My words are spirit and life.' He alone can tell us what life is, put into us the spirit in which it must be lived, give us the strength so to live it. Life takes its value from its purpose and its goal. Christ alone can give us true purpose in life and the power to work out that purpose against the constant opposition that comes from without and within.

Jesus was well aware that some would not only reject his offer but would reject it with hostility. No one can accept him unless moved by the Spirit of God to do so, but to the end of the day anyone can resist that Spirit. Such people are shut out not by God but by themselves.

ATTITUDES TO CHRIST

John 6:66–71

> After this many of his disciples turned back and would not walk with him any more. Jesus said to the Twelve: 'Surely you too do not want to go away?' Simon Peter answered him: 'Lord, to whom are we to go? You have the words of eternal life; and we have believed and we have come to know that you are the Holy One of God.' Jesus answered them: 'Did I not choose you twelve, and one of you is a devil?' He meant Judas, the son of Simon Iscariot, for he was going to betray him – and he was one of the Twelve.

HERE is a passage charged with tragedy, for in it is the beginning of the end. There was a time when people came to Jesus in large numbers. When he was in Jerusalem at the Passover, many saw his miracles and believed in his name (2:23). So many came to be baptized by his disciples that the numbers were embarrassing (4:1–3). In Samaria, great things happened (4:1, 39, 45). In Galilee, the crowds flocked after him just the day before (6:2). But the tone of things had changed; from now on there was a growing hatred which was going to culminate in the cross. Already John launches us on the last act of the tragedy. It is circumstances like these which reveal people's hearts and show them in their true colours. In these circumstances, there were three different attitudes to Jesus.

(1) There was *defection*. Some turned back and walked with him no more. They drifted away for various reasons.

Some saw quite clearly where Jesus was heading. It was not possible to challenge the authorities as he was doing and get away with it. He was heading for disaster and they were getting out in time. They were fair-weather followers. It has been said that the test of an army is how it fights when it is tired. Those who drifted away would have stuck by Jesus as long as his career was on the upward way, but at the first shadow of the cross they left him.

Some shirked the challenge of Jesus. Fundamentally their point of view was that they had come to Jesus to get something from him; when it came to suffering *for* him and giving *to* him they quit. No one can give so much as Jesus, but if we come to him solely to get and never to give we will certainly turn back. Those who would follow Jesus must remember that in following him there is always a cross.

(2) There was *deterioration*. It is in Judas above all that we see this. Jesus must have seen in him a man whom he could use for his purposes. But Judas, who might have become the hero, became the villain; he who might have become a saint became a name of shame.

There is a terrible story about an artist who was painting the Last Supper. It was a great picture and it took him many years. As a model for the face of Christ, he used a young man with a face of transcendent loveliness and purity. Bit by bit the picture was filled in, and one after another the disciples were painted. The day came when he needed a model for Judas, whose face he had left to the last. He went out and searched in the lowest haunts of the city and in the dens of vice. At last he found a man with a face so depraved and vicious as matched his requirement. When the sittings were at an end, the man said to the artist: 'You painted me before.'

'Surely not,' said the artist. 'O yes,' said the man, 'I sat for your Christ.' The years had brought terrible deterioration.

The years can be cruel. They can take away our ideals and our enthusiasms and our dreams and our loyalties. They can leave us with a life that has grown smaller and not bigger. They can leave us with hearts that are shrivelled instead of expanded in the love of Christ. There can be a lost loveliness in life – God save us from that!

(3) There was *determination*. This is John's version of Peter's great confession at Caesarea Philippi (Mark 8:27; Matthew 16:13; Luke 9:18). It was just such a situation as this that called out the loyalty of Peter's heart. To him, the simple fact was that there was just no one else to go to. Jesus alone had the words of life.

Peter's loyalty was based on a personal relationship to Jesus Christ. There were many things he did not understand; he was just as bewildered and puzzled as anyone else. But there was something about Jesus for which he would willingly die. In the last analysis, Christianity is not a philosophy which we accept, nor a theory to which we give allegiance. It is a personal response to Jesus Christ. It is the allegiance and the love which we give because our hearts will not allow us to do anything else.

NOT OUR TIME BUT GOD'S

John 7:1–9

> After these things Jesus moved about in Galilee, for he did not wish to move about in Judaea, because the Jews were out to kill him. The festival of the Jews which is called the Festival of Tabernacles was near. So his brothers said to him: 'Leave here and go down to

Jerusalem so that your disciples will get the chance to
see the works that you do. For no one goes on doing
things in secret, when he wishes to draw public attention
to himself. Since you can do these things, show yourself
to the world.' For even his brothers did not believe in
him. So Jesus said to them: 'The time of opportunity
that I am looking for has not yet come; but your time is
always ready. The world cannot hate you, but it hates
me, because I bear witness about it that its deeds are
evil. Go up to the festival yourselves. I am not yet going
up to the festival, because my time has not yet come.'
When he had said these things to them he remained in
Galilee.

THE Festival of Tabernacles fell at the end of September and
the beginning of October. It was one of the obligatory
festivals, and every adult male Jew who lived within fifteen
miles of Jerusalem was legally bound to attend it. But devout
Jews from far outside the fifteen-mile radius delighted to go
to it. It lasted altogether for eight days. Later in this chapter,
we shall have occasion to deal more fully with it. When it
came round, Jesus' brothers urged him to go to Jerusalem for
it; but Jesus rejected their arguments and went in his own
good time.

There is one unique thing in this passage which we must
note. According to the Revised Standard Version (verse 7),
Jesus says: 'My time is not yet come.' Jesus frequently spoke
about his *time* or his *hour*. But here he uses a different word,
and uses it for the only time. In the other passages (John 2:4,
7:30, 8:20, 12:27), the word that Jesus or John uses is *hōra*,
which means the *destined hour of God*. Such a time or hour
was not movable nor avoidable. It had to be accepted without
argument and without alteration because it was the hour at
which the plan of God had decided that something must

happen. But in this passage the word is *kairos*, which characteristically means an *opportunity*; that is, the best time to do something, the moment when circumstances are most suitable, *the psychological moment*. Jesus is not saying here that the destined hour of God has not come, but something much simpler. He is saying that that was not the moment which would give him the chance for which he was waiting.

That explains why Jesus later actually did go to Jerusalem. Many people have been troubled about the fact that he first told his brothers he would not go and then went. Arthur Schopenhauer, the nineteenth-century German philosopher, actually said: 'Jesus Christ did of set purpose utter a falsehood.' Other people have argued that it means that Jesus said that he was not going up to the festival *publicly*, but that did not preclude him from going *privately*. But Jesus is saying simply: 'If I go up with you just now I will not get the opportunity I am looking for. The time is not opportune.' So he delayed his going until the middle of the festival, since to arrive with the crowds all assembled and expectant gave him a far better opportunity than to go at the very beginning. Jesus is choosing his time with careful prudence in order to get the most effective results.

From this passage, we learn two things.

(1) It is impossible to force Jesus' hand. His brothers tried to force him into going to Jerusalem. It was what we might call a dare. They were quite right from the human point of view. Jesus' great miracles had been performed in Galilee – the changing of the water into wine (John 2:1ff.); the healing of the nobleman's son (John 4:46); the feeding of the 5,000 (John 6:1ff.). The only miracle that he had performed in Jerusalem was the curing of the helpless man at the pool (John 5:1ff.). It was not unnatural to tell Jesus to go to Jerusalem and let his supporters there see what he could do. The story

makes it clear that the healing of the sick and helpless man had been regarded far more as an act of Sabbath-breaking than as a miracle. Further, if Jesus was ever to succeed in winning people, he could not hope to do so by hiding in a corner; he must act in such a way that everyone could see what he did. Still further, Jerusalem was the keypoint. The Galilaeans were notoriously hot-blooded and hot-headed. Anyone who wanted a following would have no difficulty in raising one in the excitable atmosphere of Galilee; but Jerusalem was a very different proposition. It was the acid test.

Jesus' brothers could have put up a good case for their insistence; but Jesus' hand is not to be forced. He does things, not in human time, but in God's. Our impatience of one another must learn to wait on God's wisdom.

(2) It is impossible to treat Jesus with indifference. It did not matter when his brothers went to Jerusalem, for no one would notice they were there and nothing whatever depended on their going. But Jesus' going was a very different thing. Why? Because his brothers were in tune with the world and they did not make it uncomfortable. But Jesus' coming is a condemnation of the world's way of life and a challenge to selfishness and lethargy. Jesus had to choose his moment, for when he arrives something happens.

REACTIONS TO JESUS

John 7:10–13

> When his brothers had gone up to the festival, then he too went up, not openly, but, as it were, in secret. So the Jews searched for him at the festival, and kept saying: 'Where is he?' And there was many a heated

> argument about him among the crowds. Some said: 'He
> is a good man.' But others said: 'No; far from it; he is
> leading the people astray.' But no one spoke about him
> openly because of their fear of the Jews.

JESUS chose his own moment and went to Jerusalem. Here we have the reactions of the people when they were confronted with him. Now one of the supreme interests of this chapter is the number of such reactions of which it tells; and we collect them all here.

(1) There was the reaction of his brothers (verses 1–5). It was really a reaction of half-amused and teasing contempt. They did not really believe in him; they were really egging him on, as you might egg on a precocious child. We still meet that attitude of tolerant contempt to Christianity.

The French novelist George Bernaños in *The Diary of a Country Priest* tells how the country priest used sometimes to be invited to dinner at the big aristocratic house of his parish. The owner would encourage him to speak and argue before his guests, but he did it with that half-amused, half-contemptuous tolerance with which he might encourage a child to show off or a dog to display its tricks. There are still people who forget that Christian faith is a matter of life and death.

(2) There was the sheer hatred of the Pharisees and of the chief priests (verses 7, 19). They did not hate him for the same reason, because in point of fact they hated each other. The Pharisees hated him because he drove through their petty rules and regulations. If he was right, they were wrong; and they loved their own little system more than they loved God. The Sadducees were a political party. They did not observe the Pharisaic rules and regulations. Nearly all the priests were Sadducees. They collaborated with their Roman masters, and they had a very comfortable and even luxurious time. They

did not want a Messiah; for when he came their political set-up would disintegrate and their comfort would be gone. They hated Jesus because he interfered with the vested interests which were dearer to them than God.

It is still possible to love our own little systems more than we love God, and to place our own vested interests above the challenge of the adventurous and the sacrificial way.

(3) Both these reactions issued in the consuming desire to eliminate Jesus (verses 30, 32). When people's ideals clash with those of Christ, either they must submit or they must seek to destroy him. Hitler would have no Christians about him, for the Christian owed a higher loyalty than loyalty to the state. We are faced with a simple alternative if we allow Christ into our orbit. We can either do what we like or we can do what Christ likes; and if we wish to go on doing as we like, we must seek to eliminate Christ.

(4) There was arrogant contempt (verses 15, 47-9). What right had this man to come and lay down the law? Jesus had no cultural background; he had no training in the Rabbinic schools and colleges. Surely no intelligent person was going to listen to him? Here was the reaction of academic snobbery.

Many of the greatest poets and writers and evangelists have had no technical qualifications at all. That is not for one moment to say that study and culture and education are to be despised and abandoned; but we must take care never to wave people away and consign them to the company who do not matter simply because they lack the expected qualifications.

(5) There was the reaction of the crowd. This was twofold. First, there was the reaction of *interest* (verse 11). The one thing impossible when Jesus really invades life is indifference. Apart from anything else, Jesus is the most interesting figure in the world. Second, there was the reaction of *discussion* (verses 12, 43). They talked about Jesus; they put forward

their views about him; they debated about him. There is both value and danger here. The value is that nothing helps us clarify our own opinions like pitting them against someone else's. Mind sharpens mind as iron sharpens iron. The danger is that religion can so very easily come to be regarded as a matter for argument and debate and discussion, a series of fascinating questions, about which it is possible to talk for a lifetime – and do nothing. There is all the difference in the world between being an argumentative amateur theologian, willing to talk until the stars go out, and a truly religious person, who has passed from talking about Christ to knowing him.

VERDICTS ON JESUS

John 7:10–13 (*contd*)

IN this chapter, there is a whole series of verdicts on Jesus.

(1) There is the verdict that he was a *good man* (verse 12). That verdict is true, but it is not the whole truth. It was Napoleon who made the famous remark: 'I know men, and Jesus Christ is more than a man.' Jesus was indeed truly human; but in him was the mind of God. When he speaks, it is not just a man speaking to us; if that were so, we might argue about his commands. When he speaks, it is God speaking to us; and Christianity means not arguing about his commands, but accepting them.

(2) There is the verdict that he was a *prophet* (verse 40). That too is true. Prophets foretell the will of God; they have lived so close to God that they know his mind and purposes. That is true of Jesus; but there is this difference. When prophets say: 'Thus says the Lord,' their authority is borrowed and delegated. Their message is not their own. Jesus says: 'I

say unto you.' He has the right to speak, not with a delegated authority, but with his own.

(3) There is the verdict that he was a *deluded madman* (verse 20). It is true that either Jesus is the only completely sane person in the world or he was mad. He chose a cross when he might have had power. He was the suffering servant when he might have been the conquering king. He washed the feet of his disciples when he might have had people kneeling at his own feet. He came to serve when he could have subjected the world to servitude. It is not common sense that the words of Jesus give us, but uncommon sense. He turned the world's standards upside down, because into a mad world he brought the supreme sanity of God.

(4) There is the verdict that he was a *seducer*. The Jewish authorities saw in him one who was leading people away from true religion. He was accused of every crime against religion in the calendar – of being a Sabbath-breaker, of being a drunkard and a glutton, of having the most disreputable friends, of destroying orthodox religion. It is quite clear that if we prefer our idea of religion to his, he will certainly appear a seducer – and one of the hardest things in the world for any of us is to admit that we are wrong.

(5) There is the verdict that he was a *man of courage* (verse 26). No one could ever doubt his sheer courage. He had the moral courage to defy convention and be different. He had the physical courage that could bear the most terrible pain. He had the courage to go on when his family abandoned him, and his friends forsook him, and one of his own circle betrayed him. Here we see him courageously entering Jerusalem when to enter it was to enter the lions' den. He 'feared God so much that he never feared the face of any man'.

(6) There is the verdict that he had a *most dynamic personality* (verse 46). The verdict of the officers who were

sent to arrest him and came back empty-handed was that no one had ever spoken like this. Julian Duguid tells how he once voyaged on the same Atlantic liner as the physician and missionary Sir Wilfred Grenfell, and he says that when Grenfell came into a room you could tell it even if you had your back to him, for a wave of vitality emanated from him. When we think of how this Galilaean carpenter faced the highest in the land and dominated them until it was they who were on trial and not he, we are bound to admit that he was at least one of the supreme personalities in history. The picture of a gentle, anaemic Jesus will not do. From him flowed a power that sent those despatched to arrest him back in empty-handed bewilderment.

(7) There is the verdict that he was the *Christ*, the Anointed One of God. Nothing less will do. It is the plain fact that Jesus does not fit into any of the available human categories; only the category of the divine will do.

Before we leave the general study of this chapter, there are three other reactions to Jesus that we must note.

(1) There was the crowd's reaction of *fear* (verse 13). They talked about him but they were afraid to talk too loud. The word that John uses for their talking is an onomatopoetic word – that is, a word which imitates the sound of what it describes. It is the word *goggusmos* (two *g*'s in Greek are pronounced *ng*). The Authorized Version translates it as *murmuring*; the Revised Standard Version as *muttering*. It indicates a kind of growling, discontented undertone. It is the word used for the grumbling of the children of Israel in the wilderness when they complained against Moses. They muttered the complaints they were afraid to utter out loud. Fear can keep people from making a clarion call of their faith and can turn it into an indistinct mutter. Christians should never be afraid to tell the world in ringing tones that they believe in Christ.

(2) The reaction of a certain number of the crowd was *belief* (verse 31). These were the men and women who could not deny the evidence of their own eyes. They heard what Jesus said; they saw what he did; they were confronted with his dynamism; and they believed. If people rid themselves of prejudice and fear, they are bound in the end to finish in belief.

(3) The reaction of Nicodemus was to *defend* Jesus (verse 50). In that council of the Jewish authorities, his was the lone voice raised in defence. There lies the duty of every one of us. Ian Maclaren, author of *Beside the Bonnie Brier Bush*, used to tell students when they preached: 'Speak a good word for Jesus Christ.' We live today in a world which is hostile to Christianity in many ways and in many places, but the strange thing is that the world was never more ready to talk about Christ and to discuss religion. We live in a generation when every one of us can earn the royal title, 'Defender of the Faith'. It is the privilege that God has given us that we can all be advocates and defenders of Christ in the face of the criticism – and sometimes the mockery – of others.

THE ULTIMATE AUTHORITY

John 7:15–18

> The Jews were amazed. 'How', they said, 'can this fellow read when he is quite uneducated?' 'My teaching', said Jesus, 'is not mine, but it belongs to him who sent me. If anyone is willing to do his will, he will understand whether my teaching derives from God, or whether I am speaking from no source beyond myself. The man who speaks from no other source beyond himself is out for his own glory. He who seeks the glory of him who sent him is true, and there is no wickedness in him.'

WE have already had occasion to see that it is very likely that some parts of John's gospel have become misplaced. Maybe he never had time to put it fully in order; maybe the leaves on which it was written were finally assembled wrongly. This section and the one which follows form one of the clearest cases of misplacement. As these two passages come in here, they hardly make sense, for they have no connection with their context. It is almost certain that they should come after 5:47. Chapter 5 tells of the healing of the helpless man at the healing pool. That miracle was done on the Sabbath and was regarded by the Jewish authorities as a breach of that day. In his defence, Jesus cited the writings of Moses and said that if they really knew what these writings meant and really believed in them, they would also believe in him. The chapter finishes: 'If you believed Moses, you would believe me, for he wrote about me. But if you do not believe what he wrote, how will you believe what I say?' (5:46–7). If we go straight from there and read 7:15–24, it makes a clear connection. Jesus has just referred to the writing of Moses, and immediately the astonished Jewish leaders break in: 'How can this fellow read when he is quite uneducated?' We will understand the sense and the relevance of 7:15–24 far better if we assume that it originally came after 5:47; and with that in mind, we turn to the passage itself.

The criticism was that Jesus was quite uneducated. It is exactly the same accusation that was made against Peter and John when they stood before the Sanhedrin (Acts 4:13). Jesus had been to no Rabbinic school. It was the practice that only the disciple of an accredited teacher was entitled to expound Scripture and to talk about the law. No Rabbi ever made a statement on his own authority. He always began: 'There is a teaching that . . .'. He then went on to cite quotations and authorities for every statement he made. And here was this

Galilaean carpenter, a man with no training whatever, daring
to quote and to expound Moses to them.

Jesus could very well have walked straight into a trap here.
He might have said: 'I need no teacher; I am self-taught; I
got my teaching and my wisdom from no one but myself.'
But, instead, he said in effect: 'You ask who was my teacher?
You ask what authority I produce for my exposition of
Scripture? *My authority is God.*' Jesus claimed to be God-
taught. It is in fact a claim he makes again and again. 'I have
not spoken on my own, but the Father who sent me has himself given me a commandment about what to say and what to
speak' (John 12:49). 'The words that I say to you I do not
speak on my own' (14:10).

Frank Salisbury tells of a letter he received after he had
painted his great picture of the burial of the unknown warrior
in Westminster Abbey. A fellow artist wrote: 'I want to
congratulate you on the great picture that you have painted –
or rather the picture that God has helped you to paint.' All
great productions of the human mind and spirit are given by
God. If we glory in being self-taught, if we claim that any
discovery we have made is our own unaided work, we are, in
the last analysis, glorifying only our own reputation and our
own selves. The very greatest people think not of the power
of their own minds or hands; they think always of the God
who told them what they know and taught them what they
can do.

Further, Jesus goes on to lay down a truth. Only those who
do God's will can truly understand his teaching. That is not a
theological but a universal truth. *We learn by doing.* Doctors
might learn the technique of surgery from textbooks. They
might know the theory of every possible operation. But that
would not make them surgeons; they have to learn by doing.
It may be possible to learn the way in which a car engine

works; in theory we might even be able to carry out every possible repair and adjustment; but that would not qualify any of us as a mechanic; we have to learn by doing.

It is the same with the Christian life. If we wait until we have understood everything, we will never start at all. But if we begin by doing God's will as we know it, God's truth will become clearer and clearer to us. We learn by doing. If someone says: 'I cannot be a Christian because there is so much of Christian doctrine that I do not understand, and I must wait until I understand it all,' the answer is: 'You never will understand it all; but if you start trying to live the Christian life, you will understand more and more of it as the days go on.' In Christianity, as in all other things, the way to learn is to do.

Let us remember that this passage really ought to come after the story of the healing of the sick and helpless man. Jesus has been accused of wickedness in that he healed the man on the Sabbath day; and he goes on to demonstrate that he was seeking only the glory of God and that there is no wickedness whatsoever in his action.

A WISE ARGUMENT

John 7:19–24

'Did not Moses give you the law – and not one of you really keeps it? Why do you try to kill me?' The crowd answered: 'You are mad! Who is trying to kill you?' Jesus answered them: 'I have done only one deed and you are all astonished by it. Moses gave you the rite of circumcision (not that it had its origin in Moses – it came down from your fathers) and you circumcise a man on the Sabbath. If a man can be circumcised on the

Sabbath, without breaking the law of Moses, are you
angry at me for making the entire body of a man whole
on the Sabbath? Stop judging by appearances, and make
your judgment just.'

BEFORE we begin to look at this passage in detail, we must
note one point. We must picture this scene as a debate between
Jesus and the leaders of the Jews, with the crowd standing all
around. The crowd is listening as the debate goes on. Jesus
is aiming to justify his action in healing the man on the
Sabbath day and thereby technically breaking the Sabbath
law. He begins by saying that Moses gave them the Sabbath
law, and yet none of them keeps it absolutely. (What he meant
by that we shall shortly see.) If he then breaks the law to heal
a man, why do they, who themselves break the law, seek to
kill him?

At this point, the *crowd* break in with the exclamation:
'You are mad!' and the question: 'Who is trying to kill you?'
The crowd have not yet realized the intense hatred of their
leaders; they are not yet aware of the plots to eliminate him.
They think that Jesus has a persecution complex, that his
imagination is disordered and his mind upset; and they think
in this fashion because they do not know the facts. Jesus does
not answer the question of the crowd, which was not really a
question so much as a kind of bystanders' interjection, but
goes on with his argument.

Jesus' argument is this. It was the law that a child should
be circumcised on the eighth day after his birth. 'On the eighth
day the flesh of his foreskin shall be circumcised' (Leviticus
12:3). Obviously that day would often fall on a Sabbath; and
the law was quite clear that 'everything necessary for circumcision may be done on the Sabbath day'. So Jesus' argument
runs like this. 'You say that you fully observe the law which
came to you through Moses which lays it down that there

must be no work done on the Sabbath day, and under work
you have included every kind of medical attention which is
not necessary actually to save life. And yet you have allowed
circumcision to be carried out on the Sabbath day.'

Now circumcision is two things. It is medical attention
to one part of a man's body; and the body has actually 248
parts. (That was the Jewish reckoning.) Further, circumcision is a kind of mutilation; it is actually taking something
from the body. 'How can you in reason blame me for
making a man's body whole when you allow yourselves to
mutilate it on the Sabbath day?' That is an extremely clever
argument.

Jesus finishes by telling them to try to see below the surface
of things and to judge fairly. If they do, they will not be able
any longer to accuse him of breaking the law. A passage like
this may sound remote to us; but when we read it we can see
the keen, clear, logical mind of Jesus in operation, we can
see him meeting the wisest and most subtle men of his day
with their own weapons and on their own terms, and we can
see him defeating them.

THE CLAIM OF CHRIST

John 7:14, 25–30

> When the festival was now half-way through, Jesus
> went up to the Temple precincts and began to teach. So
> some of the people of Jerusalem said: 'Is not this the
> man whom they are trying to kill? And look! He is
> speaking publicly, and they say nothing to him! Can it
> be that the authorities have really discovered that this is
> the Anointed One of God? But he cannot be because
> we know where he comes from. When the Anointed
> One of God comes no one knows where he comes from.'

So Jesus, as he taught in the Temple, cried: 'So you know me? And you know where I come from? But it is not on my own authority that I have come; but he who sent me is real – and you do not know him. *But I know him*, because I have come from him, and it was he who sent me.' So they would have liked to have found a way to arrest him; but no one laid a hand upon him, because his hour had not yet come.

WE have already seen that the likelihood is that verses 15–24 should come after 5:47; so, to get the connection, we begin at verse 14 and go on to verse 24.

The crowd were surprised to find Jesus preaching in the Temple precincts. Along the sides of the Court of the Gentiles ran two great pillared colonnades or porticoes – the Royal Porch and Solomon's Porch. These were places where people walked and where Rabbis talked, and it would be there that Jesus was teaching. The people knew well the hostility of the authorities to Jesus; they were astonished to see his courage in thus defying the authorities; and they were still more astonished to see that he was allowed to teach unmolested. A thought suddenly struck them: 'Can it be that after all this man is the Messiah, the Anointed One of God, and that the authorities know it?' But no sooner had the thought struck them than it was dismissed.

Their objection was that they knew where Jesus had come from. They knew that his home was in Nazareth; they knew who his parents and who his brothers and sisters were; there was no mystery about his antecedents. That was the very opposite of popular belief, which held that the Messiah would *appear*. The idea was that he was waiting concealed and some day would burst suddenly upon the world and no one would know where he had come from. They believed that they did know that the Messiah would be born in Bethlehem, for that was David's town, but they also believed that nothing else would be known about him. There was a Rabbinic saying: 'Three things come wholly unexpectedly – the Messiah, a godsend and a scorpion.' The Messiah would *appear* as suddenly as anyone stumbles on a godsend or steps on a hidden scorpion. In the later years of the second century, when Justin Martyr was talking and arguing with a Jew about his beliefs, the Jew says of the Messiah: 'Although the Messiah be already born and exists somewhere, yet he is unknown and is himself ignorant of his Messiahship, nor has he any power until Elijah comes to anoint him and to make him known.' All popular Jewish belief believed that the Messiah would burst upon the world mysteriously. Jesus did not measure up to that kind of standard; to the Jews there was no mystery about where he came from.

This belief was characteristic of a certain attitude of mind which prevailed among the Jews and is by no means dead – that which seeks for God in the abnormal. They could never be persuaded to see God in ordinary things. They had to be extraordinary before God could be in them. The teaching of Christianity is just the reverse. If God is to enter the world only in the unusual, he will very seldom be in it; whereas if we can find God in the common things, it means that he is always present. Christianity does not look on this world as one which God very occasionally invades; it looks on it as a world from which he is never absent.

In answer to these objections, Jesus made two statements, both of which shocked the people and the authorities. He said that it was quite true that they knew who he was and where he came from; but it was also true that ultimately he had come direct from God. Second, he said that they did not know God; but he did. It was a bitter insult to tell God's chosen people that they did not know God. It was an incredible claim to make that Jesus alone knew him, that he stood in a unique relationship to him, that he knew him as no one else did.

Here is one of the great turning points in Jesus' life. Up to this point the authorities had looked on him as a revolutionary Sabbath-breaker, which was in truth a serious enough charge; but from now on he was guilty not of Sabbath-breaking but of the ultimate sin, of *blasphemy*. As they saw it, he was talking of Israel and of God as no human being had any right to speak.

This is precisely the choice which is still before us. Either, what Jesus said about himself is false, in which case he is guilty of such blasphemy as no one ever dared utter; or, what he said about himself is true, in which case he is what he claimed to be and can be described in no other terms than the Son of God. Everyone has to decide for or against Jesus Christ.

SEARCHING – IN TIME

John 7:31-6

Many of the crowd believed in him. 'When the Anointed One of God comes,' they said, 'surely he cannot do greater signs than this man has done?' The Pharisees heard the crowds carrying on these discussions about him; and the chief priests and Pharisees despatched officers to arrest him. So Jesus said: 'For a little while I am to be with you, and then I go back to him who sent me. You will search for me and you will not find me. You cannot come where I am.' So the Jews said to each other: 'Where is this fellow going to go that we will not be able to find him? Surely he is not going to go to the

Jews who are dispersed among the Greeks and teach
the Greeks? What can this word of his mean – "You
will search for me and you will not find me" and "You
cannot come where I am"?'

CERTAIN of the crowd could not help believing that Jesus was
the Anointed One of God. They believed that no one could
possibly do greater things than he was doing. That was in
fact the argument which Jesus himself used when John the
Baptist was in doubt about whether he was the one who
was to come or if they had to look for another. When John
sent his messengers, Jesus' answer was: 'Go and tell John
what you hear and see' (Matthew 11:6). The very fact that
there were those who were trembling on the brink of
acceptance moved the authorities to action. They sent their
officers – most likely, the Temple police – to arrest him.
Jesus said that he was only with them for a little time; and
the day would come when they would search for him, not
to arrest him but to obtain what only he could give, and it
would be too late. He would be gone where they could never
follow.

Jesus meant that he would return to his Father, from whom
by their disobedience they had shut themselves out. But his
hearers did not understand. Throughout the centuries, the
Jews had been scattered across the world. Sometimes they
had been forcibly removed as exiles; sometimes in the time
of their country's misfortune they had emigrated to other
lands. There was one comprehensive term for the Jews who
lived outside Palestine. They were called *the Diaspora*, the
dispersion, and scholars still use this term to describe the
Jews who live outside Palestine. That is the phrase the people
used here. 'Is Jesus going away to the *Diaspora*? Will he
even go to the lengths of going away and preaching to the
Greeks and so become lost in the masses of the Gentile world?

Is he going to run away so far that he will be completely out of reach?' It is amazing how a taunt became a prophecy. The Jews meant it as a jest, but as the years went on it became blessedly true that it was to the Gentiles that the risen Christ went out.

This passage brings us face to face with *the promise and the threat of Jesus.* Jesus had said: 'Search and you will find' (Matthew 7:7). Now as John has it he says: 'You will search for me but you will not find me' (verse 34). Long ago, the ancient prophet had put the two things together in a wonderful way: 'Seek the Lord *while he may be found*' (Isaiah 55:6). It is characteristic of this life that time is limited. Physical strength decays, and there are things that we can do at thirty that we cannot do at sixty. Mental vigour weakens, and there are mental tasks to which we can address ourselves in our youth and in our prime which are beyond us in old age. Moral fibre grows less muscular; and if we allow some habit to dominate us, there may come the day when we cannot break ourselves of it, even if at the beginning we could easily have ejected it from our lives.

It is like that with us and Jesus Christ. What Jesus was saying to these people was: 'You can awaken to a sense of need too late.' People may so long refuse Christ that in the end they do not even see his beauty; evil becomes their good, and repentance becomes impossible. As long as sin still hurts us, and the unattainable good still beckons us, the chance to seek and find is still there. But people must take care lest they grow so used to sin that they do not know that they are sinning and neglect God so long that they forget that he exists. For then the sense of need dies, and if there is no sense of need, we cannot seek, and if we cannot seek, we will never find. The one thing that must never be lost is a sense of sin.

THE FOUNTAIN OF LIVING WATER

John 7:37–44

> On the last, the great day of the festival, Jesus stood
> and cried: 'If anyone thirsts, let him come to me and
> drink. As the Scripture says: "He who believes in me –
> rivers of living water shall flow from his belly."' It
> was about the Spirit, whom those who believed in him
> were to receive, that he said this. For as yet there was
> no Spirit because Jesus was not yet glorified. When
> they heard these words some of the crowd said: 'This
> is really the promised prophet.' Others said: 'This is
> the Anointed One of God.' But some said: 'Surely
> the Anointed One of God does not come from Galilee?
> Does the Scripture not say that the Anointed One of
> God is a descendant of David, and that he is to come
> from Bethlehem, the village where David used to live?'
> So there was a division of opinion in the crowd because
> of him. Some of them would have liked to arrest him,
> but none laid hands on him.

ALL the events of this chapter took place during the Festival
of Tabernacles; and properly to understand them we must
know the significance and at least some of the ritual of that
festival.

The Festival of Tabernacles or Booths was the third of the
trio of great Jewish festivals, attendance at which was com-
pulsory for all adult male Jews who lived within fifteen miles
of Jerusalem – the Passover, the Festival of Pentecost and the
Festival of Tabernacles. It fell on the fifteenth day of the
seventh month, that is, about 15th October. Like all the great
Jewish festivals, it had a double significance.

First, it had a *historical* significance. It received its name
from the fact that all through it people left their houses and

lived in little booths. During the festival, the booths sprang up everywhere: on the flat roofs of the houses, in the streets, in the city squares, in the gardens and even in the very courts of the Temple. The law laid it down that the booths must be not permanent structures but built specially for the occasion. Their walls were made of branches and fronds, and had to be such that they would give protection from the weather but not shut out the sun. The roof had to be thatched, but the thatching had to be wide enough for the stars to be seen at night. The historical significance of all this was to remind the people in unforgettable fashion that once they had been homeless wanderers in the desert without a roof over their heads (Leviticus 23:40-3). Its purpose was 'that your generations may know that I made the people of Israel live in booths when I brought them out of the land of Egypt'. Originally it lasted seven days, but by the time of Jesus an eighth day had been added.

Second, it had an *agricultural* significance. It was supremely a harvest-thanksgiving festival. It is sometimes called *the Festival of the Ingathering* (Exodus 23:16, 34:22); and it was the most popular festival of all. For that reason, it was sometimes called simply *The Feast* (1 Kings 8:2) and sometimes *The Festival of the Lord* (Leviticus 23:39). It stood out above all others. The people called it 'the season of our gladness', for it marked the gathering in of all the harvests, since by this time the barley, the wheat and the grapes were all safely gathered in. As the law had it, it was to be celebrated 'at the end of the year, when you gather in from the field the fruit of your labour' (Exodus 23:16); it was to be kept 'when you have gathered in the produce from your threshing-floor and your wine press' (Deuteronomy 16:13). It was not only thanksgiving for one harvest, it was glad thanksgiving for all the bounty of nature which made life possible and

living happy. In Zechariah's dream of the new world, it was
this festival which was to be celebrated everywhere
(Zechariah 14:16–18). Josephus called it 'the holiest and the
greatest festival among the Jews' (*Antiquities of the Jews*,
3:10:4). It was not only a time for the rich; it was laid down
that the servant, the stranger, the widow and the poor were
all to share in the universal joy.

One particular ceremony was connected with it. The
worshippers were told to take 'the fruit of majestic trees,
branches of palm trees, boughs of leafy trees, and willows of
the brook' (Leviticus 23:40). The Sadducees said that was a
description of the material out of which the booths had to be
built; the Pharisees said it was a description of the things the
worshippers had to bring with them when they came to the
Temple. Naturally the people accepted the interpretation of
the Pharisees, for it gave them a vivid ceremony in which to
participate.

This special ceremony is very closely connected with this
passage and with the words of Jesus. Quite certainly he spoke
with it in his mind, and possibly even with it as an immediate
background. Each day of the festival, the people came with
their palms and their willows to the Temple; with them they
formed a kind of screen or roof and marched round the great
altar. At the same time, a priest took a golden pitcher which
held three *logs* – that is, about two pints – and went down to
the Pool of Siloam and filled it with water. It was carried
back through the Water Gate while the people recited Isaiah
12:3: 'With joy you will draw water from the wells of
salvation.' The water was carried up to the Temple altar and
poured out as an offering to God. While this was being done,
the Hallel – that is, Psalms 113–18 – was sung to the accom-
paniment of flutes by the Levite choir. When they came to
the words 'O give thanks to the Lord' (Psalm 118:1), and

again to the words 'O work now then salvation' (Psalm 118:25), and finally to the closing words 'O give thanks to the Lord' (Psalm 118:29), the worshippers shouted and waved their palms towards the altar. The whole dramatic ceremony was a vivid thanksgiving for God's good gift of water and an acted prayer for rain, and a memory of the water which sprang from the rock when they travelled through the wilderness. On the last day, the ceremony was doubly impressive, for they marched seven times round the altar in memory of the sevenfold circuit round the walls of Jericho, whereby the walls fell down and the city was taken.

Against this background and perhaps at that very moment, Jesus' voice rang out: 'If anyone thirst, let him come to *me* and drink.' It is as if Jesus said: 'You are thanking and glorifying God for the water which quenches the thirst of your bodies. Come to me if you want water which will quench the thirst of your soul.' He was using that dramatic moment to turn people's thoughts to the thirst for God and the eternal things.

THE FOUNTAIN OF LIVING WATER

John 7:37–44 (*contd*)

Now that we have seen the vivid background of this passage, we must look at it in more detail.

The promise of Jesus presents us with something of a problem. He said: 'He who believes in me – rivers of water shall flow from his belly.' And he introduces that statement by saying: 'As Scripture says'. No one has ever been able to identify that quotation satisfactorily, and the question is, just what does it mean? There are two distinct possibilities.

(1) It may refer to those who come to Jesus and accept him. Such people will have within them a river of refreshing

water. It would be another way of saying what Jesus said to
the woman of Samaria: 'The water that I will give will become
in them a spring of water gushing up to eternal life' (John
4:14). It would be another way of putting Isaiah's beautiful
saying: 'The Lord will guide you continually, and satisfy your
needs in parched places, and make your bones strong; and
you shall be like a watered garden, like a spring of water,
whose waters never fail' (Isaiah 58:11). The meaning would
be that Jesus can give people the refreshment of the Holy
Spirit.

The Jews placed all the thoughts and the emotions in
certain parts of the body. The *heart* was the seat of the
intellect; the *kidneys* and the *belly* were the seat of the inmost
feelings. As the writer of the Proverbs had it: 'The human
spirit is the lamp of the Lord, searching every inmost part'
(Proverbs 20:27). This would mean that Jesus was promising
a cleansing, refreshing, life-giving stream of the Holy Spirit
so that our thoughts and feelings would be purified and
revitalized. It is as if Jesus said: 'Come to me and accept me;
and I will put into you through my Spirit a new life which
will give you purity and satisfaction, and give you the kind
of life you have always longed for and never had.' Whichever
interpretation we take, it is quite certain that what this one
stands for is true.

(2) The other interpretation is that 'rivers of living water
shall flow from his belly' may refer to Jesus himself. It may
be a description of the Messiah which Jesus is taking from
somewhere which we cannot place. The Christians always
identified Jesus with the rock which gave the Israelites water
in the wilderness (Exodus 17:6). Paul took that image and
applied it to Christ (1 Corinthians 10:4). John tells how there
came forth at the thrust of the soldier's spear *water* and *blood*
from Jesus' side (John 19:34). The water stands for the

purification which comes in baptism and the blood for the atoning death of the cross. This symbol of the life-giving water which comes from God is often in the Old Testament (Psalm 105:41; Ezekiel 47:1, 12). Joel has the great picture: 'A fountain shall come forth from the house of the Lord' (Joel 3:18). It may well be that John is thinking of Jesus as the fountain from which the cleansing stream flows. Water is that without which human beings cannot live; and Christ is the one without whom human beings cannot live and dare not die. Again, whichever interpretation we choose, that, too, is deeply true.

Whether we take this picture as referring to Christ or to those who accept him, it means that from Christ there flow the strength and power and cleansing which alone give us life in the real sense of the term.

In this passage, there is a startling thing. The Authorized Version and the Revised Standard tone it down, but in the best Greek manuscript (reflected in the translation of the New Revised Standard Version) there is the strange statement in verse 39: 'For as yet there was no Spirit.' What is the meaning of that? Think of it this way. A great power can exist for years and even centuries without anyone being able to tap it. To take a very relevant example – there has always been atomic power in this world; it is not a human invention. But only in our own time have we tapped and used it. The Holy Spirit has always existed; but people never really enjoyed his full power until after Pentecost. As it has been finely said, 'There could be no Pentecost without Calvary.' It was only when men and women had known Jesus that they really knew the Spirit. Before that, the Spirit had been a power; but now he is a person, for he has become to us nothing other than the presence of the risen Christ always with us. In this apparently startling sentence, John is not saying that the Spirit did not *exist*; but that it took the life and death of Jesus Christ to open the floodgates for the Spirit to become real and powerful to all people.

We must notice how this passage finishes. Some people thought that Jesus was the prophet whom Moses had promised (Deuteronomy 18:15). Some thought that he was the Anointed One of God; and there followed a wrangle about whether or not the Anointed One of God must come from Bethlehem. Here is tragedy. A great religious experience had ended in the aridity of a theological wrangle.

That is what above all we must avoid. Jesus is not someone about whom to argue; he is someone to know and love and enjoy. If we have one view of him and someone else has another, it does not matter so long as both of us find him Saviour and accept him as Lord. Even if we explain our religious experience in different ways, that should never divide us, for it is the experience that is important, and not our explanation of it.

UNWILLING ADMIRATION
AND TIMID DEFENCE

John 7:45–52

> So the officers came to the chief priests and the Pharisees. They said to them: 'Why did you not bring him here?' The attendants answered: 'Never did a man speak as he speaks.' So the Pharisees answered: 'Surely you too have not been led astray? Has anyone from the authorities believed in him? Or anyone from the Pharisees? *They* have not; but the mob which is ignorant of the law and which is accursed believes in him!' Nicodemus (the man who came to him before) said to them, for he was one of them: 'Surely our law does not

condemn a man unless it first hears a statement of the case from him, and has first-hand information about what he is doing?' They answered him: 'Surely you too are not from Galilee? Search and see that no prophet arises from Galilee.'

WE have certain vivid reactions to Jesus.

(1) The reaction of the officers was bewildered amazement. They had gone out to arrest Jesus and had come back without him, because never in their lives had they heard anyone speak as he did. Really to listen to Jesus is an unparalleled experience for anyone.

(2) The reaction of the chief priests and Pharisees was contempt. The Pharisees had a phrase by which they described the ordinary people who did not observe the thousands of regulations of the ceremonial law. They called them *the People of the Land*; to them they were beneath contempt. 'The masses who do not know the law are accursed.' The Rabbinic law said: 'Six things are laid down about the People of the Land: entrust no testimony to them, take no testimony from them, trust them with no secret, do not appoint them guardians of an orphan, do not make them custodians of charitable funds, do not accompany them on a journey.' It was forbidden to be a guest of one of the People of the Land, or to entertain such a person as a guest. It was even laid down that, wherever it was possible, nothing should be bought or sold from one of them. In their proud aristocracy and intellectual snobbery and spiritual pride, the Pharisees looked down in contempt on the ordinary people. Their plea was: 'Nobody who is spiritually and academically of any account has believed in Jesus. Only ignorant fools accept him.' It is indeed a terrible thing when people think themselves either too clever or too good to need Jesus Christ – and it happens still.

(3) There was the reaction of Nicodemus. It was a timid reaction, for he did not defend Jesus directly. He dared only to quote certain legal maxims which were relevant. The law laid it down that all must receive justice (Exodus 23:1; Deuteronomy 1:16); and part of justice was and is the right to state a case and not to be condemned on second-hand information. The Pharisees proposed to break that law, but it is clear that Nicodemus did not carry his protest any further. His heart told him to defend Jesus, but his head told him not to take the risk. The Pharisees flung catchwords at him; they told him that obviously no prophet could come out of Galilee and taunted him with having a connection with the Galilaean rabble, and he said no more.

Often we find ourselves in a situation in which we would like to defend Jesus and in which we know we ought to show our colours. Often we make a kind of half-hearted defence, and are then reduced to an uncomfortable and ashamed silence. In our defence of Jesus Christ it is better to be reckless with our hearts than prudent with our heads. To stand up for him may bring us mockery and unpopularity; it may even mean hardship and sacrifice. But the fact remains that Jesus said he would confess before his Father anyone who confessed him on earth, and deny before his Father anyone who denied him on earth. Loyalty to Christ may produce a cross on earth, but it brings a crown in eternity.